The Calendar

by
Pah Schuck

I dedicate this book to Mona Mc-D, my wife and best friend. Without your love and encouragement, this book would not have seen the light of day.

My love to you, always.

Table of Contents

Prologue

In the finished basement of a suburban home, four men are seated at a card table while two others are standing at the bar sharing a bottle of wine.

"Arthur, how'd we do with the collection last Sunday?" Bill asked without looking up from his newspaper.

"Thirty-one hundred bucks."

"Good, that's fifteen hundred for Good Shepherd and sixteen hundred more for the William J. Nelson Community Center building fund. You know," Bill continued, "ten years ago, we could count on local businesses to come up with a chunk here and a chunk there. Now, trying to come up with a lousy two million bucks is like pulling hen's teeth."

"People are struggling, Bill. Things are tough everywhere," Arthur explained.

"Yeah? Well if things are so tough, how is it that the Catholic Church on the other side of town is always building up or adding on? Can someone answer that?"

"Don't get so worked up," Arthur cautioned. "Everybody knows the Vatican is a well-financed business. They're a Fortune 500 corporation, not a church."

"This is so friggin' frustrating. It took us years to bring old Pastor Rice around to understand the business side of Good Shepherd. I finally convince the old geyser to give up that 'save the world' crap and get on board with my plan and then, 'Wham!'" he croaks. "I mean, really, whoever chokes to death eating spaghetti? Now we're going to have to bring my son in to keep this ship afloat."

"How much longer before Billy finishes his stint in the Navy?" Tommy asked.

"Three years." Bill sighed.

"Geeez, that's a long time. What are we supposed to do until then?"

"Don't get your panties in a bunch, Arthur. I've got it all figured out. You two, grab a seat." Bill motioned to the men at the bar. "Here's the plan: we're going to bring someone in to 'shepherd the flock' while I motivate Billy to do what he has to do to get ordained. Then we'll vote him in as the pastor for Good Shepherd. Funny," Bill snickered, "I always wanted a 'man of the cloth' in the family."

"Who do you plan to be the pastor until then?" Arthur asked.

"It can't be anyone local," Bill pondered while stroking his chin. "Anyone local could be a problem."

"What do you mean?" Tommy was puzzled.

"Figure it this way," Bill explained, "If we recruit a local pastor, they'll probably come with their own people and agenda. We need to bring in someone from outside the area who has absolutely no association with any local people or organizations that can oppose us when we fire him, her, or it."

"What do you mean, 'it'?" Arthur asked.

"I mean, I don't care if it's a talking pig that occupies the pulpit until Billy arrives. As long as the flock brings their money each week and our plan stays on track, I'll be satisfied."

"So what do we do next?" Tommy asked.

"We're going to advertise the position on one or two of the national ministry websites. That way we'll be able to kill two birds with one stone. First, we can demonstrate that we've gone to the greatest lengths to recruit the most qualified applicant and, second, we'll be able to choose whoever lives the furthest distance from Scituate."

"Bill, you're brilliant!" Arthur let loose with a sinister laugh.

"I know. Thank you."

The others chimed in with kudos for Bill's plan.

"Now, let's get this ball rolling. Danny, you're good with the computer. Place the ad first thing tomorrow. I'll write it up for you tonight. Set a thirty-day time frame for accepting applications. Arthur, you'll conduct the interviews and provide us with the results at next month's meeting. Is everybody clear on their assignment?"

"I've got a question," Arthur asked, "What are we going to do for a 'stand-in' between now and the time we bring in the new hire?"

"We'll call on Pastor Rice's nephew to stand in for a stretch," Bill strategized.

"You mean that guy Reverend Bell?" asked Danny. "He sounds like a human storm drain when he talks."

"Yeah, that's the one. He won't give us any problems. After a month or so of enduring his monotone sermons with that nasal condition of his, the congregation will welcome our choice of the new pastor. And besides, if things don't go as planned with him or her, we can always bring Reverend Bell back to pinch-hit."

All in attendance agreed. The meeting adjourned after a few hours of backslapping, joke-telling frivolity.

The Chronology

Day 1
December 3ʳᵈ – Monday

Looking over at the wall clock, Horatio jumped up from his desk chair. "Five forty-five. I'm late." Quickly closing down his office, he drove directly to Scituate High School's gymnasium to attend the monthly town meeting. "Lord," he inquired, "tell me again, please, why am I even going to this meeting? I need a break from these unsaved people and all of their issues."

Arriving five minutes before the meeting was called to order, he found a seat along the front row of bleachers. He acknowledged several familiar faces with a wave and a smile. At the sound of the gavel, the meeting was called to order.

"This session of the Scituate Town Council is hereby called to order," the moderator announced. As matters concerning proposed tax increases, budgetary cuts, and zoning variances were introduced and discussed, outbursts of accusation and disdain filled the room. The congenial atmosphere had quickly turned adversarial.

Sensing the increasing tension, Horatio understood that he needed help to calm the situation. "Father," he prayed in a whisper, "Bind up the wickedness that is present in this place."

Self-interests continued to trump common sense and mutual respect. Verbal venom flowed unrestrained. Watching in disbelief, he could no longer contain himself. Rising to his feet, he spoke.

"People, please…. This conduct is most unbecoming. As God's children, we are called to walk in love…."

Before he could speak another word, a chorus of boos and heckling filled the auditorium. Vocal objection to his counsel was so loud that he could not be heard. From across the gymnasium, an unidentified voice blurted out, "Hey, Pastor, this ain't your pulpit. Take that stuff back to your church, where it belongs."

"Yeah," another voice chimed in, "Don't let the door hit you on your way out."

1

Horatio searched out the origin of the angry voices without success. He had never before heard voices so demonically influenced. Deeply shaken, he prayed, "Lord, forgive these unsaved people."

In that moment, a slide show of every frustrating incident he had experienced since his arrival to Scituate flashed through his mind, confirming his reality as an irrelevant, overwhelmed, and unappreciated servant of God. Frustrated, he quickly exited the building, refusing to look back.

"I can't do this, anymore. I hate this God-forsaken town and everything about it," he scowled.

Horatio Smiley is the Pastor of Church of the Good Shepherd located in the seaside town of Scituate, Massachusetts. Recruited from Virginia Beach at thirty-six years of age, he is perceived as an outsider who requires the counsel of the church's senior members, whether requested or not. At the same time, he is viewed by the church's youth as being too old to be trusted with their 'matters of confidence.' Each day he labors, tirelessly, in response to situations pertaining to his parishioners, in an attempt to obtain their validation as a qualified replacement for his predecessor, who died after serving in his role for forty-two years.

"Thirty-two months in this town is thirty-one too many," he muttered as he drove away from the school parking lot.

Later that night as he lay awake in bed, images of the community meeting continued to replay in his mind.

"I blew it. My chance to make a difference and I blew it," he agonized, pulling the pillow over his face. Continuing to grieve about his reaction to his dismissal by the voices at the meeting, he prayed with urgency.

"Heavenly Father, please forgive me for not standing stronger in that moment of opportunity. Help me be a better witness for you." As he continued to pray, fatigue set in. Somewhere between the states of restlessness and repentance, he drifted off to sleep.

In his darkened, quiet room, a still voice was heard addressing him by name. "Horatio, My child. I am with you. Do not become discouraged. Trust in Me. Believe in my Word."

Quickly sitting upright in his bed, he inquired, "Lord. Is it you, Lord? Lord? Speak, Lord." He attempted to engage the voice, to no avail. As suddenly as the voice appeared, it departed.

"Don't leave. Stay. Please," he pleaded.

The all-too-brief encounter left him wide awake. Any evidence of fatigue or discouragement within him, previously, had been replaced with a sense of such excitement that he had a need to share his experience with someone who could truly understand the significance of all that had just occurred. But, who could he comfortably call at one o'clock in the morning? Who, for that matter, could he call at one o'clock in the afternoon that could appreciate the gravity of his experience? A sense of profound desperation began to set in.

"Lord, your people are being overtaken by darkness. Please, show me what to do. Help me awaken your people to the reality of the spiritual warfare that has come against them." Lying in his bed, he continued to pray until fatigue returned. Eventually, he drifted back to sleep.

Day 2
December 4th - Tuesday

The morning sunlight filtered into Horatio's bedroom, bringing with it a sense of peace. To the socially conscious and spiritually dull, life in Scituate is heaven on Earth. Family-owned fishing enterprises, quaint restaurants and artsy storefronts line Front Street along Scituate Harbor. Locals take to the streets and sidewalks in a daily regimen of jogging, cycling, and strolling. To outsiders, life in Scituate is a reflection of days gone by.

At the geographical center of this bastion of tradition and tourism stands the Church of the Good Shepherd. Immediately identifiable by its majestic steeple, manicured grounds, and fresh white paint, this beacon of the community has served the residents of Scituate as host to weddings, funerals, and baptisms for the last one hundred twenty-four years. The parsonage, located adjacent to the primary church structure, is home to Pastor Horatio Smiley.

Looking in the mirror while shaving, Horatio revisited his experience with the 'voice' and all that had been communicated. Certain of how others would respond to it, he cautioned himself, "Horatio, say nothing to anyone about the voice. Not one word," he emphasized with a finger-shaking gesture.

At that moment, his focus shifted to the church's calendar project. The ordering deadline was fast approaching to ensure that the calendars would be delivered before December 31st. It was the church's tradition to distribute them at the New Year's Eve Watch Meeting. He didn't want to be remembered for breaking with that practice. On his way out the door, he grabbed a bottle of water and an apple. Walking to his office, he witnessed from across the street Sam Wooden, one of his parishioners, publicly berating his wife while their children looked on.

"What's wrong with you, Teresa? Use your head!" Sam bellowed, seemingly frustrated.

The man's voice was so loud that Horatio had to call out "Good morning, Sam" twice before he could be heard.

Sam stood six feet four inches tall and every bit of three hundred-twenty pounds. His wife, Teresa, wasn't more than five feet three inches tall, weighing in at about one hundred thirty pounds.

"Morning, Pastor," he responded, obligingly.

Sam got the hint and ceased his disrespectful behavior. He stormed off as though he had been interrupted without just cause. His wife and children acknowledged Pastor Smiley and apprehensively followed after Sam.

"So much work to do, Lord. So much work to do," Horatio muttered.

Entering his office, before being seated at his desk, he searched for a pamphlet that he had received from a calendar manufacturer. After a few minutes of moving piles of paperwork from left to right and back again, he found it. Placing a call to the company, he was directed to the Customer Service department.

"Hello. This is Adam. How may I help you, today?"

"Hi, Adam. My name is Horatio Smiley. I'm calling because I received an advertisement from your company."

"Well, thank you for your interest in our products, Mr. Smiley." Adam continued, "As you can see, we manufacture calendars. In fact, calendars are our only product. So, if it's calendars you're looking for, you've come to the right place."

"Well, Adam," Horatio chuckled, "it just so happens I'm looking for calendars."

"Great. Have you purchased calendars before?"

"Oh, yes. In fact, for the last fourteen years our church has purchased calendars from a local company. The service and quality of our previous supplier had become uninspiring and expensive so, I decided to get pricing from other vendors. After looking at your brochure, I figured I'd give you a call."

"You mentioned a church?" Adam inquired.

"Yes. I minister at Church of the Good Shepherd in Scituate, Massachusetts.

"I'm familiar with Scituate," Adam responded. "That's just off of Route 3, heading toward Cape Cod, isn't it?"

"It is, indeed."

"Beautiful part of the country," Adam continued. "So then, you're Father or Reverend Smiley?"

"Neither, actually. Pastor is fine."

"Well, Pastor, we promote our company's ability to personalize every calendar we produce to fully satisfy our customer's specific need or application. If you're not completely satisfied, you tear up our invoice."

"That's very impressive. Sounds like your company is extremely confident in your product. You know, Adam, in my line of work, I'm usually on the receiving end of a challenge. So I'm going to enjoy this time of role reversal. Where do we begin?"

"The first question, Pastor, is what would you most like to see your calendars accomplish?"

"Accomplish?" Horatio paused. "I'm not sure what you mean."

"Well," Adam explained, "We can provide inspirational themes, breathtaking photography, text that you provide, specialized formats or something with a local flair. Whatever you want."

Wouldn't that be nice, Horatio thought inwardly. "I'd love to see a calendar that would remind people that every day of life is a gift from God. That tomorrow is guaranteed to no man, woman, or child, regardless of personal standing or circumstance. That we, as God's creation, should live with a commitment to bring honor to Him in everything we say, everything we do, and everything we aspire to be."

"Wow, that's deep, Pastor. I don't think we've ever produced a calendar that has accomplished all that before. Very interesting, I must say. Would it be okay if I give you a call tomorrow? I'd like to run this by my boss, for his idea on this."

"No problem. Until tomorrow then." Bidding Adam good-bye, he hung up the phone.

Throughout the day, the matter of the calendars stayed strong on Horatio's mind. In fact, he was unable to move beyond it. He found himself, continually, praying to God for a strategy. He needed a plan that would result in growth coming to the spiritual lives of the church's congregants. Though he could not immediately discern the voice of God answering his prayer, he remembered, almost hauntingly, all that the voice had spoken to him in that early morning hour. The words "I am with you. Trust in my Word. Believe in Me" continued to echo in his head. The day concluded without the manifestation of a divine revelation or strategy. He closed down his office and headed home at six fifteen that evening.

Day 3
December 5th - Wednesday

The night turned to day, uneventfully. By eight thirty, Horatio was back at work. At ten twenty, the office phone rang. It was Adam from the calendar company.

"Good morning, Pastor. I've spoken with my boss about your calendar's objective and I've got to tell you, he is excited! He asks that you trust him with your project, or as he refers to it, our 'opportunity.' Would that be okay with you?"

"Well, I guess that's okay. I'm sure that he has a lot more experience at this than you or me."

"Great. I'll work up a proposal to include our usual satisfaction guaranty, while keeping your budget in mind."

"Sounds good to me." At that point, Horatio said good-bye. Returning to his duties, he sensed every bit of anxiety concerning the calendars lift from his spirit.

Just before noon, the phone rang. "Hello, Church of the Good Shepherd."

Pastor Smiley?" a voice on the other end of the call inquired. "Is this Pastor Smiley?" the voice asked again.

"Yes, this is Pastor Smiley. Who am I speaking with?"

"It's Loretta Andrews, Pastor."

"Oh, Mrs. Andrews. What's the matter?" he asked, sensing that something was very wrong. He knew Mrs. Andrews to be a well-grounded member of Good Shepherd who was not given to drama.

"Pastor, my son Timmy was just rushed to South Shore hospital. The police said he overdosed on drugs." She continued, "He's been in trouble before, but never anything like this. They're not sure if he's going to live. He's only twenty-two years old. Pastor, can you please meet me at the hospital?"

"I'll head over there right now," he promised.

"Thank you, Pastor. I'll meet you there. God bless you." She hung up the phone.

Within twenty-five minutes he was at the hospital. He located Mrs. Andrews in the triage waiting area. They remained seated there until a member of the medical staff could provide them with a patient status report.

As they waited, Horatio prayed, "Lord, we lift up Timmy to you and ask that you would deliver him safely through this time of affliction. Draw him to you, Lord. Silence the voices of darkness that endeavor to seduce him to seek solutions for whatever has come against him through drugs and self-destruction. Let him come to experience the perfect peace and joy that only You can provide, in the Name of Jesus."

Seated in the waiting area with Mrs. Andrews and Horatio were eight very anxious people. In the course of his vigilant prayer, others there requested prayer for their loved ones. Before long, they all had joined with Ms. Andrews and Horatio praying for God to move in their circumstance, and move He did. Each patient update, inclusive of a shooting, a drug overdose, an accidental poisoning, and a heart attack, was favorable. Horatio stayed with Mrs. Andrews until five fifteen. After assuring her that he would check back with Timmy the following morning, he returned to the church.

Every Wednesday, Good Shepherd's weekly prayer meeting was scheduled to begin at six o'clock. Horatio was responsible for making the sanctuary ready. Though poorly attended, the prayer meeting was a measuring stick that identified the church members who proved to be more than just 'pew warmers.' As he regularly reminded the faithful attendees, "We are called to pray for each other. So, pray as though someone's life or situation depends on your prayer." As he prayed earnestly, others in the group appeared to be hindered in their prayer.

Horatio continued to encourage them, "Somebody needs your prayer now. Don't cease praying. Press on! Press through! You have been given power, in the Name of Jesus. The authority is within YOU!"

The more he would try to motivate and teach them in the strategy of effective, fervent prayer, the more obvious it became that the church's prayer warriors struggled in their ability to fully grasp and apply all that was being taught them. Horatio truly loved his parishioners. Despite their shortcomings, he knew that their hearts were good and they loved God. At the end of the prayer meeting, they fellowshipped and, eventually, bade each other good-bye until the Sunday morning service. He made his way home and was in his bed before 11:00 p.m.

Day 4
December 6th - Thursday

At eight forty-five, true to his word, Horatio left to visit Timmy at the hospital. Once there, he located Timmy in his hospital room.

"Timmy. Good morning. How are you feeling today?"

"Oh. Hi, Pastor. From what my mother told me, I guess I could be doing a lot worse."

"You gave us quite a scare. What's going on?"

"I'm sorry, Pastor. I just needed to escape for a while. I didn't mean to cause such a mess. My mom told me that you came to sit with her yesterday. Thanks for being there for her. I worry about my mom. She always seems so sad."

Horatio was able to spend only a few minutes with Timmy, before the medical staff arrived to evaluate him. Timmy agreed to follow up with Horatio at his office early the following week, pending his discharge from the hospital. Horatio headed directly back to his office.

****

That afternoon, Adam called and appeared to be even more excited than the previous time they had spoken.

"Pastor, I just heard back from the big guy and he has come up with a strategy that I'm sure will get some positive results. He shared only a bit of his plan, but I've got to tell you it's awesome. From what I understand," Adam explained, "each calendar will be personalized with the church member's name, not only on the outer packaging but also somewhere within the pages of the calendar. My boss says this added touch will confirm to the reader that the calendar was created specifically for him or her."

"That is an interesting approach," Horatio acknowledged. "Truly interesting. What about the cost?"

"Now, this is where it gets really weird," Adam continued. "My boss sent an email saying that the cost has been fully covered. I'm not sure how this could be, given that I haven't even prepared a job quote or received a purchase order from you giving us the go-ahead. Have you been in touch with my boss, or something?"

"Adam, do you know God?"

"Do I know God?" Adam responded defensively. "Of course, I do. Doesn't everybody? I mean, He's the man upstairs, right? The One who decides who goes to Heaven and who goes to hell, right? Let me tell you, I was the youngest altar boy in my church, attended catechism, and I still pray from time to time. Who knows God better than me, right?"

"Adam, I seem to have struck a nerve," Horatio offered apologetically. "Please understand that was not my intention. My question was in response to you asking me if I had any communication with your boss. As you and I have never met, it would be difficult for you to fully understand just how much I believe God is involved in all that is going on with these calendars. The favor that God has given me with your boss is something that I, in my flesh, could never expect. Yet the voice of God spoke to me only a few days ago telling me to trust him, and now he is moving in answer to my prayers to confirm his word. And I've got to tell you, Adam, this experience has God's signature all over it"

"Whoa, Pastor! This is getting a little heavy for this old altar boy," quipped Adam. "Well," he continued, "the calendars should be delivered ahead of your deadline and, to be honest, I am very curious as to what the old man has in store."

"Yes, Adam. I think we both are. I'll get you a list of names for the calendars," Horatio promised. Saying good-bye, he returned to addressing the pile of paperwork that had accumulated on his desk. Included in correspondence personally addressed to him were letters from church members and others who were laden with situations involving desperation, isolation, frustration, and financial devastation. All afternoon it was like being hit with one body blow followed by another as he read each request. Eventually, a sense of grief overtook him and he could no longer contain himself.

"Oh, God," he cried out. "Where are you in all of this, Lord? Why are you not moving in the circumstances of your people? Have I so failed in my assignment that you have withheld your blessing from the people you have given me to shepherd?"

Tears flowed freely as he bared his soul.

"I'm sorry, Lord. Please forgive me for my selfish desire to be far away from this place. I didn't understand," he acknowledged. "It's not me who needs a break, it's your people." The prayerful monologue continued as he held up the handful of letters above his head.

"Please, send relief. You are their present and only help in their time of need. You, oh Lord, can do all things."

The Lord was silent. Emotionally spent, Horatio returned home around nine thirty that evening.

Later, as he lay awake in bed, he continued to grieve. Again, the quiet, still voice appeared.

"I have heard your prayers, each and every one, and I have responded to them. Trust in Me."

Uncertain as to whether he was dreaming or awake, he remained still. The voice departed.

Day 5
December 7th - Friday

The new day was ushered in with the sound of starlings singing outside Horatio's bedroom window. Refreshed by a restful sleep, he was eager to get back to his office to begin working on the list of names for the calendars. He was out the door in record time. Going directly to his office, Horatio got busy searching through church files and address books. Not wanting to exclude any adult church member from receiving a calendar at the New Year's Eve Watch Meeting, he painstakingly reviewed and revised his distribution list. Once completed, the list totaled one hundred fifty-seven names of church regulars and a few others who attended church services when their health challenges permitted.

Convinced that he had performed a diligent job of ensuring that there would be no confusion or disappointment, he prepared to send the document to Adam. Before he could scan the document, the phone rang.

"Good afternoon, Pastor." It was Adam.

"Wow, Adam. This is truly amazing. I was just about to send you the list of parishioners who I'd like to receive a calendar."

"That's great. I was concerned about letting another day go by without scheduling your order for production. As you can understand, given the time of year, everybody wants their order yesterday."

"I certainly understand." Horatio continued, "I've got to tell you that I truly appreciate your help in keeping this project on course. I can confidently say that I would have been hard-pressed to complete this without your help. You are a blessing from the Lord."

"Pastor, I'm flattered. But I've got to be honest, all credit goes to my boss. I mean, he's amazing. I've never worked for anyone like him. He never makes a promise that he doesn't keep. Just being around him, watching him operate, motivates me to represent him the absolute best that I can. You should get in touch with him, when you get a moment, and see if he affects you in the same way he does me."

"I'd like that, Adam. I could certainly use an influence like that in my life, right about now."

"If there is one guarantee that I can give, it would be this, Pastor: you will not be disappointed." Saying good-bye, Adam explained that he had another call on hold and had to take it.

Horatio continued to review the listing before moving on to the next matter of business. As he did, he recalled the names and circumstances of several people on the list. Other names he remembered vaguely, as they were of parishioners who attended Good Shepherd, sporadically. For those whose circumstance he could recall, he began to pray as the Spirit of God led him. He prayed according to the instruction given in the scripture, John 15:16 ("Whatever you ask the Father in My name, He may give it to you"), to be sure that God would hear and respond to his prayer. He began praying for the first name on the list. The more passionately he prayed, the more he was blessed with the ability to recall details about other church members' situations.

The presence of God was tangible. Horatio ebbed and flowed between weeping and rejoicing as he continued to pray. He sensed that the Spirit of God had already begun to move in the circumstances of those whom he prayed for. He gave thanks. He didn't stop until he had prayed for every name on the list. It was eight o'clock. Exhausted, he closed down the building and went home.

Day 6
December 8th - Saturday

The morning sky was gray. The approach of an impending snowstorm could not be ignored. Horatio was slow to get up. Usually by this time, he would be preparing for his trip to the local nursing home to visit Widow Spence, Clara Thomas, Charlie Sheehy, and a host of others. The gloominess of the weather had served to slow his pace. Nevertheless, he was determined not to let the oppressive feeling deter him from making his rounds. Within five minutes of being ready to head out, his phone rang. It was Arthur Mutton, a church trustee board member.

"Good morning, Arthur. How are you doing on this fine Saturday morning?"

Seemingly caught off guard, Arthur responded, "Ah, oh yes. Good morning to you as well, Pastor."

"Great thing, this caller ID," Horatio chided.

"Yes. Great thing, indeed," Arthur muttered.

Like others who served on the trustee board with him, Arthur never laughed and seldom smiled. It was as if a great penalty would be assessed them should any evidence of joy or levity be reflected in their demeanor. Horatio, on the other hand, loved a good laugh. Arthur appeared to be a happily married man. He and his wife had three beautiful children, now grown, with children of their own. Wherever Arthur went, the atmosphere would seem to shift toward one of heaviness. He was the trustee who Horatio sat with at the time he interviewed for the position as senior pastor for the church. At the conclusion of his interview, because of Arthur's emotionless disposition, Horatio was certain that he would not be considered further. Now, each time he had an opportunity to make Arthur crack a smile, Horatio would attempt to lighten the moment.

"Arthur," Horatio began, "can I call you back? I've got to get down to the police station and post bail."

"What's going on now?" Arthur asked with a sigh.

"Well, it seems a cook was arrested for beating an egg." Horatio chuckled.

Arthur wasn't amused.

"Look, Pastor, about the sabbatical you requested last month. Well, I was calling to let you know that the board approved your request."

"Thanks, Arthur. Let the board members know that I am appreciative. Arthur, be blessed and, if the Lord is willing, I'll see you in church tomorrow morning."

"You as well, Pastor. See you then." Arthur hung up.

Unbeknownst to Horatio, his detractors had been posturing to bring in Bill Nelson's son, Billy, to replace him permanently. The trustees agreed that this would be the perfect time to bring in Rev. Bell as Horatio's temporary replacement and set the stage for the nonrenewal of his employment contract with Good Shepherd. In Horatio's mind, the sabbatical could not have come at a better time. It was scheduled to take effect on January 15th and last thirty days. Within a few minutes of concluding his conversation with Arthur, he was on his way to the nursing home.

****

Every time Horatio entered the Driftway Nursing Home, it was as though a celebrity had come to visit. Pleasant, grateful faces would greet him as he walked the halls, praying a blessing over anyone who requested one. The nursing home staff and residents considered him a part of their family and, consequently, it became necessary for him to learn the names of everyone there. He managed to accomplish that task within two weeks after his initial visit. In preparation for each of his visits, the staff and residents gathered in the community room so everyone would have the opportunity to join in on the fun.

If, for any reason, a resident couldn't make their way to the gathering, Horatio would seek them out, in their room. He valued the time that he spent there and it showed.

Typically, Horatio's visits would end at four o'clock, just before dinner was to be served. Afterward, he would return to his office to fine-tune his Sunday sermon notes. His Saturdays usually ended with a quiet, solitary dinner and an early lights out.

Day 7
December 9th - Sunday

"No!" Horatio screamed as his body jerked into an upright position. He had awakened from a deep sleep. His body was sweaty. His head was pounding. His hands trembled. Feeling a bit disoriented, he looked over at the clock beside his bed.

"Three thirty-three. The witching hour."

Horatio understood that witchcraft was not to be taken lightly. The dark powers of witchcraft are spoken of in Old Testament Scripture. The witch of Endor conjured up spells and communicated with the dead in the book of Samuel. There were several times before that Horatio was certain someone was working witchcraft against him. His dream, just concluded, confirmed his suspicion that someone or something had put a curse on him. He was scared.

"Who, Lord? Tell me, please. Who or what is behind this spiritual attack?"

His dream began in the high school gymnasium, just as he was earlier in the week. Everything that occurred in the gym the night of the community meeting was repeated in his dream, to a point. The circumstances of his actual experience differed, in that, this time he was able to locate the source of the demonically influenced voices. As he perused the crowd, angry faces of men and women were transformed into faces of demons. Hideous, angry beings that were coming after him. Most of them held bibles above their heads, as if intending to beat him down with them. Several hundred Bible toting demons chased him out of the building, down the street and out of town. It was at that point he woke up.

Unable to return to sleep, he continued to ponder his dream. Burdened by all that took place in the dream, a familiar spirit of oppression that routinely attacked him each Sunday morning was there in added measure. Discouraged and exhausted, he wrestled with the feeling of being incapable of ministering to others at today's service. In his three years of serving the church as pastor, he had never missed a worship service or prayer meeting.

Convicted not to "wimp out," he attempted to motivate himself. "C'mon, Horatio. Rise and shine," he commanded without success.

Recognizing the futility in his attempt, he prayed, "Lord, in the name of Jesus, I take authority over every dark, demonic affliction that has come against me this morning. Let Your light enter in and dispel all darkness that seeks to oppress, frustrate, and hinder your word from going forth to your people, with full effectiveness in today's worship service. Amen."

Immediately, he sensed the lifting of the heavy, oppressive spirit that was present before his prayer.

"Thank you, Lord," he remembered saying as he headed out the door.

****

The morning church service was excellent. Horatio couldn't recall one better. The presence of God was strong. Several parishioners experienced it for the first time in their lives. Some wept, others shouted 'Halleluiah,' confirming that the Spirit of God was moving in them.

During the service, he noticed a young man sitting in the front row who had come to give God another try. It was Timmy Andrews who, only days before, stood at death's door as the result of a drug overdose. Horatio was excited because the Word that God had placed in his heart to deliver was found in the book of John, chapter 8, verse 7: "Let him who is without sin, cast the first stone…." While ministering the Word, he noticed tears in the eyes of Timmy and several others. It was clear that the message was not intended exclusively for Timmy.

At the conclusion of the service, several church members gathered around the pulpit and confirmed that the impact of today's Word had blessed them tremendously. As the crowd thinned out, Horatio sought out Timmy but, he had left. After the church sanctuary had emptied, he closed down the building.

****

Later, he stopped by the Village Mart before heading over to the Heywoods' home for Sunday dinner. George and Mattie Heywood were pillars of the community and historically generous to a fault. Anytime someone needed a place to stay or a few dollars to get them by, the Heywoods were there to help. Now up in years and struggling to keep food on their own table, Horatio would join them for Sunday dinner twice each month.

"Well, good afternoon, Pastor. Come on in." George smiled as he held the door open wide.

"George. My friend. How are you and Mattie doing today?"

"Pastor, you should know by now that Mattie and I are a couple of tough old birds." George chuckled. "Looks like you bought some of everything from the store by all those bags you're carrying."

"George, I'm a sucker for a sale. Just can't say no to a deal." Horatio laughed loud enough for Mattie to hear the banter from the upstairs bedroom,

"What are you two doing down there?"

"C'mon down, Baby girl, and find out for yourself," George said.

Mattie made her way to the kitchen quickly enough to witness the boyish grins on George's and Horatio's face.

"My, oh my," Mattie said as she counted four bags of groceries on the kitchen table.

"I hope you're not going to give me a tough time about my spending, too," Horatio chided.

"Pastor. You know this is much too much." Mattie cut her eyes. "How many times do I have to tell you to stop spending so much of your hard earned money on George and me? The next time you do something like this…. Well, you may be my Pastor but you're not too grown to be put over my knee and paddled, don't you know?"

"Don't think she won't do it, Pastor. She almost took me over her knee a time or two before." George blushed.

They all laughed.

"Now, you two go on in the other room and make yourself comfortable while I see what I can do with what you brought," Mattie instructed.

"Well, can I at least sneak a peek at what's in the bag before you send me away?" George asked with a convincing smile.

"Just one peek. Then skedaddle, you charmer," Mattie said.

"Woman, you have such a way with words!" George laughed while reaching for a bag to look into.

"You two are poster children for God's idea of marital bliss," Horatio said. "George, I'll wait up for you in the living room."

"Okay, Pastor. I'll be there in a minute."

Horatio would never provide advance notice of what he would bring when he visited, so it was like a Christmas morning surprise as George and Mattie unpacked the bags. They would "ooh" and "ahh" and giggle like young children. Mattie would spend the next hour or two in the kitchen 'creating' while George and Horatio enjoyed good conversation.

George was a quiet man who, through the years, had become increasingly burdened with a sense of not having used wisdom with the family finances. He was guilt-ridden seeing his wife scraping by in life when it seemed everyone else their age was living comfortably. George valued his time with Horatio and considered him a dear friend.

The Heywoods were challenged with health and mobility issues, so Horatio was their primary link to community goings-on. The time that the three spent together laughing, reminiscing, philosophizing and eating passed quickly. At six thirty it was time for Horatio to leave. After the usual group hug he was out the door, headed home.

Day 8
December 10th - Monday

The church's Christmas pageant is less than two weeks away. Horatio held little hope of change trumping tradition. Christmas, as celebrated at Church of the Good Shepherd, is considered to be a sacred program that serves the church "perfectly well," according to the trustees. Previous attempts to introduce minor program tweaks had resulted in a near church split, resignations, emotional tantrums, and relational breakups. This event was perfect for photo ops of children reenacting the nativity scene and various choirs belting out seasonal favorites, concluding with a surprise visit from Santa Clause. This festive celebration routinely yielded the largest offering of the year for Good Shepherd.

In the first year of his tenure, Horatio attempted to create an atmosphere of deeper praise and worship than what he understood Good Shepherd's traditional Christmas pageant to include. The wrath that followed was something that he had never before or since experienced. Since then, his participation in the pageant has been limited to welcoming comments and the prayer of dismissal.

Recognizing that his sabbatical is scheduled to begin January 15th and understanding that he will be gone for one month, he endeavored to craft a powerful Watch Meeting message that will convict the church's members to live an uncompromising, reverent lifestyle. It was increasingly clear, by all that was going on in the lives of his congregants, that until they understood the reality of spiritual warfare, there would be no victory in battling against dysfunction in families, relationships, finances, health issues or generational curses. He prayed that God would bless him with the perfect message.

As he continued to pray, something very unusual occurred: light flooded his office with such intensity that he looked up from his praying position. Searching the room, he tried to identify the light source. He couldn't locate anything that would cause it, but he did observe that as the light came into contact with the far wall of the office, it did so in the form of a cross. Reflexively he swung around, searching, yet, again for something that would explain the image. The image remained there for only a moment and then disappeared. Certain this was a sign confirming that God was listening, he increased the intensity of his prayer. The more he prayed for a word from God, his focus would increasingly shift to the calendars. He was reminded of how God had moved in that situation. Recognizing that he was directing the flow of his sermon rather than giving God the ability to minister to him, he set aside the scriptures and notes that he chose to include in his message.

"Lord, forgive me. I have tried to create, in my flesh, a life-altering message for your people. I have seen the plight of your people and I have responded with my natural understanding. I should have responded according to my faith in you. Again, I ask to be forgiven. Have your way in me. Prepare my spirit that your word and your word alone will go forth. May those you bring to the New Year's watch meeting be greatly blessed, in Jesus' name I pray. Amen."

For the remainder of the day, he chose to disconnect from the usual business of paperwork, telephone calls, and sustenance. He remained in his office until the light of day had passed, praying for every person and circumstance that the Spirit of God placed upon his heart. He closed his office and headed home at five forty-two that evening.

Just after seven thirty, Horatio decided to go outside for some fresh air. He walked to the Village Mart to pick up something from the dessert section to satisfy his sweet tooth. The cloudless sky revealed a brilliant display of stars and a winter moon. The beauty of God's creation was breathtaking. He was so busy looking skyward that he would, occasionally, stumble as he walked along.

"Lord, you are so amazing. You are so good," he thought aloud.

On his way home, practically tasting the Boston Crème cake and chocolate ice cream he purchased, he noticed one of his church members, Sara Reynolds, walking in his direction. As she came nearer to him, he could see that her eyes appeared red and swollen.

"Sara, are you all right?"

"Yeah, I'm fine, Pastor," she responded unconvincingly.

"Where are you headed?" he asked, attempting to keep the conversation going.

"Nowhere. I mean, anywhere. Any place far from here would be fine with me," she said while trying to hold back a sob.

"Sara, please. Tell me what's going on."

She took a deep breath. "Well, I went to the clinic two weeks ago and was told that I'm two-and-a-half months pregnant. Pregnant! Can you believe it? I can't stay at home much longer before my mother figures out what's going on. I don't know what to do. I can't let her find out. After everything she's been through, this will devastate her." She began to cry.

Horatio was familiar with Sara's home life circumstance. Her mother, April, had a difficult life. At age nineteen, she married a philandering, abusive alcoholic twelve years her senior who, by all accounts, did her a favor by leaving her for another woman. Their marriage produced four children. After her husband's abandonment, April made it her mission to raise her children to know that they would always be first in her life and know that they were loved.

As the eldest child, April relied on Sara to set the example for her younger siblings. She understood just how much her mother loved her. Since the age of five, Sara bore witness to the sacrifices that her mother would make to ensure that her children were clothed, fed, and housed. Through all the family's difficulties, Sara remembered most the way that her mother would always give God thanks for keeping them together, protected, and provided for. There were countless times, growing up, when there was no money, food, or heat in their apartment. Her mother would always call the children to her side, in prayer, and God would move in their circumstance. It might have been a donation of food for a meal or a sewing or cleaning job that allowed an immediate financial need to be met.

Whatever the situation, April taught her children the importance of giving thanks to God, always. As a result, the Reynolds family was well represented in the church. They were actively involved in a variety of ministry programs.

"Mom has always trusted me to do the right and responsible thing. I let her down, Pastor. Can you speak to her? Let her know how sorry I am for what I've done."

"Sara, only you can express to your mother all that your heart is experiencing. I can't tell you what to say or how to say it, but I can refer you to one who can best counsel you in this time of hurt and uncertainty."

"I know what you're going to say, Pastor, but...." Sara paused. "You're right. I need God's help in this. Thank you."

"Sara, would you allow me to pray with you before you head home?"

"I'd appreciate that, Pastor."

Locating a bench on Front Street, they sat down and prayed. A sudden dampness in the night air caused a chill to come over Sara and Horatio as they concluded their prayer. As they stood to part company, Horatio presented her with the bag containing the cake and chocolate ice cream.

"This brings me comfort in difficult times. Take it home and share it with your family," he offered with a smile.

"Cake and ice cream, huh?" Sara managed a chuckle. "Guess I can get used to this. Cravings and all, you know. Thanks, Pastor."

With that, she was off. Horatio headed home without any cake or ice cream. He understood his errand had nothing to do with the sweets he desired. It was for God to use him to bring comfort to Sara in her time of need.

"You're good, God." He laughed. "You're really, really good."

Day 9
December 11th - Tuesday

Seated behind his desk on this sunny morning, Horatio revisited his conversation with Sara. He would occasionally pause to lift her situation in prayer. In that time, he retrieved a voicemail message from Mrs. Andrews, Timmy's mother.

"Good morning, Pastor. This is Loretta Andrews. I called to thank you, again, for responding to my son's hospitalization like you did. I'm so thankful to God. It looks like Timmy has finally given up his careless lifestyle. God bless you and see you at prayer meeting tomorrow night."

Horatio was delighted with the update, and he especially appreciated that Mrs. Andrews had committed to attend the weekly prayer meeting. With all that families in the church were going through, he understood the importance of a strong prayer covering for them. He believed that the greater the number of church prayer warriors, the better. Later that morning as he was working at his desk, the phone rang.

"Good morning, Church of the Good Shepherd," he greeted.

It was Sara Reynolds.

"Hi, Pastor Smiley. It's Sara."

"Well, good morning, Sara. How are you doing today?"

"Not so good, Pastor. I'm not sure that I can continue with this pregnancy."

"Sara, what are you saying?" Horatio was stunned.

"Well," she began, "I read about a pill…."

"Sara, you can't be serious?" he interrupted. "We're not talking about a case of acne or diarrhea. A child's life hangs in the balance, here."

"Pastor, you don't understand what I'm dealing with…"

"You're right, Sara, I don't…. Please explain it to me and your baby so we can understand." He could hear the frustration in his voice, so he toned it down. "I apologize, Sara."

She attempted, unsuccessfully, to hold back her tears. "I'm sorry, Pastor. I have to go now. Goodbye." She hung up the phone.

"Lord, forgive me," Horatio muttered. "What's wrong with me?"

Realizing that he had just shattered any measure of strength that Sara should have been able to find in him, he hung his head. Thirty seconds seemed like thirty minutes. Unaware that he hadn't, yet, hung up the phone handset, the call disconnect signal sounded. *I need to call Sara and apologize right away*, he processed. He tried calling three times, only to have his call go into a voice mail system. On his fourth attempt, she answered.

"Sara, please don't hang up," he pleaded. "My response was, absolutely, the worst that I could have offered. I was being judgmental. I know in my heart that is the last thing that you need right now. Can you forgive me?"

"It's okay, Pastor. I just wanted to call and thank you for the time and prayer that you blessed me with last night. I appreciate your passion for the unborn. Your response to my indecision caused me to consider my situation from an entirely different perspective. No harm done."

"Thank you so much, Sara. Now it's you who is blessing me." He breathed a sigh of relief.

"So, have you had the opportunity to speak with your mother yet?"

Sara told him that she had not yet spoken with her mother about the situation, but promised to do so later that day. Horatio assured her that he would be available to her and her mom should they need him.

"I appreciate that, Pastor. I'll keep that in mind. Thank you." The call ended.

He prayed that the Spirit of the Lord would enter in and instill joy and strength in the lives of the Reynolds family members. That in this time of testing, Mrs. Reynolds, Sara, and the other children would be given to hold on tightly to each other. He prayed that the father of the unborn child would honor Sara with marriage and, he would love her and their child with a perfect love. This he prayed in the name of Jesus.

"So many people are hurting. They need help and encouragement," he pondered aloud. "Lord, please show me how I can make a difference."

His heart was moved to send out Christmas cards. Horatio remembered a time in his life when he needed encouragement to stand strong in a time of testing. Someone, unknown to him this day, mailed him a handwritten Christmas card. The card read: "Be anxious about nothing, but in every circumstance and in everything, by prayer and petition with thanksgiving, continue to make your wants known to God." (Philippians 4:6) The card was a huge blessing to him.

28

Who cares this much about me? he remembered thinking to himself after reading the card. He was motivated to do exactly as the card instructed and was delivered supernaturally from a valley-low situation in his life. In the years that followed, he would say when sharing his testimony, "I know what God's handwriting looks like."

Horatio wasn't much of a card writer. In fact, he couldn't remember the last time that he sent a card, let alone handwrote one. He left his office in search of Christmas cards to follow through with his plan. Forty-five minutes later, he returned with cards in hand. He handwrote thirty-eight cards that afternoon and dropped them in a mailbox on his way home. He continued to pray for Sara and her situation.

Day 10
December 12th - Wednesday

Throughout the night and into the next morning, the Lord had placed Timmy Andrews on Horatio's heart. Seeing Timmy in church on Sunday and later receiving a call from his mother convicted Horatio to seek him out. He remembered that Timmy told him that he had just taken a job as a short-order cook at a restaurant the next town over. Timmy hadn't provided Horatio with his telephone number, so he decided to stop by Timmy's workplace later that afternoon.

Walking to his office to prepare for a nine o'clock meeting with his detractors, Bill Nelson and Arthur Mutton, Horatio noticed a Nexstar service vehicle exiting the church parking lot.

"I wonder what they're doing at the church?" he processed as he continued walking toward the building.

Arriving at the front door, he saw an orange service tag hanging on the doorknob. The notice read: "Service Temporarily Disconnected. Please contact our Collections Department at the number below to arrange for service restoral."

"What the heck is this about?" he asked, as if someone was there to respond.

Placing the key in the lock and turning the doorknob, he entered the building. It felt as though the heat had been off for days and, sure enough, the building was dark. The sun, hidden behind a barrier of ominous clouds, did little to bring any natural light or heat into the building.

"This is great. Just great," he muttered.

He went directly to his office and found the electric company's invoice. He noticed that the invoice had been paid well before the payment due date. A PAID stamp inclusive of the check number, date, and amount of the payment provided all the ammunition he needed to confirm his position that the utility company was in error. Using his cell phone, he called the Customer Service number on the notice. Six minutes later, after navigating his way through a maze of teleprompts and musical holds, he was connected with a Credit & Collections representative.

"Thank you for calling Nexstar. My name is Mary St. Fleur. May I help you?" a smoker's voice asked.

"Hello, Manny," Horatio began.

"Sir, my name is Mary," the voice responded with a bit of attitude.

"I'm so sorry, sir, I mean ma'am," he offered apologetically. *Man, this isn't starting off very well*, he sensed inwardly.

"Mary, I need your help."

Explaining that the power had been erroneously disconnected at the church, he informed the woman that he had documentation to support his position.

"Well, sir, I can't help you until I see some proof. You need to fax or email your documents, along with proof of payment from your bank that your check was honored when presented."

I get it, Horatio thought to himself: *payback for calling her Manny, no doubt.*

"Mary, we have no power here," he continued, "How do you expect me to fax or email the documents to you? There must be some other way."

"Sir, you're right," Mary began, "and I'm sure you will come up with it. Have a nice day." She hung up the phone.

"Demon seed," Horatio muttered.

Before he could devise a plan to forward the documents to the utility company, he heard a man's voice calling out.

"Pastor. Pastor Smiley, are you in there?" It was Bill Nelson.

"Great. From the frying pan, into the fire," he muttered. "Bill, I'm here. Come on in."

He could hear the voices of two men chuckling as they made their way toward his office. It was Bill and Arthur Mutton. Bill entered the office first. Folding his arms across his chest and his head shaking repeatedly from left to right, he spoke, "What have you done to the power?"

Arthur Mutton just stood there doing his best imitation of a bobblehead dashboard ornament. "Yeah, what happened to the electricity?"

"Don't worry, guys," Horatio responded. "I've already contacted Nexstar and they're aware of the problem. I expect it should be resolved quickly."

"Good," Bill continued. "We don't want to have to conduct tonight's prayer meeting by candlelight."

"Yeah, candlelight. Good one, Bill." Arthur chuckled.

"That's awesome. You gentlemen will be joining us for prayer meeting tonight?"

It had been at least six months that Bill or Arthur had made an appearance at the church's weekly prayer event.

"We'll try, but we can't make any promises." Bill continued, "We have to stop by the lodge first for an important matter. If we can get out of there in time, we'll make our way to your prayer meeting."

"Yeah, we'll try," Arthur echoed.

"Listen, Pastor," Bill began, "The members of the trustee board would like to schedule a meeting with you after the first of the year. We've formulated a business plan that we believe will set the course of this church's growth for the next decade."

"Yeah, the next decade," Arthur repeated while still doing his best to imitate a bobblehead doll.

"Tell you what, I'll give you a call the first week in January to set it up."

"I'd like that, Bill."

With that, Bill and Arthur excused themselves and left the building.

As soon as their car cleared the driveway, Horatio grabbed the Nexstar file and drove to the office of the church's insurance agent to fax the documents to Mary. In less than one hour the paperwork was received by Mary, and her commitment to correct the utility company's oversight was given.

She instructed Horatio to return to the church and power off the main breaker so the electricity could be safely turned back on. By the time he had accomplished that task, it was approaching eleven o'clock. He endeavored to stay at the church as long as he could tolerate the absence of heat and light. By twelve forty-five, he had waited long enough. Cold and hungry, he decided to pay a visit to Timmy Andrews. He confirmed the name and address of the diner by letting his fingers do the walking through the phone book. With the information necessary to program his car's navigation system, he went in search of Timmy. He arrived at the Stuffed Pig Diner twenty minutes later.

Entering in, he could immediately discern that the food had to be good. From one end of the service counter to the other, every seat was occupied. He further noticed that every customer there, both in booths and at the counter, was a flannel shirt-wearing, bearded, outdoors-type of man. He felt out of place. Timmy was working the grill with his back to the counter, so it took a few minutes before he noticed Horatio. While he waited, the cashier observed him standing off to the side.

"Are you here for lunch, sir?"

"Yes, thank you."

At that moment, a booth became available along the window wall of the restaurant. As Horatio made his way to the booth, he heard a voice call out.

"Pastor, is that you?"

Immediately, he recognized the voice as that of Timmy Andrews'.

"Timmy, how are you?"

"I guess I'm okay," he said as he removed the apron from around his waist. He walked over to shake Horatio's hand.

"I was hoping to catch up with you," Horatio explained. "In fact, the Sunday you came to church I tried to get your attention afterwards, but you left before I could get to you."

"Wow, Pastor, I didn't think you noticed me. In fact, at first I kept asking myself why I had even gone. Corey, can I take a break?" Timmy called out to the restaurant manager behind the counter.

"Ten minutes," the man responded.

Timmy sat at the booth and continued his conversation without breaking stride. "The message you gave that day made me glad that I did come."

"Thanks, Timmy. That blesses me more than you know."

"Pastor, how are things going for you at the church?"

"Well, to be sure it's interesting." Horatio chuckled.

"Really?" Timmy appeared surprised. "I thought it would be boring. I mean dull. Strike that," he offered, trying to extract himself from the hole that he was digging himself into. "Let me rephrase that. I thought that life as a pastor in Scituate or anywhere would be uneventful."

Horatio smiled. "You know, Timmy, I entered ministry somewhat reluctantly because while I wanted to help people, I didn't want to die of boredom doing it."

Timmy laughed.

Horatio continued, "Believe it or not, in the course of a day I might experience very few waking hours of quiet time."

Timmy appeared unconvinced.

"Pastor, other than Sunday church service and Wednesday night prayer meeting, what keeps you so busy?"

"Timmy, I've got to tell you people are hurting everywhere you look. They're desperately searching for answers or solutions to life-altering situations without success. Episodes of addiction, divorce, homelessness, sickness, depression, and fear have become a daily reality for people who have always believed that they had the solution or the ability to rely on themselves, only to realize that they do not. Being in the people-helping business, it's my profound privilege to be available to them in the way God leads me. Timmy, with all due respect, my role, my schedule is anything but boring or routine."

"Wow. I never thought about it like that," Timmy acknowledged. "So, I guess your trip to the hospital to see me was no big deal?"

"Nonsense," Horatio responded. "Every call, every visit is a big deal to me, and it's a big deal to God. Speaking of which, how have you been doing since the last time we spoke?"

"Things are getting better," Timmy began. "It's no secret that I was living recklessly. Nothing mattered more to me than having fun. As a result of my selfish attitude, I was hurting people. I hurt my mom. I hurt friends. It was like I was watching my life through an out-of-body experience and it was like a train wreck with a lot of casualties. I began to see my father in me. He was a miserable, miserable piece of work. He was especially abusive to my mom, my sister, and me. His own flesh and blood. Can you believe it?"

"Timmy, I'm sorry to hear that. I didn't know your father or your family history," Horatio offered apologetically.

"No problem, Pastor. He's long gone. Good riddance to bad rubbish, I always say." Timmy was aggravated by the memory. "Like I was saying, as soon as I realized that I was becoming more and more like my father, the better I understood that my family, my friends, the world would be better off without me."

Horatio understood Timmy's need to open up, so he listened as Timmy went further into detail. "Pastor, you don't know what it's like to actually hear voices day and night convincing you that you have no future. That you're better off dead. Or that God is never going to forgive you for stuff you've done, even though you've asked for forgiveness, time after time, after time."

Timmy's eyes began to tear up.

Horatio reached across the table and took Timmy's hand. "Timmy, do you understand what I'm doing?"

"Yeah. You're holding my hand," Timmy responded while looking around the restaurant, hoping that none of his coworkers or customers were paying close attention to what was taking place.

"Timmy. I am doing now what God will always do when you ask him," Horatio explained. "God, our Father, never fails to take us by the hand when we ask. His promise to us is that He will never ever leave us alone or forsake us. Do you believe that, Timmy? Have you ever known God to lie or make a promise that he didn't or couldn't keep?"

"I guess not."

Horatio continued, "I'll bet that looking back, you can recall situations or circumstances that you've found yourself in the middle of that, in all honesty, you can't remember how you safely made it out."

"Yeah," Timmy perked up. "Like the time you came to see me in the hospital. I knew I screwed up. I'm sorry. I meant to say 'messed up,' really bad. There I was lying on the floor of my friend's place all alone, after a night of partying. My heart started racing and everything in the room began to go in and out of focus. I was sure that I was gonna die without seeing my mom and sister again. My life flashed before my eyes. I could see the faces of people I had hurt who I wouldn't get to apologize to for things I'd done. I could see my mom standing over my casket, blaming herself for my death." Timmy paused as his eyes began to well up with tears.

"Timmy, let me ask you a question: do you believe that God loves you?"

"I hope so."

"Do you know that God's plan for your life is good?"

"After all the stuff I've done, I don't know how much 'good' there can be in me," Timmy replied, shaking his head from side to side.

"Timmy, break's over. We need you on the grill," his boss called out from behind the service window.

"Sorry. Timmy. I didn't mean to keep you so long. Please do this one thing for me…."

"What's that, Pastor?"

"Sometime, later today, when you're alone and it's quiet, ask our heavenly Father, in the name of Jesus, to show you his love. Discuss with Him all that you shared with me this afternoon: your fears, your regrets, and your doubts. That's all I'm requesting of you."

"Okay, I will."

"Let me know how it goes," Horatio requested as he signaled to the waitress that he was ready to place his order.

"I promise." Timmy stood to return to the kitchen.

Horatio ordered a Blue Plate special to go. When his order was ready, he paid the bill and returned directly to his office.

****

As he drove onto the church parking lot, he noticed that the lights were not yet on in the building.

"Great. This is just wonderful," he said sarcastically.

His focus turned to the prayer meeting scheduled to take place later that evening. "I'd better call everyone and let them know not to come tonight. It's going to be too cold in there. I don't want to be responsible for anyone getting sick."

At that point, he decided that two actions were necessary. First, call the utility company and give them a piece of his mind and, second, write out and place a note on the church's front door informing the church members who were not reachable by phone of the prayer meeting cancellation. Sitting behind the steering wheel of his car, he called the customer service telephone number listed on the orange disconnect notice that was left at the church earlier. After a minute or two of following telephone prompts, he was connected to a company representative. Immediately, he went on the offensive.

"Yes, thank you. My name is Horatio Smiley and I'm the pastor of the Church of the Good Shepherd in Scituate, Massachusetts. I'd like to be connected to a supervisor, please."

"Good afternoon, Pastor; perhaps I can help you. What seems to be the problem?" the service representative inquired.

"No, I'd like to speak to your supervisor," he responded, digging in his heels.

"Yes, sir. Hold one moment, please."

The service representative returned after a moment to inform him that a supervisor would assist him shortly.

"Hello, Pastor Smiley, this is Peggy Cogswell. How is everything at Good Shepherd today?"

"Not so good, Peggy," he sighed. "I'm not one to be easily frustrated, but today your company has really tried my patience."

"I'm so sorry to hear that, Pastor. What seems to be the problem?"

He took Peggy through the events relating to the disconnection of electric service at the church.

"Hold on; just a moment, please, Pastor Smiley. Let me see what the notes to the account read."

He heard an occasional, "Uh-huh" as Peggy reviewed the account.

"I see the problem here." Peggy explained, "There hasn't been a payment posted to your account since Sept. 22nd."

He could no longer contain himself. "Peggy, somebody needs to get their act together over there. I can't believe a company the size of Nexstar isn't able to accurately record payments to customer accounts. And then, to make matters worse, you take your own sweet time correcting the problems that you create. This is unbelievable!"

"Pastor, let me tell you what I see in your account history," Peggy continued, respectfully. "We did receive payments from you for the months of October and November. The problem is that the checks issued in payment to your account were payable to the gas company," Peggy continued, "Each time we returned the checks to the church along with a letter requesting that a replacement check be issued to avoid service interruption. Further," she noticed, "several calls were placed through our automated system requesting that someone from the Church's office would contact our collections department to resolve the problem. No one returned our calls, so eventually the account was scheduled for shut off."

Horatio was silent.

Peggy continued, "You submitted the paperwork that was requested to restore service, and even though what you submitted confirmed the information that we have in our system, we dispatched one of our service vehicles to restore power to the church within one hour of your call this morning, as a courtesy."

He had a sick feeling in the pit of his stomach.

"Peggy, I apologize," was all he could think to say. "Are you telling me the power is restored?" he asked with humility.

"Yes, sir," Peggy continued. "Did you turn the main breaker on at the panel?"

"No, not yet," he answered sheepishly.

"Well, Pastor, what would make you think that the power wasn't restored? Didn't you read the white service restoral card left at your front door?"

Now, it was Peggy's time to become agitated.

"Peggy," Horatio began, "I haven't even made it to the front door of the church yet," he confessed. "Please, hold on for just a moment." He walked from his car to the front door of the church.

There hanging on the doorknob was a white card, identical in size to the orange disconnect card that he received earlier. Reading the card while Peggy remained on the phone, he was instructed to return the main breaker on the electric panel to the "on" position to power up the building.

"Peggy, what can I say to redeem myself? This is so unlike me."

"Pastor, we all have days we'd like to forget." Peggy chuckled. "I've visited your church before and I promise to not let this episode deter me from visiting again. Don't worry. Have a great day, and always remember the scripture that says you may be entertaining angels unaware."

For the remainder of the afternoon, Horatio repented for his poor witness as God's representative. Church meeting began promptly at six o'clock. The building was warm and well lit. Loretta Andrews was present, as promised, with fourteen other prayer warriors. The meeting concluded at seven thirty. Horatio returned home immediately thereafter.

Day 11
December 13th - Thursday

At seven fifteen, Horatio awoke from a restless sleep. Experiencing episodes of tossing and turning throughout the night, he continued to dwell on his ordeal with the utility company. Convicted by his conduct, he decided to send flowers and a note of apology to Peggy Cogswell, the Nexstar Customer Service supervisor.

He was showered, dressed and on his way to the office before eight o'clock. Having a renewed sense of appreciation for electricity, he thanked God for everyone who shared in the ability to harness and mass-distribute it. Nexstar's corporate office was fifty miles away, so he ordered a floral arrangement to be delivered by a flower shop near Peggy's office. He received a confirming message that the flowers would be delivered before noon. With that task completed, he turned his attention to the pile of paperwork on his desk. Separating the Christmas cards from the remaining paperwork, he opened and strategically placed the cards that were hand-signed throughout his office. Other cards that appeared to be signed mechanically were placed in the trash. He was a bit old-fashioned. Before the last few cards were put into place, the office phone rang.

"Good morning, Good Shepherd."

"Hi, Pastor. Its Timmy. Timmy Andrews."

"Oh, good morning, Timmy. And how are you doing today?"

"Man, oh man, Pastor! I couldn't wait to call and tell you what happened." Timmy was excited.

"What's going on?"

"Well, remember what you told me to do yesterday? You know, you told me to ask God to show his love for me."

"Oh, yes. I remember," Horatio recalled. "Did God move on your request?"

"He sure did. It was amazing."

"Tell me what happened." Horatio was caught up in Timmy's enthusiasm.

"Pastor, I'd rather tell you in person. Are you gonna be in your office today?"

"I expect to be, but you remember what I told you, yesterday: I'm on call." Horatio chuckled, continuing to emphasize that there is nothing "boring" about ministry.

"I get your point, Pastor. I'm not working today. Is it okay if I stop by for a few minutes?"

"Timmy, my door is always open to you. By all means, c'mon over." His invitation was quickly accepted.

"I can be there in thirty minutes."

"Great. I'll be here waiting for you. See you soon."

The call ended.

There was something about Timmy that reminded Horatio of himself when he was younger. He considered the time he would spend with Timmy as an opportunity to make amends to God for his poor witness the day before in the Peggy Cogswell situation.

Not long thereafter, he heard a car pulling onto the parking lot. Looking out the window, he recognized Timmy behind the wheel. He met Timmy at the door and escorted him back to his office.

"Tell me, Timmy, what happened to get you so excited?" he asked, before settling back into his chair.

"Pastor, it was like something out of a movie," Timmy explained. "I prayed just like you instructed me. I said, 'Father, in the name of Jesus, please show your love for me.' I apologized for things that I had done that I knew were selfish and wrong. Anyway, while praying, I began to get a headache. I'm not sure whether the headache was there before I began praying or not. Anyway, I didn't have anything for the pain, so I decided to go to the store."

Horatio listened as Timmy continued. "The intensity of the pain in my head spiked as I put on my coat to leave. Something within me said, 'Just stay here and lie down.' I decided to go anyway, since I already had my coat on. I remember how another spike of headache pain doubled me over as I reached for the door handle to leave. Anyway," Timmy continued, "I made it to the store and found what I was after, when this little girl appeared at my side. 'She looked up at me and said, 'Jesus loves you.' Then she turned around and waved good-bye as she walked away. Pastor, I never saw that little girl before. I have no idea who she was or why she said Jesus loves me. Then, it clicked. God answered my prayer. And then I came to understand that whatever that thing was that came against me through the headache pain was to try to keep me from receiving His answer. Wow! The more I thought about it, the more I understood that something very dark had been assigned against me and it doesn't want me to know that God loves me. He has forgiven me. God has really forgiven me." Timmy's eyes welled up with profound relief.

Horatio was excited. "Timmy, God is so good. I can tell you from personal experience that His love is perfect and unconditional."

"Pastor, this experience has opened my eyes to see that it's not too late for me. The night I ended up in the emergency room from the overdose, I was convinced that there was nothing good left in me. I believed, like I told you yesterday, that I and everyone else would be better off with me dead. I need to discuss some things that I'm dealing with. Is that okay with you?"

"Absolutely, Timmy. The scripture in James 5:16 instructs us to confess our sins one to another, that in that day we would pray for each other that we might be healed. Please," Horatio continued, "tell me what's going on."

"Pastor," Timmy began, "the reason that I tried to check out by overdosing was because I had crossed a line that I was sure I was going to burn in hell for. I wrecked a girl's life and nothing I could do would undo the damage that I had caused. The sweetest, kindest person I've ever known trusted me to return the kindness and respect that she showed me and I took advantage of her. Something within me caused me to seduce her and then disconnect from her, as if she was just another notch in my belt."

Horatio's eyes grew wide. Inwardly, he processed: *Could this be Sara Reynolds he's talking about?* Saying nothing, he allowed Timmy to speak without interruption.

"All I knew, Pastor, was I had no future with this girl. I remembered how my father treated my mother. I wanted no part in bringing devastation to anyone's life like he did over and over again. The greatest favor I could do for Sara was to disappear."

Unaware that he had revealed that it was Sara, Timmy continued on. Horatio was positioned on the edge of his seat, trying to remain silent.

"When she came to tell me that she was pregnant, I told her to do what she had to do but, forget about me," Timmy recalled with a heavy heart. "Pastor, the fact of the matter is that I do care a great deal for her. I want to marry her and be a family." Timmy hung his head. "But I'm so afraid of doing more damage than good to any chance that she and the baby might have for a better life." Again, his eyes filled with tears.

"Timmy, why are you so convinced that you can't be a good husband to the young lady and father to your child?"

"I don't know, Pastor. I guess I don't expect things like that to come into my life because, after all, I am my father's seed." He continued, "I've always been told that, as the old saying goes, an apple doesn't fall far from the tree."

"Timmy, are you familiar with the scripture that reminds us that the power of life and death is in our tongue? You need to believe in your heart that God desires a blessed future for your life, not a cursed one. And, to be sure, that blessing doesn't usually come magically. We have to be obedient and fully yielded to God's will. We have to trust that He knows what's best for us better than we know for ourselves."

"Wow, that's deep, Pastor."

Horatio emphasized, "There is One who is able to do more for you than you could ever expect. His name is Jesus. After all, He loved you so much that He gave His life for you before you were formed in your mother's womb. And God, Our Father, has given you His Holy Spirit as a Comforter and Counselor to lead you through all that you experience every minute of every day. God wants to be first in your life."

Timmy could only respond, "Wow. Pastor, how do I begin to clean up this mess I've made? I want to do better."

"Well, let's begin with your situation with the young lady. I believe you said her name was Sara." He was seeking confirmation that Timmy was in fact speaking of Sara Reynolds.

"Where is your heart in all of this?" Horatio asked.

For the next two hours, he listened as Timmy discussed his feelings for Sara and the joy that he experienced whenever they were together. He told Horatio that he would give everything to share the rest of his life with her.

At that point, Horatio asked, "Have you told Sara this?"

"I don't know how I can," Timmy processed. "With the money I'm making at the diner, I can't afford to provide for her and the baby. I can't expect her to get excited about scrimping, saving and trying to make ends meet for the rest of her life, or" Timmy paused, "looking to our mothers for help when they're struggling themselves."

"Timmy, have you asked Sara how she feels about all of this?"

"Umm, no. Not yet"

"Timmy, are we speaking about Sara Reynolds?" By now it was obvious that it could only be her.

"How did you know that?" Timmy was stunned.

"Well, not to betray a trust, but I ran into her the other day. She was distraught about sharing some news with her mother," Horatio continued. "You really need to have a deep, heartfelt conversation with her. I believe that she deserves that much honesty from you, at the very least."

"Pastor, I feel like such a fool," Timmy confessed. "She's been trying to reach me at my job but I haven't returned her calls. I didn't know what to say."

Horatio was becoming frustrated with Timmy.

"How in God's name can you justify that?" he asked, trying not to be critical of him.

"I don't know. I don't know." Timmy hung his head.

"You're leaving this precious young lady alone to clean up a sensitive situation that you have an equal share in." Horatio was dumbfounded. "Why would you do such a thing?"

"At the time, it seemed to be the best thing to do," Timmy explained. "But now I see how selfish and cowardly a thing that was." He pleaded, "Pastor, please help me to make this right."

"Timmy, has Sara discussed any of this with her mother yet?"

"I'm not sure," Timmy responded. "The last message she left for me said that she was waiting for a good time to tell her mom. I think her mom was dealing with something, so Sara held off."

"I suggest that you call Sara immediately," Horatio instructed. "Ask her to meet with you before saying anything about this to her mother. Go ahead," he said, handing Timmy the phone.

Timmy took the phone and called Sara.

"Hello, Mrs. Reynolds, this is Timmy Andrews. How are you, ma'am? That's good. I'm fine, ma'am. Thank you for asking. Is Sara home? No. Could you please let her know that I called and I'll try her again later? About six o'clock, you say? Okay, I'll call back after six. Oh, yes. My mom's doing fine. Yes, I'll let her know you were asking about her. Thank you again, Mrs. Reynolds. Bye." Timmy hung up the phone.

Turning back to Horatio, he said, "She won't be home until sometime after six o'clock."

"Well, Timmy," Horatio suggested, "let's use this time to figure out what the Lord wants us to do next."

"How do we do that?" Timmy asked.

"We get down on our knees and pray."

Timmy knelt beside him and they prayed. Timmy wasn't big on prayer at that point, but that was all about to change. As Horatio took the lead, Timmy came to understand that there was nothing more that God required in coming before His Throne of Grace than the confession of Jesus Christ as Lord and a sincere heart. Timmy's prayer was touching. The presence of God's Spirit was undeniably present in that room. Emerging from their time in prayer, Horatio confided what he heard the voice of God saying to him as they prayed.

He said, "In my spirit, I heard the Lord telling me to go with you to buy Sara an engagement ring."

Timmy's mouth was agape. "How did you know what I was thinking?"

"I didn't, but God knew," Horatio replied.

"Amazing," was all that Timmy could offer in response.

"Yes, He is," Horatio confirmed with an "I told you so" chuckle. "What do you say we take a walk over to the jewelry store on Front Street?"

"Pastor, I can't afford a ring."

"Timmy, it doesn't cost anything to look at rings last time I checked. Has something changed in the practice of window-shopping?"

"No, I guess it wouldn't hurt to look," Timmy acknowledged.

They put on their coats and walked to the jewelry store. Ten minutes later, they were looking at engagement rings.

"Wow, that's a nice one there," Timmy said, pointing to a ring with a one-half carat solitaire. "How much for that one?" he asked the jeweler.

Removing it from the case for closer examination, the jeweler looked at the price tag and said, "Nineteen hundred ninety-five dollars."

Timmy's enthusiasm quickly departed. "I'll never be able to afford something that nice," he muttered.

"Timmy, have you already forgotten our discussion about the power of life and death being in the tongue? Don't limit the Lord's ability. Ask Him to take charge in this." Horatio winked.

"You're right," Timmy acknowledged. "That's one bad habit that I've got to break."

"Amen to that," Horatio agreed.

Speaking to the jeweler, Horatio asked, "Sir, if we pay cash for this ring right now, what is the best price you can give us?" He gave Timmy a look as if to say, *Let me show you how it's done, little brother.*

"I can take fifty dollars off," the jeweler responded.

"Can you give us a moment, please?" Horatio requested of the jeweler.

Taking Timmy to the side, he reminded Timmy of their prayer before coming to the jewelry store. He then instructed Timmy to stand off to the side and silently pray that as Horatio continued to speak with the merchant, God would bless him with great favor with the man. Timmy complied.

"Sir, that young man," Horatio said, pointing to Timmy, "is about to propose marriage to a fine young lady this evening. He isn't able to afford the nineteen hundred forty-five dollars that you are asking for this ring. Can you do any better than that?"

The man stroked his chin and responded, "I can take another fifty dollars off, but that would be the best I can offer."

"I'm afraid that's beyond this young man's reach."

"You know," the jeweler said, as if remembering something that he had not considered earlier, "I have some rings back in the office that I have taken in from customers as credit toward the purchase of new rings. I can give you a really good deal on those."

"May we see them?" Horatio asked.

The merchant retreated to a room off to the side of the showroom and returned with two trays of rings.

"Take a look at these and see if anything interests you," he suggested.

By this time, Timmy was standing alongside Horatio. At first glance, the rings appeared to be old and dull. Not something that would be pleasing to a recipient.

"I don't see anything here that I like," Timmy said.

"Young man," the merchant said, addressing Timmy. "Look very carefully at what is before you. Sometimes we have to examine opportunities to recognize a hidden blessing." He winked at Horatio.

The rings, as presented, had not yet undergone the process of cleaning and restoration.

"Rings are like great classic books," the jeweler began, "They don't make them like they used to."

"Timmy," Horatio instructed, "use your imagination and try to envision how these rings looked when they were new. Do you see anything here that might be of interest to you?"

Timmy looked again.

"I suppose this one could have been nice," he responded, pointing to one of the rings.

"How much for this one?" Horatio asked.

"I can clean this one up nicely and have it in a box for you by the end of the day for, let's say, one thousand dollars," the merchant offered.

"One thousand dollars?" Timmy responded. "Pastor, I don't have a thousand dollars right now."

"Timmy, that's what I like to hear," Horatio responded.

"What, that I don't have one thousand dollars?" Timmy asked.

"No, that you don't have one thousand dollars, RIGHT NOW."

The jeweler, bearing witness to the exchange, understood what was taking place.

"Young man," the jeweler interrupted, "you look very familiar. Don't you work at the Stuffed Pig Diner?"

"Yes, sir,"

The jeweler continued, "I was there one day last week ordering lunch for my wife and I to bring back to the shop. When my order was ready, I reached for my wallet, only to find that I had left it here on my desk."

"Oh, yeah," Timmy remembered. "I thought you looked familiar. I couldn't place your face."

The jeweler continued, "You covered my tab. You paid my bill and you didn't even know me." The man continued, "I told my wife what had happened and how the cook paid for our food. She thought I was pulling her leg. Please, stay right here. This will only take a minute."

The jeweler reached for the phone behind the counter and quickly dialed a number.

"Amber. It's me. You'll never believe this. Remember the other day I went to get us lunch and forgot my wallet? Yeah. The young man who I told you paid my tab is here in the store. Yeah, seriously." Turning to Timmy, the jeweler passed the phone to him, "My wife has something to ask you."

Timmy shyly took the phone, "Hello. Yes, ma'am. I'm here with my pastor looking at engagement rings. Yes, ma'am. No, I expect to propose to her tonight. I couldn't afford a new one so we're looking at a used one. Yes, ma'am. Okay. Thank you. Nice speaking with you also." Timmy, passing the phone back to the merchant, said, "Your wife wants to speak with you again."

Timmy and Horatio waited patiently as the jeweler and his wife spoke. After the man hung up the phone, he returned and took the trays of used rings to the back office.

Unclear as to what was going on, Horatio asked, "Is everything okay?"

The jeweler, returning to his position behind the counter, reached into the showcase and, removing the ring that Timmy first liked, placed in on a blue velvet display cloth.

Looking at Timmy, the jeweler asked, "Can you afford to pay fourteen hundred dollars for this ring?"

Timmy was in disbelief. "Why would you lower your price like that?" he asked.

"Son, someday after you've been a married man for a while, you'll understand."

Horatio chuckled as he thanked God for the favor Timmy had been given with the man.

"Well, I don't have the money yet, but I'll work extra hours at my job to get it as quickly as possible."

"That might not be necessary," the jeweler began. "My wife wants me to ask you about working for us here, you know, part time, until we can make sure that it's going to be a good fit. Are you interested?"

"Yes. Definitely," Timmy responded. "How much do you pay an hour?"

"How's twelve-fifty an hour?" the jeweler asked.

"Awesome," Timmy continued. "I'll have that ring paid off in no time."

"By the way," the man added, "I'll box up the ring and you can take it with you. Pastor, you'll vouch for Timmy?"

"Absolutely," Horatio responded.

The man quickly cleaned the ring and placed it in a fancy box and bag. Timmy agreed to report for work the following Monday. Before leaving the store, the jeweler, familiar with Good Shepherd, promised to visit the church with his wife. He asked Timmy to give him a call the next day to let him know how his fiancée liked the ring.

"My fiancée. My fiancée," Timmy repeated. "I like the sound of that." He agreed and thanked the jeweler for his help in making this a very exciting time in his life. Timmy and Horatio returned to the church after picking up a sandwich along the way.

Back at his office, Horatio and Timmy continued to revisit the way that God responded to their prayer. Timmy was like a child who had just witnessed a rabbit being pulled from a magician's hat. They agreed that the following order of business would be the most honorable:

Timmy would ask his mother to accompany him to Sara's home that evening. Horatio would not be present but would be available if needed. Timmy would apologize to Sara, Mrs. Reynolds, and his mother for the hurt and disappointment he had caused. With Sara's consent, he would break the news to everyone about her condition. As Sara's mother was her only parent, he would ask her for Sara's hand in marriage. All of this would begin after he and Horatio spent the rest of the afternoon in prayer. Timmy left Horatio's office at four fifteen, after promising to call at the first opportunity and apprise him of the evening's events.

The call came at six forty-two that evening. It was Timmy, Sara, Mrs. Reynolds, and Mrs. Andrews on a speakerphone. Everyone was laughing and celebrating with tears of joy. Timmy's proposal of marriage to Sara was enthusiastically endorsed by Mrs. Reynolds and blushingly accepted by the bride-to-be. They all thanked Horatio for the role he played in helping Timmy and for bringing so much joy to their families. Before the call ended, Horatio scheduled a December 19th premarital counseling session for the soon-to-be newlyweds. Timmy and Sara asked Horatio to be their baby's godfather. He graciously accepted.

"Thank you Lord for the do-over," he said as he turned off the lights and headed home. He was in bed by eleven o'clock that evening.

Day 12
December 14th - Friday

At nine fifteen as Horatio was walking to his office, he noticed an older model pickup truck parked at the curb in front of the church. He observed two heads, one of a man and the other a woman, in the cab of the truck. Sensing that the people in the truck were watching and perhaps waiting for him, he acknowledged them with a wave. Reaching to put the key in the door of the church, he heard car doors opening and closing and then footsteps walking up behind him. Turning around, he noticed a man, woman, and two young children approaching.

"Are you Pastor Smiley?" the man asked.

"Good morning. Yes, I'm Pastor Smiley. How may I help you?"

"Pastor, my name is Ted Willis. This is my wife, Ellen, and our children, Noah and Becky." The man continued, "We were evicted from our place four days ago. Everything we own is in the back of our truck."

"I'm so sorry to hear that. How can I help you?"

"I was wondering if you know of a shelter or facility that we could stay at until I can get my bearings on what to do?" Ted explained. "We've been going through hell for the past fourteen months ever since I lost my job at the boatyard. We've been through some tough situations before but never anything this bad."

"Well," Horatio replied, "Come on inside and let's see what we can find out."

Once inside, he asked Ted if they had a church home. In cases where someone in need has a church home, he would redirect them to their church. This was a policy to ensure the church's resources would first be used to assist Good Shepherd's church members or others who were 'unchurched.' Ted assured him that his family did not attend church. At that, Horatio continued on to his office with the Willis family in tow, to make phone calls in search of emergency assistance. With each phone call, he noticed a look of desperation registering on Ted's face. Although help was available for food and clothing, four empty beds could not be located at any of the shelters within twenty miles of Scituate.

"Pastor? Would it be okay if my wife and the children wait in another part of the building for a while? Perhaps somewhere where they can stretch out on the floor and rest?"

"Sure." Horatio added, "They can wait in the sanctuary. There are sheets and blankets around here somewhere. Let me see if I can locate them. Come with me."

He led Mrs. Willis and the children into the sanctuary and invited them to sit down. Within a few minutes, he returned with blankets draped over his arms.

"Mrs. Willis, you, Becky, and Noah make yourself comfortable while Ted and I work to locate shelter for you."

Mrs. Willis, fragile from all that had taken place in the course of the last four days, gave Horatio a hug and managed a heartfelt "Thank you, Pastor."

Back in his office, Horatio and Ted placed calls to more distant homeless shelters. A bed was available in Plymouth, another in Woburn, and two in Haverhill. The Willis family had a decision to make. The choice was an easy one. They did not want to be separated. Ted confided in Horatio that he and Ellen considered giving temporary custody of their children to the state's foster care system to, at the very least, ensure that they would be together. Earlier in the week, Ted had placed a call to the state agency that manages the foster care system and learned that there would be no guaranty that Noah and Becky would remain together. While Ted and Ellen could live in the truck, it would be unacceptable for their children to endure that hardship. They prayed for an answer to their dilemma.

Today, while driving through Scituate, Ted explained his truck stalled in front of the church. Sitting on the side of the road, they noticed the sign identifying "Horatio Smiley, Senior Pastor."

"Well," Horatio offered, "It certainly appears that the hand of God brought you here and I can understand the choice you made, not wanting to be separated. In light of the fact that your family is probably exhausted and hungry, how about spending the weekend at my house, next door? It's highly unlikely that any decent shelter will be located before Monday morning."

"Oh, Pastor. Are you sure that's okay?"

"Ted. If I did anything less, I would be a hypocrite in the eyes of the Lord. The house is small, but I think that it will do for a few nights."

Ted gave him a great big bear hug and ran out to tell his wife the news. "Ellen, Pastor will let us stay with him the weekend. We'll be together."

Ted and Ellen hugged each other. It was an answer to their prayer, albeit short-lived. The children, understanding that this was a moment of celebration, joined in to form a group hug. Horatio directed Mrs. Willis and the children to go and wait on the front porch of the house while Ted parked his truck in the church parking lot.

Ted motioned sheepishly to Horatio, but he didn't understand what it was that Ted was trying to say. Walking nearer to Ted, he could hear Ted whisper, "My truck is out of gas."

Horatio gave a nod to let Ted know that he understood.

"Ted. On second thought, why don't you leave the truck where it is. It will be easier to unload from there rather than from the parking lot."

Ted gave Horatio a wink and a very grateful smile.

Inside the parsonage, two bedrooms were set up for the Willis family. Towels and washcloths were provided so that each family member could begin their stay with a nice hot bath. While they took turns cleaning up, Horatio cooked a large pot of pasta and sauce. Sitting around the dinner table, Ted and Ellen shared much of what had taken place in their lives since Ted lost his job as a shipbuilder fourteen months ago.

The family's home was foreclosed after falling behind in mortgage payments. Eventually they moved into a small run-down apartment that Ted agreed to repair as partial payment toward the monthly rent. According to Ted, an agreement with their former landlord to install three new kitchens and bathrooms, miscellaneous electrical repairs, and some exterior painting would allow them to pay $500.00 monthly for the first year of their tenancy. Ted expected that within that time, he would be able to find employment and subsequently get back on sound financial footing. He was unable to find employment, so he worked seven days a week for five months in completing all that his agreement with his landlord required. Unbeknownst to the Ted and Ellen, their landlord sold the property and left them to fend for themselves with the new owner.

Understandably, the new owner of the property did not honor the arrangement with the previous owner. Receiving only $730.00 monthly in unemployment benefits and unable to afford the $1,250.00 monthly rental rate, the new landlord moved quickly to evict them.

They, then, relocated to a local motel until their money ran out. With no money and no gas, they found themselves sitting in front of the Church of the Good Shepherd.

"Pastor, I've got to tell you," Ted began, "a church is the last place I thought we'd end up getting any help. Every day I see so many people who go out of their way to let you know that they are Christians. At the same time, these same people gossip, judge, and take advantage of people in need. I've felt more love inside a wrestling ring than I have in most churches. If I had gas in my truck, I probably would have just kept going."

"Ted, all that you're saying is much of what is wrong in churches these days. For so long, Christians have viewed their salvation as a coronation rather than a calling. For years, I have tried as a layperson and a pastor to open people's eyes to the damage we do by not seizing every opportunity to let the Lord move through us and not in spite of us. We have to learn to truly walk in love. Not only when it's comfortable or convenient, but always. I haven't given up and I pray that I never will. There are so many hurting people in the world."

Dinner was "delicious" according to Noah and Becky. After, they watched television in their bedroom while Ellen, Ted, and Horatio talked about everything from childhood experiences, religion, politics, the economy, to personal aspirations. The day was spent laughing, crying, and encouraging each other.

Horatio thoroughly enjoyed his time with his guests. He hadn't realized how much he missed having company in his home. They continued to talk until eleven thirty. Bidding each other a good night, they retired for the evening.

Day 13
December 15th - Saturday

Uncertain if it was the sound of hammering outside or the smell of coffee brewing and bacon frying in the kitchen, Horatio woke up at eight fifteen. Quickly getting dressed, he made his way to the kitchen to see all of what was going on. Poking his head inside the door opening, he saw Ellen and Becky engaged in bit of mother and daughter conversation. Becky was telling her mom how much she liked being in a house and not at that "scary" hotel. She asked her mom if she thought they would ever again have their own house.

"Becky, I believe with all my heart that there is a beautiful house somewhere just waiting for us to find it. It might not be very big. It might need a lot of fixing up, but I know that as long as Noah and you and your daddy and I can be together, it will be the happiest home in the whole wide world."

As Ellen finished her reply, Horatio entered in.

"Good morning. Did everyone sleep well last night?"

"Perfectly," Ellen responded. "In fact, Ted slept well beyond his usual five thirty wake up time. He's been dealing with so much, lately, that he doesn't rest well anymore."

"I'm happy to hear that he managed to get some rest," Horatio continued. "It's got to be mighty tough to go through all that he's been dealing with." Changing the subject, he asked, "So what's going on in the kitchen this morning? This old stove hasn't seen this much activity since I've lived here."

"I hope you don't mind, Pastor," Ellen explained, "I had a couple of dollars in change, so Ted and Noah walked to the store and picked up a can of coffee, a few eggs, and some bacon. We wanted to fix you breakfast as a token of our gratitude."

"Thank you so much." Horatio was touched. "What are Ted and Noah up to outside?"

"Ted noticed a few broken spindles on your porch railing yesterday, so he and Noah went out to fix them."

"That's not necessary," Horatio explained, "those spindles were like that before I moved into this house. Please, have Ted and Noah come in and have some breakfast."

"Pastor, we want you to eat. We don't need breakfast," Ellen explained. "We usually eat one meal a day, about noontime. We'll be fine, thank you."

"Ellen, I will not eat breakfast alone," he insisted. "As my guests, I am asking you all to have breakfast with me." Horatio was sticking to his guns.

"Maybe I can convince Ted to have some coffee," Ellen postured.

"Coffee and eggs and bacon," Horatio insisted.

"Pastor, we weren't able to buy but enough for you," Ellen responded with a bit of embarrassment.

"Ellen, the Willis family is in this house as my guests. If I am to eat, we all are to eat." He remained insistent. "Now, I'd like you to tell me about the best breakfast that you and Ted ever had. Leave nothing out."

Uncertain as to the reason why he was asking this question, Ellen indulged him. "Well," she began, "it was Christmas morning nine years ago. Mr. Collins, the owner of the boatyard, gave Ted a bonus. It was the biggest check Ted had ever received. There was a restaurant that we used to go to before we got married. Each time we went there, on the way we would tell each other everything that we were going to order. We were like kids in a candy store." Ellen paused to smile, as she reminisced. "Ted would order up ham steaks, bacon, fried potatoes, biscuits, and honey. I ordered pancakes with strawberries, and a western omelet. We ate so much that we couldn't eat again for two days." She began to laugh.

"I haven't eaten like that in years myself." Horatio recalled with a smile. "Ellen, make a list of everything we need to make a meal exactly like the one you just described," he instructed. "Leave nothing out. While you get the pots and pans ready, I'll head for the market and gather up the ingredients. We're going to fix Ted a breakfast that will make him forget everything that has come against him for the last fourteen months, if only for a little while."

Becky, getting caught up in the excitement, began to leap up and down, while clapping her hands.

"Shhhh, Becky," Ellen cautioned. "We're going to surprise Daddy. Okay?"

Becky nodded her head and put her finger to her lips.

Within a few minutes, Ellen had prepared the list.

Horatio perused it. "What about some juice?"

"Mercy, I forgot the orange juice," Ellen acknowledged.

"I'm off." Slipping out the side door so he would not be noticed by Ted and Noah, Horatio headed to the Village Mart. Twenty-five minutes later, he returned with four bags of groceries. He could hear Ted and Noah still at work. Ellen had begun preparing the pots and pans, with Becky as her helper. Horatio went outside to keep Ted occupied for the time that Ellen indicated that she would need to pull off the surprise. To ensure that Ted and Noah didn't come inside the house until it was time, he walked Ted around the exterior of the church building, asking for pointers about repairs that needed to be budgeted for the main structure. Before time for the work assessment to be completed, Becky came looking for Ted and Noah.

"Daddy. Mommy said she needs you and Noah, and you have to come now."

"Well, Noah, I guess we better see what your mom wants us for," Ted chuckled.

Noah seemed thankful for the break. Picking up the tools, they headed back to the house. Before they got inside the door, the smell of fresh brewed coffee and home cooking greeted them.

Walking in, Ted couldn't help but ask, "What's that cooking? Do I smell ham and fried potatoes? Ellen, what are you up to?"

Seeing a table set before him with all of his favorite foods, he stood there speechless with his mouth wide open.

"Please sit down, honey. Let us take care of you today" was all Ellen needed to say. A few words, yet a mouthful.

"Oh, Ellen," Ted whispered as he embraced her, "I love you so much. Thank you."

For the next thirty minutes mouths were moving nonstop, but not many words were being spoken. An occasional, "Please pass this" or "Please pass that" broke the silence, but that was the extent of conversation. Horatio enjoyed every minute of it. From time to time he would just start laughing. The laughter was contagious. After breakfast, Ted, Noah, and Horatio praised Ellen and Becky for preparing the best breakfast any of them could remember eating, ever. They cleaned up the kitchen while Ellen and Becky relaxed. Horatio encouraged Ellen to seriously consider cooking as a profession.

After the kitchen work was completed, Horatio prepared for his usual Saturday afternoon visit to the nursing home. Prior to leaving, he offered Ted fifty dollars for the porch repairs. Ted refused the money, so he handed it over to Ellen. The Willises prepared to leave the house while Horatio was out, but planned to meet him back at the house at five o'clock that evening.

At the nursing home, Horatio caught up with all that had happened with his "extended" family, since he last saw them. Christmas decorations were prominently displayed for all to see. As everyone gathered together in the community room, seasonal songs were sung and later, he read Matthew Chapter 1:18 through Chapter 2. At four thirty, his visit concluded with a nursing home tradition: the reading of the poem "The Night Before Christmas" by one of the nurses. After that, he bade everyone good-bye and promised to return the following weekend. He headed directly home to meet the Willises.

Pulling into his driveway, he noticed that the Willises' truck was already there. Becky and Noah waved. Ted and Ellen exited the truck with a stack of papers in hand.

"Hi, guys," Horatio greeted with his familiar smile. "Looks like you've had a busy afternoon. What's all the paperwork?"

"We went to the library to use their computer," Ted began. "I found a few leads in the 'Help Wanted' listings that I'll follow up on first thing Monday morning."

"That's great, Ted. You are a very gifted man. I watched the attention to detail you demonstrated in repairing the porch spindles. If you need a reference, put my name on those applications."

Ted laughed. "Well, I tell you, Pastor, you won't get to spend the greater portion of your life building boats if you don't pay attention to detail. You'll be out of a job real fast."

"I see your point." Horatio chuckled. "Let's go on inside. It's getting cold out here." Horatio boiled a pot of water. He and Ted had tea while Ellen and the children had hot cocoa. Noah and Becky were watching television in another room while the grown-ups continued talking in the kitchen.

"Pastor," Ted began, "Ellie and I aren't sure whether we're ready to return to church. We don't want to go out of obligation. It would feel … you know, phony. We appreciate everything that you've done for us, but I gotta tell you we have had a real problem sitting in a room full of hypocrites trying to look like we're happy to be there."

"When I opened this house to you and your children, I did it because that is what the Word of God tells me to do. I honor my father and my mother because, again, that is what the Word of God instructs me to do." He continued, "Scripture tells me that I am not to lean to my own understanding but inquire of God first in every situation. I, too, often make decisions without waiting for confirmation from God. Does that qualify me as a hypocrite? The short answer is absolutely. It also qualifies me as human and imperfect." He explained, "Our church, like any other church, is comprised of imperfect human beings. Now, if I made the decision to open up the church exclusively to people who are perfect, the pews would be empty, the Sunday School would be empty, and the pulpit would be empty. Interestingly, where the highest level of 'acknowledged' imperfection exists, the Spirit of God is able to move best. Jesus came to save us all because we all need saving. There is no such thing as a perfect human."

"Uncle, Uncle. Okay. I get the point." Ted laughed. "I give. I give. Ellen, I guess we need to head up to bed. We don't want to be late for church in the morning."

Ellen chuckled.

"Thanks, Pastor. You're good," Ted acknowledged.

"Anytime," Horatio responded while unsuccessfully trying to maintain a straight face. "Church begins at ten thirty."

Day 14
December 16th - Sunday

Horatio and the Willis family were in church by ten o'clock. He noticed that the familiar spirit of heaviness he experienced most Sunday mornings was absent today. Entering inside, he greeted a few parishioners while introducing the Willises before heading to his office. Before the start of morning service, he prayed for the presence of God to manifest in the church and dispel all darkness from the people, the building, and the community. He left from his office, believing that God had heard and would respond to his prayer.

Promptly at ten thirty, he stepped behind the lectern. Looking out into the congregation, he noticed George and Mattie Heywood among others who had been such a blessing to him. It had become increasingly difficult for the Heywoods to attend church as regularly as they once did because of George's chronic arthritis. It was difficult for him to walk or drive without discomfort.

As the praise and worship went forth, Horatio silently thanked God for every one of the church members present and absent. The headcount numbered between 125 and 150, which was above average for the Sunday service before the annual Christmas event. That service headcount averaged 250. Horatio ministered as God gave him instruction. At the conclusion of the service, several people confirmed that the message he gave was meant personally for them. He remembered one parishioner telling him, "Someone must have told you all about what I've been struggling with."

"No," Horatio replied, "I have no personal knowledge of your situation. But," he continued, "nothing is hidden from God. He knows what you're going through."

Horatio sensed that God was moving somehow in Good Shepherd and in him. The Heywoods made their way over to him before he could get to them.

"Hello, Pastor," George began. "Wonderful message today."

"Thanks, George. I think that I was blessed by it even more than you were." He continued, "George and Mattie, there's someone I'd like you to meet."

Motioning to Ted and Ellen, they came together at the front of the church.

"Ted and Ellen, meet my dear friends, Mr. and Mrs. Heywood."

"Hold on," interrupted George. "My parents were Mr. and Mrs. Heywood. I am George and this is my bride, Mattie. Ted and Ellen, we are pleased to know you."

Laughter erupted.

"Forgive me, George." Horatio continued, "Now, as I was saying, these are my dear friends, George and Mattie Heywood, and these are my new friends, Ted and Ellen Willis."

"Willis, huh?" George asked. "I was in the Army with a fella named Willis. We were based out of Fort Bragg together back during the Vietnam war. He was a quiet guy. In fact, I didn't even know he was from Scituate until the day he got shot up. As we waited for the medics to come, he kept talking about how bad he wanted to make it back home to his wife and son. Then, he mentioned something about climbing to the top of Scituate Light. That's when it connected. He was a real nice guy."

"That was my father," Ted acknowledged. "He never made it home. From what I was told, he died before they could get him to the military hospital in Landstuhl."

"I'm so sorry to hear that, Ted. I wondered from time to time what ever happened to him. Your dad was a good man and an excellent soldier."

"So, what brings you to our church?" Mattie inquired.

"We've been going through some difficult times and well, to tell you the truth, it seems that God has brought us here," Ted explained.

"We had very little, if anything, to do with it," Ellen added.

"Funny how God does that to us," mused Mattie.

"The pastor opened his home to us for the weekend, to give us a break." Ellen continued, "We have been so encouraged by God's act of kindness through him that we've gained a renewed sense of hope and strength that we believe will sustain us in the days ahead."

"Now, now," quipped Horatio, "I'm watching my calorie intake, so please take it easy on the butter." Everybody laughed.

"I know that this is 'winging it' but George and Mattie, would you like to join us for dinner?" Horatio asked.

"We'd love to," George replied. "What's the plan?"

"We can go back to my house," Horatio offered.

"Nonsense," Mattie insisted. "Come to our house. I'm sure I can come up with something."

"Has the pastor treated you to his pasta and sauce, yet?" George asked.

"Oh, yes. We had that the first night that we stayed with him," Ted recalled.

"You are aware that's the only dish he knows how to cook?" Mattie ribbed.

At that, Noah and Becky laughed along with the grown-ups.

"I'm busted," Horatio confessed. "That's why I could only invite them for the weekend. One more day in the house and they would have figured out my culinary limitations. I guess it would be better to have dinner at your place after all." He chuckled. "Ted, can you give me a hand locking up? Is it okay if Ellen and the children ride back with you, George and Mattie?"

"Ellen, we would be delighted to have you and the children ride back with us," Mattie said.

Ellen kissed Ted good bye and walked to the car with the Heywoods.

Horatio and Ted closed down the building and prepared to make a stop at the Village Mart to pick up a few items before heading to the Heywoods' home. At the store, they picked up a couple of chickens, sweet potatoes, salad ingredients, rolls, and ice cream. They were at George and Mattie's home just a few minutes after the Heywoods had arrived. Mattie was already at the kitchen sink preparing the pots and pans. Ellen was at her side, graciously accepting instruction. The children were outside playing with Cliff, the Heywoods' dog.

"Come in, Ted. Welcome to our humble home," George said as he reached for Ted and Horatio's coat.

"Thank you. You have a nice place here."

"Mattie and I have called this 'home' for forty-seven years. At one time, this house was the busiest place in town. Through the years, Mattie and I were blessed with eighty-six children who kept this home buzzing with excitement."

"Never a shortage of excitement that's for sure." Mattie chuckled.

"Eighty-six kids. How'd you manage that?" Ted asked.

"Well, it all began with a mission that Mattie and I took on after our son died. Geo was a good boy. Only eight years old when he was run over by a drunk driver. Hurt like hell, but we had a choice to make. Do we hold onto his death by grieving for the rest of our days, or do we celebrate life? We chose to celebrate life. Well, sir, in that time God blessed us with an awesome opportunity to be a stable, loving foundation for children in the state's foster care system. So many of those kids were strangers to love and stability. Anyway, the agency sent us two children at first. Mattie, you remember the Gessler boys?" George asked.

"How could I ever forget those poor boys?" Mattie recalled. "Those boys came from a family that truly needed a lot of prayer." She continued, "Clinical therapists prescribed medication as the only answer to their being made manageable. Before the first month had passed, the boys were so happy, calling us Nana and Poppa, working at Bill Murphy's Hardware store and medication-free."

"Wow. That's amazing," Ted responded. "How did you accomplish that?"

"It was all God. He brought them to us." George continued, "He instructed us in what to do and how to do it. Well, sir," George went on, "the people at the agency couldn't understand the transformation these children experienced. Pushing the envelope, they tested our mettle by sending us their 'problem placements.' All these children needed was structure, love, and someone to show an interest in them."

As the discussion continued about the state of foster care, Mattie and Ellen worked in the kitchen like a finely tuned machine preparing the perfect Sunday dinner. Sitting at the dinner table, the conversation continued.

"We were immersed in foster children for thirty-two years," Mattie explained. "We actually had to renovate our barn to increase capacity. The agency compensated us well for the care we provided. In fact, the money that we were paid was enough to completely renovate the barn to include five bedrooms, two full bathrooms, and a kitchen. We even set up a scholarship fund in our son Geo's name, so that other children would be blessed long after they left our care. We managed to pay for six of the children to go to South Shore Community College."

"In all the time that we've spent together," Horatio acknowledged, "I was not aware of your experience."

"Well, Pastor," George said, "after we stopped caring for the kids, our excitement for life seemed to wane. The joy that came with every challenge each child brought was gone. That season of our life had ended," George continued. "Instead of moving forward, Mattie and I found ourselves returning to a place of grieving the death of Geo, almost as though it had just happened."

"God understood your grieving and your heart to be a blessing to the Body of Christ, so in your time of loss he added to your joy," Horatio offered. "You can't help but love him."

"That's exactly what he revealed to us and, yes we do love him for every opportunity that he has blessed us with." George continued, "Well now, enough about us. Ted, tell us about you and Ellen."

"Wow, where to begin?" Ted pondered. "After seventeen years of working as a shipbuilder at Marina Boatworks, business was slow and I was laid off. I had been unemployed from time to time before because of the nature of my work. Usually for a month or two, at most. When I was laid off fourteen months ago, I was told that the yard was closing down for good. Since that time, I've applied for work at other yards, on fishing boats, construction companies, and retail stores without success. We were living on my unemployment checks, trying to make ends meet. Our home was foreclosed after we fell behind in our mortgage payments. We found a small apartment that I had agreed to fix up in exchange for a discount on our rent. As soon as the repairs were completed, our landlord sold the property. The new owner raised our rent to $1,250.00. When I told him that I couldn't afford that, he evicted us." Ted continued, "It seemed as though every time we got settled, something happened to move us again."

"My, that's a lot to go through," George said. "What's your plan?"

"Well, Ellen and I are talking about relocating," Ted began. "I wanted to stay close to this area because my mother is in a nursing home, and Ellen's dad is dealing with health issues. We hoped to remain in this area because we want Noah and Becky to spend time with their grandparents. I guess, at this point, we'll have to wait and see what opens up first."

"Ellen," Mattie began, "you certainly know your way around a kitchen. Do you like to bake?"

"No, I don't like to bake. I *love* to bake." She laughed.

"What do you say we whip up a cake to go with the ice cream that Pastor brought?" Mattie asked.

"Count me in, Mattie." Ellen continued, "What do you suggest we create?"

Mattie was quick to respond, "I'm thinking a three-layer chocolate cake with…."

"Don't tell me butter crème frosting," Ellen interrupted, completing Mattie's thought.

"How did you know that?" Mattie laughed.

"Birds of a feather, you know," Ellen confirmed.

As they got busy "creating," Horatio, George, and Ted went outside to get some exercise with Noah and Becky in tow. George showed Horatio and Ted the renovated barn that he mentioned earlier. It had been left unused for several years and, as a result, needed a thorough freshening up before it could be occupied again. Ted offered George his help if ever he needed a hand doing repairs around the house. Ted didn't have a cell phone or home telephone number, so he took George's phone number and promised to check in with him from time to time. George appreciated Ted's gesture. Noah and Becky played on a tree swing while the men continued to inspect the structural and mechanical condition of the barn. After a short while, Ellen's voice could be heard summoning everyone into the house. Sitting around the kitchen table, the remainder of the evening was spent laughing, eating, and poking fun at each other as everyone filled up with cake and ice cream. The day came too soon to an end.

Bidding farewell to the Heywoods, Horatio and the Willises headed home. Noah and Becky were fast asleep in the backseat, one on either side of Ellen. In the front seat, Ted told Horatio of his plan to get through this difficult time. Horatio listened without interrupting. Ted ran through his plan step by step, day by day. When Ted had completed mapping out his strategy, Horatio shook his head in disagreement.

"Ted, I see why you are in this position."

"Pastor, what are you saying?" Ellen asked.

"Can't you see? Don't you understand any of this?" He continued, "Everything that you have done, every choice you have made over the last fourteen months, you have undertaken without consulting God. The Word of God cautions us: 'Unless the Lord builds the house, we labor in vain.' Have you ever heard that scripture, before?"

Ted acknowledged that he had not, let alone understood it.

"Guys," Horatio began, "before you plan to do anything more, agree to spend tomorrow with me. I want to show you something that you sorely need to understand in trying to get back on your feet."

Ted was puzzled. "What are you saying?" he asked.

"I'm saying that I believe I understand what you need to do," Horatio continued. "All I ask is that you give me one day to share my understanding with you. Will you allow me that much?"

"Pastor, no disrespect intended," Ted began, "but I believe that nobody can handle my business or my responsibility for my family better than me. We can't afford to lose another day in getting our lives back on track," Ted said with conviction. He continued, "I appreciate your hospitality, but I've got to do what I've got to do in terms of my family's future."

"Ted, Ellen," Horatio said, "I count you as friends and as your friend, I am asking you to reconsider your position."

"Ted, maybe we should…." Ellen began.

"Ellen, let me handle this, please," Ted froze her midsentence. The remainder of the ride home was uncomfortably quiet.

Back at Horatio's house, Ted broke the silence. "Pastor," he began, "we can never thank you enough for all that you've done for us over the course of this weekend."

Ellen nodded agreeably.

"I have to give our situation one more try before I can be convinced that I'm doing something wrong," Ted explained. "If my plan fails; if what I understand to be the solution falls

short, I promise to come back, sit with you for a day, a week, a month or whatever it takes to try it your way. Are you good with that?"

"Ted, I only want what's best for you and your family," Horatio assured. "I hope that if I do see you again, it won't be because your plan didn't work out. But," he continued, "I'd welcome the opportunity to share with you understanding that has not only blessed me but, changed my life forever."

"You've got a deal," Ted promised. The two hugged and headed to their rooms for the evening.

Day 15
December 17th - Monday

The Willises were up and knocking at Horatio's bedroom door with their bags packed at seven fifteen. Ted and Ellen were determined to get Noah and Becky to school on time because they had missed four days of school the previous week.

"Be right out," Horatio called out as he hurried to get dressed. Opening his bedroom door, he could see that Ted, Ellen, Noah and Becky were dressed and ready to go. "My goodness. You certainly aren't wasting any time getting on the road."

"We've got to get the kids to school by eight o'clock," Ted continued. "Pastor, we can't thank you enough for all you have done for us. I was thinking about what you said last night and I promise that if my plan fails, I'll give God's way a try. I do believe, though, that I've got it covered this time."

"I hope so, Ted. And whether your plan succeeds or fails, I will be disappointed if you don't come back and visit."

"Consider it done," Ted affirmed with a hug and a back pat.

The Willises headed out the door. Horatio watched as they placed their belongings into the back of the truck and drove away.

Looking around, he considered returning to bed for an hour or two. *After all*, he pondered, *this is the first time in three days that I can relax and enjoy the quiet and privacy of my home*. Without a second thought, he chose to get ready and head for his office.

Forty-five minutes later, he was back at his desk sorting through voice mail messages and paperwork. One message was from Kelli Brock, a staff member at the Driftway nursing home. Kelli was not a member of Good Shepherd, so she identified herself to make sure that Horatio remembered her. She left her cell phone number. Horatio returned her call, immediately.

"Good morning, Kelli. This is Pastor Smiley. I just received your call. Is everything all right with everyone at the nursing home?"

"Hi, Pastor. Thank you so much for calling me back. Everyone's fine at the nursing home." Kelli continued, "Pastor, I have a sister who is in a bad situation. She needs help that I'm not able to give."

"What seems to be the problem?"

"Too much to go into now. I've got to get back to work, but can I call you tomorrow? It's my day off."

"By all means give me a call. I should be in my office tomorrow, between ten o'clock and two thirty."

"Thank you so much, Pastor. I'll call around noontime, after I've finished my exercise class. Bye, for now." She hung up.

Horatio remained at his desk working until one o'clock. He decided to take a break and go for a haircut. He remembered that a new hair salon had recently opened at a mall in a neighboring town. He figured he'd give it a try because his regular barbershop was closed Mondays.

Arriving at the mall, he parked his car in front of Walmart. Business appeared to be brisk for a Monday afternoon. At the mall's main entrance, he noticed a man, dressed in Santa Clause garb standing alongside a holiday donation kettle, ringing a bell as shoppers passed by. Many people entering and exiting the mall made an obvious effort to avoid making eye contact with the man. Other shoppers looked at the man with disdain, as if to be repulsed by his declaration of "Merry Christmas! Merry Christmas!" Horatio walked over to encourage the man at the kettle.

"Merry Christmas. Jesus Christ is Lord," he called out, waving a twenty-dollar bill above his head fifteen feet from the man. Several people within range heard the exchange but did not respond. They kept walking with their eyes toward the ground. The Santa figure responded with a hearty "Ho! Ho! Ho!" He understood what Horatio was doing. Placing the money in the kettle, Horatio encouraged the Santa to keep up the good work.

As he walked inside the mall searching for the salon, he noticed a recurring pattern of interaction between mothers and their preschool-age children. Mothers would routinely bribe their children with promises of a toy, candy, etc., if only the child would do as they were asked.

"My Lord," Horatio thought aloud, "what has this world come to?" Continuing on to the salon, he walked by several window displays projecting seductive images that called out to every man's flesh. "My Lord, your people are going to hell tattooed and wearing thongs," he muttered as he passed a women's intimate apparel store.

Finally, having located the salon, he nearly collapsed into a chair in the waiting area. Immediately a "technician" with streaks of purple and white through his hair greeted him.

"Hi. My name is Thad. What can I do for you today?"

Lord Jesus! Horatio recognized immediately that he had made a grave mistake coming to this place. *How do I make a graceful exit from this place, Lord?* he processed, inwardly.

Just then, the Spirit of God spoke to him. Horatio. You are my ambassador. The still voice reminded him, *Be slow to speak and quick to listen.*

Yes, Lord, was his only response. Seeming as if time had stopped while Horatio received correction from the Lord, there stood Thad before him awaiting his response. "Thad, I'd like a light trim if you will."

"Are you sure? That's all? I'd love to try something a little bit different. Will you trust me on this?"

"Thad, the only one I trust is God."

"Yeah, been there, done that," Thad acknowledged.

"Where have you been and what did you do, if I may ask?" Horatio inquired.

"The whole church routine." He covered Horatio's neck and chest with a bib as he settled into the chair. "You know what I mean, sir." Thad explained, "The family piles into the car on Sunday morning headed for church. Mom and Dad are arguing right up to the time we drive onto the parking lot. Mom accuses Dad of whoring around, while Dad calls her an insecure alcoholic. Sadly, they're both right. Walking into the building with my sisters, we are warned: 'Be on your best behavior, or there will be consequences later.' Yeah, brings back a lot of great memories. NOT! I quit going to church when I was fourteen. I'm figuring all those people and the hypocritical sideshow hasn't changed much. In fact, my parents still go to that church, faithfully, every Sunday. And let me tell you, this experience is not exclusive to me. My boyfriend, Carlos, told me that he witnessed the exact same thing in his family when he went to church."

"Thad, I'm so sorry to hear that." Horatio was grieved. "Your experience is not unusual, and neither is your response." He continued, "The tragedy of it all is that people get angry with God and turn away from him, instead of praying against the demonic, seductive spirits that manipulate the people we love."

"I don't understand what you mean, sir. What demons and spirits are you talking about?"

"First, Thad," Horatio explained, "you have to understand that God gave us the Bible as our instructional manual. Think of it this way: when you buy an automobile, you are provided with an owner's manual. The manual, written by the creator of your automobile, instructs you on what you must do to get the most out of your vehicle. Think of the Bible in the same way. The Bible, made available to you by your Creator, tells you how to get the most out of your life."

"Wow. That's deep!" Thad paused.

"Yeah, really deep, yet so simple." Horatio continued, "The Word of God tells us that a double-minded man is unstable in all of his ways. Believe me if your parents knew the Word and committed their lives to it, your church experience would have been awesome."

"Sir, can you repeat that thing about the double-minded man again?" Thad asked. "I like that."

For the next half hour, Thad and Horatio got so caught up in their discussion they hadn't noticed that other customers and staff were listening. After Thad had finished Horatio's "trim," he expressed his appreciation for helping him to understand some things that he acknowledged had messed with his head since he was a child. Refusing to accept payment from Horatio for the haircut, Thad asked if Horatio had a business card or contact information. Reaching into the pocket of his coat, Horatio produced a business card.

"You're a pastor?" Thad's eyes opened wide. "You didn't mention that."

"At your service," Horatio smiled.

Thad inquired about Good Shepherd's worship service schedule. As he prepared to leave the salon, other customers approached Horatio and requested his business card.

It was three thirty and Horatio was hungry. Before returning to his office, he stopped at a drive-thru for some tacos, nachos, and a bean burrito. This was a welcome change of pace in his diet, as there were no restaurants in Scituate that offered Mexican food.

Back at his office, Horatio returned to his paperwork. Sitting at his desk, he revisited his time and conversation with Thad and gave God thanks for trusting him with that assignment. He remained there until six thirty that evening. He went home and watched television until eleven o'clock.

Day 16
December 18th – Tuesday

Before going to his office, Horatio stopped at the post office to buy stamps. Katie Hitchins stood at her window directing him over.

"Good morning, Pastor. What can I get for you today?"

"Hi, Katie. One roll of stamps will do nicely, thank you."

"Flags or Forever stamps?" she asked.

"I'm trusting more in 'Forever' than flags these days," he quipped.

"I know what you mean," she continued. "Isn't it a shame about the financial mess this country is in? And it's getting worse by the minute. I hear talk of more government layoffs and cutbacks if things don't change. All this foreign aid. We keep going deeper and deeper into debt. We can't even take care of our own. How can we expect to pay the freight for every country on the planet? What the heck is Washington thinking?"

Katie was off and running, as usual. Horatio wanted to say good bye, but he had to wait for her to stop and take a breath. Just then, Katie's cell phone rang. At that, Horatio said, "Gotta go." Before Katie could say another word, he was out the door.

Entering the church, he could hear his office phone ringing. He rushed to get to it but picked up the receiver one ring too late. The call had disconnected. He went through his caller ID and was able to determine that it was Kelli who had called. Her call was well ahead of schedule, so he immediately called her back to confirm that there was no change in their scheduled meeting. Kelli picked up her phone on the first ring.

"Hello. This is Kelli."

"Good morning, Kelli. This is Pastor Smiley. I apologize for missing your call."

"No problem, Pastor. Thanks for getting back to me so quickly."

"Are we still on for today?" he asked.

"Yes, absolutely. In fact, I skipped going to the gym today, because my sister's situation has gotten worse."

"Well, what's going on?" he asked.

"It's a very long, very upsetting story," Kelli paused. "Can we meet somewhere and discuss it? I'll explain it all when I see you."

"Sure. What time and where?"

"How's the coffee shop on the Driftway?" Kelli suggested.

"Great. That's just up the road from my office. What time?"

"Eleven okay?" Kelli asked.

"Eleven it is. See you there. Bye, bye." He hung up.

Before long, Horatio was out the door headed for the coffee shop. Walking in, he spotted Kelli sitting at a booth and motioned to her to sit with him at the counter. There were only a few customers in the coffee shop, so he explained his request for sitting at the counter. "Kelli," he began, "thank you for indulging me."

"Indulging you, Pastor?" she asked. "What are you referring to?"

"You appeared to be comfortable in the booth, but I asked you to sit with me at the counter. Please, it's just an occupational safeguard that hasn't failed me, yet."

"Occupational safeguard?"

"Oh, yes," he explained, "I believe that when unmarried members of the opposite sex meet, they should be chaperoned. And if a chaperon isn't available, sit in plain view of everyone."

"Sounds old-fashioned. You'd get along great with my father." Kelli chuckled. "Well, whatever your reason, this is fine." She continued, "I'm, just so thankful that you were able to meet with me." Kelli Brock is an attractive woman, about thirty-two years of age. She had long autumn brown hair and pretty brown eyes. Her presence seemed to bring joy to the, otherwise, depressive atmosphere at the nursing home. Kelli truly appreciated the time that Horatio had set aside for her today.

"Kelli, it's my pleasure. All this mystery about your sister's situation. What's going on?"

"Well, it's a long story and a very stressful situation that began for my sister six years ago." Kelli went on to explain the circumstances that led her to reach out to him.

"Pastor, Rene is a good person who fell in with some unsavory people. She became involved in a lifestyle that included drugs, alcohol and, eventually, time in jail. Growing up as my older sister, she rebelled against the 'rules' that our parents set for us. By the time Rene turned twenty-one, her rebellious attitude was more than my parents could tolerate, so they sent her packing. For the next eight years, Rene's life as she described it was a 'living hell.'

"Weakened by addiction, she couldn't put that lifestyle behind her. Abused and depressed, she considered herself beyond redemption, so she continued down that road to ruin.

"Five years, ago, Rene was admitted to the emergency room at South Shore Hospital for treatment of a broken arm she sustained from yet another incident of physical abuse." Kelli's eyes began to well up. Horatio passed her a napkin and asked if she was all right. She nodded her head and continued.

"I'm sorry, Pastor. Please forgive the tears," she apologized.

"As I was saying, during Rene's examination, the doctor determined that she was four months pregnant. She was committed to carry the baby to term, so arrangements were made to place her in a rehabilitative program for the duration of her pregnancy. The program was a blessing for a number of reasons: It removed Rene from a living situation that would have probably ended with her getting killed, and it gave her access to medical care to help the baby develop, as well as could be hoped for. Best of all, the program brought structure and healing into Rene's life. She remained in the program until time for the baby to be born."

Kelli continued, "On the day that she was scheduled to be discharged, somehow her boyfriend, abuser, or whatever he was, came and checked her and the baby out of the hospital. After one day back with that guy, she overheard him talking on the phone to someone about selling them the baby for five thousand dollars. Rene knew that she had to do something to protect the baby but she was trapped. Her loser boyfriend didn't allow her or the baby to leave his sight. According to Rene, while the piece of crap was napping that afternoon, she slipped out with her baby and took him to a local firehouse, where they sponsored a 'safe baby' program. When she returned to her boyfriend's place, he beat her so badly that the court put him away for fifteen years. It took her every bit of a year to heal physically. She's still trying to heal emotionally."

"Oh, my Lord," was all that Horatio could think to say. "So what's going on now?"

"Well," Kelli continued, "after all of four years, my sister was able to find out where her son is. Pastor, from what she's told me, he's a beautiful five-year-old boy. His name is Daniel. Anyway, he is a ward of the state and he is living at Mercy Ministries Home for Children. Rene learned of his whereabouts some time ago, and every day since then she parks her car in the parking lot near the play area, hoping to get a glimpse of him. Several trespassing complaints filed against her by the orphanage have resulted in a restraining order being issued against her. She misses Daniel so much that she has no peace. She worries about him day and night. Rene certainly poses no threat to anyone. She's just a loving mother who misses and cares about her baby." Kelli sighed.

"Any chance of Rene regaining custody of Daniel?" Horatio asked.

"I don't think so, Pastor. At her boyfriend's trial, he told the judge that it was my sister who wanted to sell Daniel. At the time, Rene had returned to smoking marijuana or drinking or something. She knew that she couldn't pass a blood test or urine screening. Her arrest record confirmed that she had previously been caught with drugs. She didn't dispute the accusation because she knew that her boyfriend would arrange to have her or Daniel killed if she didn't go along with his story. The judge agreed to give her probation instead of jail time for her complicity if she signed over her parental rights for Daniel to the state. The fact of the matter is that, as much as Rene loves and misses Daniel, she's convinced that she isn't worthy of having him in her life. She believes with all her heart that God gave her Daniel as a gift and she didn't honor that responsibility. She's tormented with guilt all day, every day."

"What can I do to help?" he asked.

"I'm not sure, Pastor. I know that the orphanage is a Christian organization and I was hoping that you might know someone there who can help to reunite Rene with Daniel. She has a job and an apartment. I know that she would be an excellent mother to Daniel, if only she could forgive herself for her past."

"Has any effort been made by Rene to begin this process?"

"Not to my knowledge." Kelli continued, "As much as my parents and I encourage her, she believes that God is angry with her. She doesn't think of herself as worthy of a second chance."

"That's a lie from Satan himself." Horatio shook his head. "A friend of mine says it best: 'God doesn't throw us away when we make mistakes.' That's the reason God gave us Jesus. Through His crucifixion, resurrection, and our confession of faith, by Grace we were delivered from God's condemnation. Rene must believe that. Do you or your sister attend church, Kelli?"

"No. We don't. We used to but not for a long time." Kelli explained, "When I started working at the nursing home, I decided to work Sundays to get the higher pay rate. I guess I never thought about missing church as being that important."

"Believe me, Kelli," Horatio explained, "if where you are going to spend your eternity is important to you, then you need to be in church. Join a word-based teaching ministry and you will be amazed how God will reveal to you all that you will need to know, so that you can live and appreciate life now and eternally."

"Revelation, huh?" she reflected. "That's a book in the New Testament, right?"

"That's right," Horatio continued. "But don't start with the book of Revelation. If you have the opportunity, start with the book of Genesis and work your way through to Revelation. If not, you can begin by reading the Gospel John. Believe me, Kelli, the knowledge and understanding that you'll receive is worth every minute of reading time that you invest. The Bible is the true account of God's love for us, His creation.

"Knowledge and understanding, huh?" Kelli paused. "Sounds like that 'New Age' enlightenment stuff that those afternoon television talk shows promote."

"Not at all," Horatio continued. "Biblical principles such as confessing Jesus Christ as Lord, salvation, repentance, and grace are clearly explained in scripture that God divinely communicated to man thousands of years ago. To be sure, there's nothing 'New Age' about scripture."

"Thousands of years ago?" Kelli asked.

"That's right. And you know what's really exciting about it all?" Horatio chuckled, "Today, scientists, geologists, archeologists, astronomers who previously challenged the validity of scriptural accuracy are now acknowledging that they were wrong in their positions. It only makes me want to honor God all the more."

"You make quite the case for God, Pastor."

"That's what we all should be doing." Horatio continued, "He's our Creator. Take some time today and get to know Him. He knows you!"

"I'm sold." Kelli appeared to be sincere. "Would it be okay if I visited your church the Sunday after next? I have to ask my supervisor for the day off."

"Kelli, that would be awesome!" Horatio continued, "But please…. I don't mean to pressure you to come to Good Shepherd. You should go where God's Spirit leads you."

"Pastor, for you to be as excited as you are about God, I want to drink from the same well that you're drinking from. No, it has to be Good Shepherd for me," she made clear, as if to let him know that there was no way he was going to change her mind.

"Then it's settled. See you the Sunday after Christmas. Now, back to Rene," he continued. "I would very much like to meet with her. Anything you can do to arrange for that to happen?"

"That's going to be a tough one." Kelli sighed. "The one place where I know you can catch up with Rene would be at the orphanage parking lot. She goes there just about every day during her lunch break and sits in her car. Aside from that, I haven't a clue where you'd be able to catch up with her. Yeah, I'd say the parking lot would be your best chance." Kelli described Rene's features and a description of the car she drove.

"I'll pray for God's guidance in this." Horatio continued, "I promise to keep you informed, Kelli."

"Thanks again, Pastor. I believe that if anyone can help my sister, you are the one to do it." With that, she hugged him and left the coffee shop.

Unbeknownst to Horatio, trustee board member and ally to Bill Nelson, Joe Thomas, was seated in a blind spot inside the coffee shop, taking pictures with his camera phone of Horatio's meeting with Kelli.

Driving back to his office, Horatio prayed for the Lord to move in Rene's situation and bless her with the opportunity to reunite with Daniel. Checking the dashboard clock, he noticed that it was twelve fifteen. He pulled his car onto the shoulder of the road and programed his GPS for Mercy Ministry's Home For Children. The system coordinated the route of travel. *Next stop, Mercy Ministry's Home for Children, 1215 Centre St., Brockton,* he thought aloud. Unsure of what awaited him, he sensed, in his spirit, that God was directing him there. During the next twenty-five minutes, Horatio was proficiently guided to his destination.

The parking lot was positioned to the right of the main building. Driving through the lot, he observed who he deduced was Rene. She was seated behind the steering wheel of her car, far removed from other vehicles, with her face in her hands. Obvious to anyone watching, she was sobbing. He pulled his car alongside hers and prayed, *Lord, what should I do next?*

He shut his car off, got out, and walked over to Rene's driver side window, waving as if he were an old friend. He motioned to her to roll her window down. At first Rene ignored him. Then he spoke to her by name. Rene wiped the tears from her eyes and rolled her window down about two inches.

Looking up, she asked, "Do I know you?"

"No, but I know you," he replied. "My name is Horatio Smiley, and I'm a friend of your sister, Kelli."

"What do you want?" she asked.

"I learned about you and your situation. I was so interested in meeting you that I took a chance and drove by, hoping to introduce myself. I'm so happy that I was able to connect with you."

Rene didn't respond.

"Is it okay if I come by tomorrow and speak with you?" he asked.

"No. Don't. I'm not interested in talking to you," she replied.

"Oh, I understand," Horatio said. "I'm sure you'll want to call Kelli and check me out. You can't be too careful these days."

Rene began to roll her window up.

"Rene. How about Thursday?" he asked. "Can I stop by and speak with you Thursday? I'd really appreciate it. I'll bring lunch."

She didn't respond.

"Great, then." Horatio continued, "See you Thursday," he said as he walked back to his car, waving good-bye.

Back at his office, he called Kelli to report on his interaction with her sister. He expected that Rene would contact her to confirm their relationship. His call went directly to her voice mail. He left a message asking Kelli to contact him at her earliest opportunity.

At four thirty-five, Kelli returned his call. She was excited that Horatio had responded to Rene's situation so quickly. "I have to call my parents and let them know that you actually spoke with her. I'm telling you, Pastor, I believe in my heart that if anyone can get Rene to respond, it's you. Thank you so much…."

"Kelli, you are giving me credit where credit is not deserved," he began. "To be sure, I prayed that God would speak through me because I had absolutely no clue what to say to her. I'm convinced that it was God who spoke through me because I honestly would have not chosen that approach, if left to me."

"Really? How can something like that happen?" Kelli was puzzled.

"Simple," Horatio explained, "just ask Him. Let Him know that you need His help."

"That's all?" she asked.

"That's all."

"Wow. I never would have believed it could be that simple."

"Well," Horatio offered, "I'll give you a call as soon as my meeting with Rene is over."

"Sounds great. Thanks again, Pastor. Speak with you then." The call ended.

Horatio remained in his office until a few minutes after six o'clock and then went home for the evening. He heated up a frozen pizza and watched the Travel channel until retiring for the night.

Day 17
December 19th – Wednesday

Before going to his office, Horatio stopped by the Village Mart to pick up a can of coffee, tea bags, and snacks in anticipation of Timmy and Sara's four o'clock appointment. He stood in the checkout line behind an elderly Asian woman who labored to gather her bags and carry them outside. She appeared to have limited movement in her right side and slurred speech, perhaps the consequence of a stroke. The young people who served as the store's cashier and two of the baggers were annoyed by the woman's delayed movement. Gesturing to each other, they mimicked the woman's mobility and speech. Snickering to each other as they watched her leave the store. Horatio was angered.

"What, may I ask, is so amusing about that poor old woman to you, kids? You get your manager out here right now!"

The store manager heard the commotion and hurried over to address what was going on. "Pastor Smiley," the manager, recognizing him, asked, "is something wrong?"

The expressions on the faces of the store employees telegraphed the element of shock when they learned that Horatio was a pastor.

"Good morning, Caleb. Yes, there is something very wrong here." Horatio continued, "An elderly woman who is physically impaired just left from this register. Your employees treated her in a manner that no one deserves to be treated."

"I'm so sorry," Caleb apologized. "What exactly did they do?"

"I would suggest that you review your security cameras and see for yourself," Horatio instructed. "What you do from there is up to you."

Horatio paid for his purchase and left in pursuit of the woman to assist her. He caught up with her at the far end of the parking lot, making her way home.

"Excuse me, Miss. Excuse me, please," Horatio called from behind. The woman seemingly was unaware that he was calling out to her. She kept walking. Again, he called out to her, "Hello, ma'am."

At that, the woman turned around to see that it was Horatio who was calling to her.

She smiled and asked, "Young man, do you need help with something?"

Horatio was taken aback. Here before him was this elderly woman, on a cold winter morning, struggling to make her way home, carrying bags of groceries asking him if he needed help?

"Ma'am, I noticed you leaving the grocery store with those heavy bags and I wanted to assist you in making it home safely," he explained.

"My goodness. That is so kind of you, young man." The woman continued, "In all my years in Scituate, no one has shown such consideration for me as you have today. Thank you. I would appreciate your help."

The woman's name was Lu Chang. She lived half a mile away from the Village Mart. As he drove her home, she discussed much about her time living in Scituate. Daily she experienced the absence of warmth and a haunting presence of loneliness. Her husband died five years ago. He liked to fish, so he convinced her to move to Scituate.

Mrs. Chang was Buddhist, so she did not accept Horatio's invitation to visit Good Shepherd. She didn't want to make a promise that she knew in her heart she could not honor.

Horatio thanked Mrs. Chang for sharing her time with him. He told her that she could call on him anytime she needed transportation to the market or a doctor's appointment. He also invited her to accompany him on Saturday afternoons when he visited the nursing home. He told her it would give him someone to talk with along the way.

Mrs. Chang promised to ride shotgun for him, but only if he was sure that it wouldn't be an imposition for him. They parted laughing. Horatio returned to his office to prepare for his four o'clock appointment.

****

Precisely at four o'clock, voices entering the church foyer could be heard. Immediately recognizable as those of Timmy and Sara, Horatio summoned, "Come on in, Mr. and Mrs. Andrews-to-be." They giggled in response to the way that he addressed them. They were happy and in love. Entering his office, Sara gave him a hug and Timmy followed that up with a hug of his own.

"You guys look great. What's your secret?"

"Pastor," Timmy began, "everything that I've always wanted, I have; the love of the world's greatest girl who is about to become my wife, our first baby on the way, a new job, and best of all, God's forgiveness. It doesn't get much better than this."

"Isn't he cute, Pastor?" Sara asked with a smile.

"Well, I'm not going to call you 'cute,' Timmy, but I will agree that you are blessed." Horatio laughed. "So, tell me: what's been going on with you two since the engagement?"

"Pastor," Timmy began, "I'm working full time at the jewelry store and part-time at the diner. I've kept clear of drugs, liquor, and parties since my episode in the hospital. Sara and I are reading the Bible together every day. Our mothers are happier than Sara or I can remember."

"That's awesome." Horatio was impressed. "And how about you, Sara?"

"Pastor Smiley, other than the morning sickness, I couldn't be more excited." She laughed. "I'm excited about our future as husband and wife, as parents, and as friends who love each other as we do. Understanding what our mothers had to endure as single parents, Timmy and I are committed to do everything within our ability not to allow that to happen to us. We pray together every day and save every nickel we can. I'm continuing my night classes and working more hours at my job. I am so excited about our future."

Horatio began the session with a prayer. Next, he counseled Timmy and Sara in God's love for marriage and family according to scripture. The study focused on the roles of Godly husbands and wives as established in the Books of Proverbs, Song of Solomon, and First Corinthians. Timmy and Sara had never fully understood or appreciated the relevance and extent of the wisdom God had given to mankind for victorious living. They didn't want the counseling session to end. At five-thirty, Horatio explained that prayer meeting was scheduled to begin at six o'clock. Timmy and Sarah ate the snacks that he offered. Together, they agreed to attend prayer meeting.

Prayer meeting was well attended, and the presence of the Lord was undeniable. Horatio could sense that those present were growing in their prayer life. He was very pleased. The prayer meeting ended at eight o'clock. Afterward, he went home and watched a Boston Celtics basketball game until ten thirty.

Day 18
December 20th – Thursday

The morning passed quickly. Looking over at the wall clock in his office, he noticed that it was after eleven o'clock. His plan was to wait in the orphanage parking lot with sandwiches and hot cocoa when Rene arrived. Beyond that, he had no plan. He didn't want to appear weird or imposing in his first opportunity to speak with her. He prayed that Rene would be comfortable with him because of his friendship with Kelli.

Horatio got in his car and headed in the direction of the orphanage. After making a quick stop at a sandwich shop, he arrived at Mercy Ministries on schedule. Parking at a vantage point, he was able to clearly see every vehicle coming into the lot.

He made himself comfortable and waited. And waited. And waited. Twelve thirty. One o'clock. One thirty. It became obvious that Rene wasn't showing. Disappointed but not discouraged, Horatio got out of his car and walked to the facility's administration building.

As he entered the reception area, he noticed that the walls were adorned with children's artwork. The receptionist was busy with a phone call. In the time that he waited, he prayed that God would give him great favor with the receptionist. His attention was drawn to a flier on a bulletin board advertising the next 'Foster Parent' orientation session.

"Hi. Can I help you, sir?" the receptionist asked, looking up.

"Good afternoon. Yes, thank you. My name is Horatio Smiley and I just stopped by for some information on the next 'Foster Parent' orientation group."

"Let me give you one of these," the receptionist offered, handing him one of the brochures from a file on her desk. "The next session is December 26th at six o'clock." She continued, "You'll have to register for that session by December 21st, because of the holiday weekend. I can give you the registration materials to take with you if you'd like."

"I'd like that," Horatio continued. "You are Sheila?" he asked, observing the name plate on the desk.

"That's me. Sheila Vega."

"Sheila, are you a foster parent?"

"No. I'm not married. But if I was able, I'd adopt all of the children. They're so precious."

"That's very interesting that you mentioned adoption. Why adoption instead of foster care?"

"I was in foster care from the time I was seven until my eighteenth birthday. During that time, I lived with four different families."

"That's a lot of moving around," Horatio acknowledged.

"For the most part the families gave me the care and support that I needed, but I never believed that I was loved enough to be reunited with my bioparents or adopted by my foster parents." Sheila continued, "I want to show every one of these children that they are worthy of an unconditional 'never gonna leave you' kind of love."

"You speak from your heart."

"Yeah," Sheila replied. "I'm guilty of wearing my heart on my sleeve, I guess."

"Well, Sheila, I have truly appreciated our time together and I hope to see you again."

"Thank you, Mr. Smiley."

"Horatio," he said with a correcting gesture.

"Sorry. Horatio." She laughed.

"Sheila," Horatio continued, "it's been a pleasure. Take care."

Lord, you are amazing, Horatio thought to himself as he walked away. He understood what God had done. Had Rene shown up, he wouldn't have gone inside and met Sheila. As a result, he came away with an ally, within the organization, who appeared to be passionate about family reunification and adoption.

He was back at his office before two o'clock. Checking his voice mail, the system reported, "You have one new message." The message followed:

"Pastor Smiley? Hi, this is Rene, Kelli's sister. I was supposed to meet you today at the orphanage. My car had a flat tire so, I wasn't able to come. I'm sorry. I didn't know that you were a pastor. Kelli told me about you and if you could return my call, I would really appreciate it. You can reach me at the number showing up on your caller ID after six o'clock. Thank you, Pastor. Bye."

A smile formed on Horatio's face and evolved into a hearty laugh. "Lord. You never cease to amaze me," he thought aloud.

****

Later that afternoon still in his office, he received a telephone call for help. Former Scituate High School Prom Queen and Miss Massachusetts pageant third runner-up MaryLou Gannon has had it with her "heathen" husband.

Married for six years, her husband, Paul, loves her dearly, but has no interest in hearing anything more about Jesus, God, or scriptural quotes. Marylou, on the other hand, loves the Lord. All through their courtship, she labored diligently to 'save' Paul's soul. As part of their marriage ceremony, Paul publicly confessed Jesus Christ as his Lord and Savior.

Friends of Paul confirmed that he would have agreed to do whatever it took to make MaryLou his wife. The true Paul surfaced shortly after their honeymoon ended. As persistent and tenacious as MaryLou was, the demonic spirit that was influencing Paul to remain firm in his defiance was equally determined.

Whenever she hosted prayer meetings in the family home, Paul would leave and vow to return only when, "the coast was clear." Other times, he would request overtime work at his job when he saw MaryLou's notes on the kitchen calendar about a prayer meeting scheduled to take place in their home.

Marylou was certain that the birth of their first child would move her husband to honor his spiritual commitment. It was well after the birth of their third child that it became clear that she was not going to change Paul. Once again, she is reaching out to her pastor to vent.

"Good afternoon. Church of the Good Shepherd," Horatio announced.

"Good afternoon, Pastor. This is Marylou Gannon."

"Hi, Mrs. Gannon. And how are you doing this fine day?"

"Pastor, I wish I could say that everything is fine, but that's not the case." She sighed.

"Oh, my. I'm sorry to hear that. Would this call be about your husband, Paul?"

"It certainly is," Marylou confirmed. She was frustrated to the point of tears. "Pastor, I thought that he was finally changing. Last week he took one of our Bibles to work."

"Well, that's certainly a step in the right direction. Wouldn't you say?"

"That's just what I thought," she continued. "I didn't let on that I saw him. I was so happy that I got down on my knees and cried tears of joy unto the Lord. My husband didn't say a word about it to me. As much as I wanted to ask him about it, I was determined not to. Then, this morning, after he left for work, I noticed the Bible was back on the dining room table. I went to pick it up to see if he had left any study notes in it and, Pastor, I couldn't believe my eyes. That heathen hollowed out the center of the bible and put a ring box in there. The ring was for our seventh wedding anniversary and it was the most beautiful ring that I've ever seen, but Pastor, how could anybody do such a wicked thing?"

"Well," Horatio suggested, "I'm sure that was his way of making sure you found his surprise."

"Surprise! Surprise!" Marylou was livid. "I'm sure the Lord has a surprise waiting on him for that wicked thing that he did. Pastor, I love Paul very much but I am deeply concerned for his soul. What more can I do to get him to understand that his eternal destiny hangs in the balance?"

"Mrs. Gannon. We've discussed your husband's situation more times during the last three years than I'm sure you or I can recall. I think that it's time for you to take a step back and let God move unencumbered in Paul's life. You have given it your very best. Now, give God a chance."

Horatio explained, "At times, in our determination to see our loved ones experience salvation, we interfere with God's plan. We then become complicit in prolonging Satan's grasp on the very ones we love. John 8:36 clearly tells us: 'Who the Son sets free, is free, indeed.' It doesn't mention anything about MaryLou or Pastor Smiley setting anyone free but, the Lord and only the Lord is He who sets us free. Do you understand my point?"

"Loud and clear," Marylou acknowledged. "Well, is it okay if I continue to focus my energy on at least praying for Paul?"

"Of course. That's the best thing you can do," Horatio encouraged. "God will move in Paul's salvation according to His way and time. Just rest in the Lord's ability to do what you haven't been able to. We don't call Him 'Great God' without reason."

"Thank you, Pastor." Marylou was appreciative. "You are a blessing to the Body of Christ."

"You have a great day, Mrs. Gannon. I promise to continue to pray for your husband. Goodbye."

"Goodbye, Pastor," Mrs. Gannon hung up and Horatio returned to his paperwork.

****

At three o'clock, Horatio heard members of the church's youth choir entering the building for another practice session for the Christmas pageant. From his office, he could discern a spirit of confusion in the overall tone of conversation that was taking place amongst the choir members. Voices were being raised in frustration.

"For eight years I've been in the choir and not once has anyone given me the opportunity to sing solo," complained Angela Hightower. "How is it that Sharon gets to solo after being here less than two years?"

"Now, Angela. Let's not go down that road again." Mrs. Munsey, the choir leader, continued, "When you can commit to coming to rehearsal on a regular basis and on time, I will consider you for a solo opportunity. Until then, I have to rely on those who honor a sincere commitment."

"You know, Mrs. Munsey, I try to get here when I can get a ride. It's not my fault when I miss practice."

"Angela, you live only two blocks from the church," Stanley Dalton chimed in.

"Stanley, no one was speaking to you! No one ever speaks to you. Can't say that I blame them," Angela responded rudely.

Hearing all of what was taking place in the sanctuary, Horatio decided to go out and calm the situation down.

"Good afternoon," he said, as he entered the Sanctuary.

"Good afternoon, Pastor Smiley," the group responded in unison.

"I hope everyone is ready for a truly awesome Christmas pageant. Mrs. Munsey, there's a lot of energy in these young people. More than I remember in the past two years. However, do you manage to harness all this energy and have it result in the heavenly, angelic chorus that you do?"

"Pastor, if you only knew," she sighed.

"Angela," Horatio continued, "I understand that you have been a part of the choir longer than most here. As an experienced member of the group, I expect your full support in helping Mrs. Munsey show the newcomers how we do it. Okay?"

"Yes, Pastor Smiley," Angela responded.

He gave a look to Mrs. Munsey to let her know that he understood all that she had been dealing with. Mrs. Munsey appeared appreciative. He stayed put for the remainder of the rehearsal. During that time, there were no further disruptions. After the rehearsal had concluded, Horatio returned to his office. Realizing that it was after six thirty, he called Rene.

"Hi, Rene. This is Pastor Smiley."

"Oh, hi, Pastor."

"Sorry we weren't able to connect this afternoon," Horatio began. "Did you manage to get your tire repaired okay?"

"Yes, thank you. Everything's fine." Rene appeared to be pleased to speak with him. She continued, "I'm so sorry for acting the way that I did the other day."

"That's okay," he replied, "I think that you responded the way most women would react to a strange man approaching them in a secluded location. Believe me I completely understand and I'm not in the least offended."

"I just felt vulnerable. Thank you for understanding, Pastor"

"Rene, Kelli made mention of your situation the other day. An interesting dilemma, to be sure. Kind of like a lioness protecting her cub."

"Really?" Rene seemed relieved. "Pastor, from what Kelli has told me about you, I would really appreciate the opportunity to sit with you. There is so much that I need to confess."

"Rene," Horatio began, "I'd be happy to counsel with you, but your confession should be to God. He wants to hear your confession from you, not by proxy. You have complete access to Him twenty-four hours a day, seven days a week, fifty-two weeks every year. I'm certain that as your Heavenly Father, he would be pleased to hear it from you directly." He continued, "Rene, I know that Kelli couldn't tell me everything about your past because, after all, how can she tell me what she doesn't know? Would you object to her being present when we meet? I'd like someone else to be present at the session," he explained.

"I don't know what you've been told about me, but I'm not dangerous," Rene responded.

"Oh, no Rene, I didn't mean to suggest that you're dangerous." He chuckled. "God's Word advises us that unmarried members of the opposite sex, when together, should be chaperoned. It's a policy that I have learned to appreciate."

"Oh, I understand," she continued. "I wish I had followed that order of discipline growing up. God knows my past would have been a whole lot different."

"So, when do you want to meet?" he asked.

"Monday afternoon, if you're available." She continued, "I know that's Kelli's next day off. It's Christmas Eve but maybe we could schedule a time early enough in the day so it doesn't interfere with your holiday plans."

"I can be available early afternoon," Horatio offered.

"Thank you, Pastor. I really appreciate that," she said with a sense of relief.

"Well, then, Monday it is. Let's say twelve thirty at my office?"

"That will be great," Rene confirmed.

"Well, until then, have a nice weekend. Bye, bye."

****

Horatio had a taste for Chinese food from Pho Ho Ho, his favorite Asian restaurant. It was always worth the trip to a neighboring town for some perfectly prepared Gai Poo Lo Mein, Crab Rangoon, and Spring Rolls. Along the way, he noticed a travel agency displaying pictures of tropical destinations. *Hmmm*, he thought to himself, *I might as well stop to pick up some brochures and see if anything interests me. After all, January 15th is not that far away*.

After thirty minutes of conversation with the travel agent, he was leaning more towards a Caribbean cruise than anything else. *That's about as complete a change from my daily routine as I know*, he pondered. With brochures in hand, he continued on to Pho Ho Ho.

At the restaurant, as Horatio sat in a booth perusing the travel literature sipping from a cup of hot tea, he reflected back to the situation that Kelli's sister, Rene, was dealing with. His heart grieved for her because he understood firsthand how poor choices in relationships can cause disconnect from family. Horatio hadn't kept in contact with his family or friends in Virginia Beach since moving to Scituate. His parishioners weren't aware that he struggled with occasional bouts of loneliness.

It was three years ago when his heart was broken by the callous rejection of his proposal of marriage to the love of his life. Despite concerns held by his parents, family and friends about his marital intentions, he continued to pursue his plans undauntedly. In the end, the woman of his desire showed herself to be everything but virtuous. Embarrassed by the realization of his mistake, he chose to distance himself from everything that reminded him of his family and hometown.

Looking back at the heartache and separation that God allowed him to experience, he convinced himself that it all was necessary to prepare him for his next assignment as pastor to Church of the Good Shepherd. God was going to use him to bring change to the church community. At least, that's what he believed when he received the offer letter from the church's trustee board. Now he finds himself inquiring of God, "Will it ever get any easier, Lord?"

After finishing his meal, he returned home. He ended his day by reading from I Corinthians, chapter 13, the "Love" chapter.

Day 19
December 21st - Friday

It was Horatio's last full day of work in his office before the church's Christmas pageant. Historically this was the day when phone calls, letters, and visitors would pour into the church office requesting help in making this a "Merry Christmas" for family members and friends. Requests for emergency assistance would range from traumatic to truly foolish.

Whenever a phone request was received, the first question Horatio would ask is: "What church do you attend?" At that question, more than half of the callers would slam the phone down. Others would give the name of a church but couldn't easily remember the address or the name of the pastor who shepherded the church. For those he believed to be genuinely in need, he would direct them to one of several philanthropic agencies or organizations.

During his tenure as pastor, Horatio wasn't able to convince the trustee board to establish a fund to assist Good Shepherd's church families who were experiencing difficult times. The financial focus of the church's trustee board was limited to feeding its Building Fund.

The first call came in at eight ten. Horatio didn't get the chance to say a single word before he heard:

"Good morning and God bless you," the caller began. "I need some help with buying my son the computer that he wants for Christmas. I see it on sale for eleven hundred dollars and was wondering what your church can do to help me get it. I don't want my boy to be disappointed."

"Well, good morning to you," Horatio responded. "Let me ask you a question, if you don't mind: what church do you attend?"

CLICK! was all he heard. Ten minutes later, another call came. It was bolder than the first call.

"Good morning," Horatio greeted. "Church of the Good Shepherd. Pastor Smiley speaking."

"Pastor, my name is Ned Clemmons and I live in Providence, RI." The man continued, "I've fallen on hard times and I'd like a plasma television to kind of, you know, get me in the holiday spirit."

"Ned," Horatio started, "I can't help you with the television but…."

CLICK was Ned's response.

Calls continued to come in. Some of the calls were so outrageous that he began documenting them. By the end of the eighth call, Horatio realized that he had to respond to the calls differently. After a few minutes in prayer, he devised a strategy. When the next caller requested assistance, he would inform them that they would be placed in queue on the prayer line, until a representative was available to respond to their request. To the caller, it would appear that they had been redirected to a recorded message when, in fact, Horatio would begin praying for them.

After a few minutes of hearing his prayer, most callers would disconnect. He was able to pray for more than thirty callers. Seven callers gave their hearts to the Lord. Horatio was so excited about souls being saved that he refused to break for lunch. Callers who remained on the phone through the prayer received the full measure of his assistance in referring them to organizations that were positioned to help.

At four o'clock, members of the church's youth choir began to arrive for their final rehearsal for the Christmas pageant. Horatio greeted the children and Mrs. Munsey as they entered the sanctuary. Taking a seat at the rear of the church where he could be easily noticed, he remained for the duration of the practice session. Mrs. Munsey later laughed and acknowledged that after the kind of day she experienced, his presence was the best Christmas gift anyone could have given her. Horatio closed down the church at six forty-five that evening.

A messy snowstorm was predicted to arrive overnight so, he stopped by the Village Mart for some storm provisions before going home. His basket was brimming with frozen clam chowder, bread, tea, chocolate chip cookies, and milk as he made his way to the checkout area. He paid for his groceries and went home. After some quiet time, spent reflecting on the events of the day, he went to bed.

Day 20
December 22nd - Saturday

At three thirty, Horatio was awakened by the sound of gale force winds knocking over trash barrels beneath his bedroom window. The commotion was so loud that he had difficulty returning to sleep. As he lay awake listening to the cold, stormy weather outside, his attention moved to the warm sunny scenes that were prominently displayed in the Caribbean vacation brochures he had picked up at the travel agency.

Reaching into the top draw of the nightstand, he began flipping through the cruise ship literature. Sun-filled skies, sandy beaches, Vegas shows and endless buffets adorned each page of the brochure. This was as far from winter in Scituate that he could ever expect to be. He decided then and there that he would book a cruise vacation that afternoon. Eventually returning to sleep, Horatio remained in bed until eleven o'clock.

At twelve noon, he left for his weekly visit to the nursing home. Inside the nursing home, the Christmas party was in full swing. Horatio had prepared goodie bags inclusive of yoyo's, paddle balls, sugar-free candy, and bookmarks that delineated the Ten Commandments. He distributed the gift bags to the residents and staff members. They each responded to their gift as if someone had given them a bag filled with money. Most of the male residents, having a natural white beard, donned red stocking caps and played the role of Santa Claus. Twenty-plus Santa Clauses were packed into the community room.

To reduce the confusion, the nurses held a contest to 'crown' the true Jolly Old Saint Nick. The contestant who could correctly name each of Santa's reindeer would be crowned Santa Claus. All others would be relegated to the role of Santa's helpers. The contest was hilarious. The participants did well to remember the name of Rudolph. The names of Comet, Vixen, Cupid, and Donner were seldom mentioned. At the conclusion of the contest, Vinny Johnson was declared the winner. Having remembered seven reindeer names, he managed to better his closest competitor by two.

At three o'clock, the Christmas party was still going strong when Horatio apologized for having to leave. He explained that he had a stop to make before returning home. After a brief prayer, he said good-bye.

Upon leaving the nursing home, Horatio stopped by the travel agency to make arrangements for his Caribbean cruise. Entering the agency, he was greeted by an older man.

"Good afternoon, sir. How may I help you today?" the man asked.

"Good afternoon, indeed. I am interested in booking a cruise vacation with a mid to late January departure date," he specified.

"I'm pleased to meet you. My name is Tony. I'm the owner of this agency. And, your name is…?"

"Hi, Tony. My name is Horatio Smiley."

"Hello, Horatio. Thank you for trusting me with your travel plans." Tony continued, "May I ask you a few questions to determine which cruise package would be the best fit for you?"

"Please, ask away," Horatio invited. During the next ninety minutes, Horatio received an education in the intricacies of cruise itineraries and accommodations that assured him that he had made the right choice in vacation options. With travel documents specifying a January 22nd departure date in hand, Horatio stopped at a department store along his way home to pick up a couple of bathing suits. He was so excited about his travel plans that he forgot that swimwear wouldn't be back on the store shelves for at least four months. Still he thanked the Lord and reminded Him, *Even though I will be on vacation, I am still available and on call for whatever you have need of, Lord, even while at sea.*

He ordered some Chinese food and carried it home, where he remained for the rest of the evening.

Day 21
December 23rd - Sunday

At nine thirty, Horatio looked out his window to observe the activity taking place in front of the church. From his vantage point, he could see that the Christmas Sunday event was well underway. Vehicles lined both sides of the street in either direction, as far as the eye could see. The church parking lot was quickly filling in. Parishioners streamed toward the church, where they were met by holiday greeters. Cameras and camcorders were busy memorializing special moments as members of the Children's Choir arrived adorned in costumes of fluffy angel wings and halos. "Lord, your people are lost. So lost." His heart was grieved.

Relieved of his usual sanctuary opening responsibility and having no sermon notes to review, Horatio planned to delay his arrival at the church. Inwardly, he discerned God's Spirit ministering to him.

"The Shepherd must protect his flock, or they will be overtaken." The check in his spirit brought such conviction on him that he repented for his poor attitude and made his way quickly to the church. To an observer, by the way he was running, it would appear that someone was chasing him. After some time spent greeting parishioners, he took his position at the lectern and prayed the commencement blessing. He remained at the rear of the sanctuary until he was called upon to deliver the benediction.

In secular terms, the pageant was a great success. The headcount, the offerings and the organizational effort exceeded the trustee's expectations. The choirs sang, the parents cried, and Santa arrived on cue. So joyous an event, yet so painful to watch. Spiritually, the opportunity to honor Jesus Christ was a complete failure. There was absolutely no evidence that God's Holy Spirit was present anywhere in the sanctuary. Throughout the event, Horatio prayed earnestly that God would touch the hearts of those present to recognize and give thanks for the greatest gift ever afforded mankind: Jesus Christ. After all, this was the occasion to honor the Lord's birth and, seemingly, he was the only one there who was aware of this. As the last of the parishioners exited the church building, he closed the building down and went home.

Sitting at his kitchen table, the familiar spirit of depression overtook him. The Christmas holiday season used to be his favorite time of the year. Family, friends, and laughter were never in short supply. Admittedly, it was his decision to isolate himself from those who loved him dearly. Voices of heartache, concerned for his well-being, continued to leave phone messages pleading with him to call. The last call came two years ago. His need to be left alone was, at last, received and respected. Now he has only himself to confide in, laugh with, and cry to each and every day of the year.

Lifting his eyes to look outside, he could see the sun setting.

"Where did the time go? I can't believe I've been sitting here this long. Lord, please give me the courage to make things right with my family. I miss them so much." A tear rolled down his cheek and onto the table.

In times past when he experienced similar episodes of loneliness, he would go to a pay phone on Front Street and call his parents' home. His mother was always the one to answer. The sound of his mother's voice brought conviction to him but he lacked the ability to manage a single audible syllable in response. He would remain silent until she would hang up.

At times, in the aftermath of a failed attempt to reconnect with his parents, he would grieve for days and sometimes weeks that followed. Horatio understood that his parents loved him and wanted only the best for him. He accepted that his inability to end his self-exile caused hurt and worry to be borne by his parents unjustly. He wanted more than anything else to gather the strength to say, *Mom and Dad, I'm sorry*, but every time he mustered the courage to call and he heard a loving voice on the other end of the call say, "Hello," a mute spirit would come upon him, causing him to become unresponsive. He recognized that his battle was a spiritual one and only the Lord, through prayer, could help.

"Lord, I need your help. I am incapable of overcoming these demonic forces that have been assigned against my relationship with my family. Because of my pride and unforgiveness towards my parents, I have given authority to these dark spirits to enter in and harden my heart against them. This is sinful. I am wrong. Please, Lord, forgive me. I repent for every part that I played in causing division and hurt to come to my parents. They are wonderful parents. They don't deserve the pain I've caused. Deliver me from this wickedness. Bind up the mute spirit that hinders my ability to speak to my parents each time that I struggle to let them know how much I love and miss them. This I pray in Jesus' name. Amen."

At the conclusion of his prayer, Horatio felt as though a spiritual burden had lifted. He had, at last, given his burden to God. In that moment, he remembered the assurance that the still voice had spoken: *I am with you. Trust in Me. I have heard your petitions and I have responded to them.*

Day 22
December 24th – Monday

Horatio awoke from a refreshing night's rest. The powerful spirit of depression that hung over him, as if it was the Sword of Damocles, had departed. In preparation for his meeting with Kelli and her sister, he hastened to complete his daily regime of errands before their arrival. At twelve noon, Kelli called to let him know that she and Rene were on their way and expected to be on time. She hadn't been to Good Shepherd before, so Horatio gave her directions.

Kelli and Rene arrived promptly at twelve thirty. Horatio greeted them as they entered and gave them a brief tour of the church. At the conclusion of the tour, Kelli and Rene were invited to join Horatio for sandwiches and hot cocoa in church kitchen.

"I hope you don't mind eating while we talk." Horatio chuckled.

"Rene and I thought about bringing some snacks, but we weren't sure how long you would be available to meet with us today," Kelli explained.

"My time is your time. I am very interested in hearing more about your situation, Rene."

"Well, Pastor, it's a great big mess," Rene replied. "Where would you like me to begin?"

"Do you attend a church?" he asked.

"I haven't been inside a church for years," Rene confessed.

"Why not pick it up from the time that you stopped going to church," he suggested.

"Wow. That seems like a lifetime ago." Rene paused. "I was eighteen and, having just graduated high school, I declared myself 'emancipated' from every tradition and obligation that got in the way of my ability to be the 'me' that I wanted to be." She continued, "Every Sunday morning for as long as I can remember, my parents would have me sitting in the fourth pew for another dose of "church." I saw no consequence in missing a Sunday or three so; I went when I felt like it. By the time I turned twenty-one, I had disconnected from church, altogether."

"What were some of the things that you did in those days of declaring your freedom, Rene?"

"Oh, my God," she reflected , "sex, drugs, alcohol was pretty much what I lived for. I was out of control. If it didn't feel good, I wasn't interested. My parents tired of my rebellious behavior so, they told me I had to leave."

"Any regrets?" Horatio asked.

"More than I care to remember," Rene sighed. "Aside from my total screw-up with Daniel, I've slept in boarded up buildings, aborted unwanted pregnancies, watched friends die, been beaten, robbed, jailed; you name it and I'm pretty sure I've got the trophy." An expression of agony registered on Kelli's face. Clearly she was hearing much of her sister's testimony for the first time.

Rene continued, "I never realized that the more I rebelled, the deeper I descended into a living hell. At the lowest point in my rebellion, I got pregnant, again. Just before that happened, I was beginning to tire of the lifestyle that had become routine. Actually, I remember praying once or twice for a strategy to get out of this place in my life, alive." She recalled, "I thought this was God's way of telling me, 'I am giving you one last chance, Rene. Take care of this baby and show me that you are redeemable.' He gave me my chance and I blew it."

Looking over at Kelli's face, Horatio noticed a stream of tears. "Kelli, are you all right?"

"Yes, I'm good, thank you. I'm sorry. Rene, I didn't know that all this stuff was going on with you. I had no idea things were so bad." She sobbed as Rene tried to console her.

"It's okay, Sis." Rene gave her a hug. "I'm glad it's all coming out. Don't apologize for your tears. God knows I've cried my share."

"Rene," Horatio began, "you said God told you to take care of your baby as the way to show that you were worthy of His redemption. From what I understand, you did for Daniel exactly what was required for his safety. And," Horatio continued, "you didn't disappoint God. In fact, I expect that He was well pleased with the courage and sacrifice that you displayed in that situation."

"I'm sorry, Pastor. I don't see it your way." Rene explained, "I gave up my baby. When I had the opportunity to fight for him, I couldn't. The drugs and alcohol that I retreated to following Daniel's birth would have shown up in any blood test." She paused, remembering that pivotal moment in court. "If only I had stayed clean. No, I'm sorry, I didn't respond the way I should have." Rene's eyes began to fill with tears.

"Rene," Horatio paused, "where is Daniel?"

"He's at the Home for Children," she responded.

"Let me ask you another question: where would Daniel be if you allowed your boyfriend to do what he wanted with him?"

"I don't know."

"Is it possible that Daniel might have ended up in a situation of abuse, molestation, even as a sacrifice in some occult ritual?" he asked.

"I suppose anything is possible."

"I'm not here with you, today, for the purpose of giving you warm and fuzzies." Horatio continued, "I agree that, yeah, you made some shortsighted choices. And every choice you made, God knew before you chose." He could see that Rene was listening.

He continued, "God didn't tell you that you're beyond redemption. You allowed yourself to believe that. God's love is a perfect love. He doesn't abandon us because we abandon Him. He's not interested in keeping a scorecard of our sins. God's intention for your life, Kelli's life, my life, is good, not evil."

"Then why did He allow all this wicked stuff to happen to me?" Rene challenged.

"God is not a monster. He is patient and loving," Horatio explained. "Just like the time you rebelled against your parents' counsel, they didn't disown you. They didn't lock you in the basement of their home until you came to your senses. They told you that because you chose rebellion over respect, you had to experience the consequences of living in rebellion. And, I'm certain that, because of their love for you, they continued to pray for you every day."

"Amen. You can say that, again. We all did," Kelli confirmed. Rene smiled.

"God loves you with a love greater than even your parents are able to give," he said, "like the parable of the 'Prodigal Son' demonstrates; after we've come to the end of our living in rebellion, God will be there waiting to receive us, with outstretched arms and a love that never fails. We all go through a rebellious period in our life."

"Pastor, were you ever rebellious?" Rene asked. Kelli perked up.

"Oh, my Lord, yes," he continued. "But, that's another story for another day." His face reddened. Everyone laughed.

It was after three o'clock. Horatio had to call the counseling session to an end. "Rene. Kelli. I know it's getting late, but can we spend a few minutes in prayer?"

"I'd like that," Rene said.

"Me too," Kelli agreed.

Joining hands, he prayed for Rene to be blessed with healing, strength, and for her reconnection to God. The room temperature appeared to soar as palms and foreheads perspired. Horatio initiated the prayer but before long, Rene and Kelli were praying, also. At the conclusion of the prayer, everyone acknowledged the strong presence of God.

Unbeknownst to Horatio, Rene and Kelli were groomed to be prayer warriors at an early age. Life circumstances caused them to move away from spending any time with God. They had forgotten how good it felt to be in the presence of the Holy Spirit.

As they prepared to leave, Kelli asked, "Pastor, do you have plans for Christmas day?"

"Nothing concrete. I usually make the rounds to homes of some of the church members. I expect that's what I'll be doing."

"Pastor, how do we become members?" Kelli asked.

"Yeah," Rene chimed in.

"There's no ceremony or test," he chuckled. "If you choose to become a part of the church, you just say so."

"So," said Kelli.

"Double so," said Rene.

"Well, I guess that makes it official enough." Horatio laughed.

"So, what time will you be stopping by our parents' house?" Rene continued, "That's where we'll be."

"How's two o'clock?" he asked.

"Two o'clock is perfect," Kelli responded.

"Pastor, by the way, what do you like to eat?" Rene asked.

"Anything except my own cooking."

"That bad, huh?" Kelli asked.

"Don't ask," Horatio confessed.

Laughter filled the kitchen as Kelli and Rene prepared to head out. Horatio stayed behind just long enough to close down the building.

****

Experiencing a surge of Christmas cheer, Horatio stopped by the Village Mart one last time before the holiday arrived. Not wanting to show up empty-handed when making his rounds, he picked up some flowers and three Boston Crème cakes. He returned home directly after leaving the store.

Sitting in his favorite chair watching a holiday movie, he revisited his conversation with Kelli and Rene. The comment that he made to Rene regarding her shortsighted choices continued to resonate. After all, it was he who chose to separate from his family and friends three years ago. So many times, he longed to share with family members and friends about things that were taking place in his life; good, bad, or indifferent. Yet, every time his phone identification device displayed incoming calls from the people he loved, he would choose to ignore their reaching out to him. It was his way of administering justice to those he believed had betrayed him in his time of need. In that time, he came to justify that it was the Lord's way of drawing him into a closer relationship with Him. Even though he knew that his justification contradicted scriptural teaching, he chose to rebel against divine instruction.

Horatio cried out to God, "Please, Lord, heal me. Forgive me of my unrighteousness. Please." He understood that the spirits of unforgiveness, pride and anger, within him were not of God. Again, he remembered the times that he picked up the phone to call his parents. He knew that he needed to apologize and tell them how much he loved them. But how? Once again, as he sat in solitude remembering so many previous Christmas Eve celebrations spent with his family, he grieved. The clock on the wall showed the time to be eight thirty-five.

As if experiencing an out-of-body moment, he realized that he was reaching for the phone one more time. His eyes watered as he keyed in the telephone number that he would never forget. The phone handset didn't feel right. It's dripping with sweat. It's uncomfortable. He senses the need to set it back on the cradle, before the call goes through. He doesn't want this attempt to reconnect with his parents to fail, like so many times before. He bites his lower lip. His stomach is becoming unsettled. *Don't hang up,* he tells himself. First ring. Second ring. The phone is still in his hand. Third ring.

Thank you, Lord. Nobody home. He expelled a sigh of relief. *I'll leave a message*, he strategized. *Just hang in there for two more rings*. He's counting as he remembered that the voice messaging system is programmed to pick up on the fifth ring. Another ring was heard. *That's four*. Preparing to leave a message, he anxiously awaited the fifth ring.

"Hello. Smiley residence." It was his father.

Caught off guard, he responded.

"Hi, Dad. It's Ace." A moment of hesitation. "Merry Christmas."

The silence seems to last forever.

"Son? How are you? Is everything all right?" His father was concerned.

"Everything's good. Is Mom okay?" It was unusual for his father to answer the phone.

"She's fine, son. She's upstairs in bed. Please, hold on. Let me get her. Don't hang up."

"Dad. Don't wake her. Let her rest. I can call back another time."

"Son, it's been three years. Please, hold on. She needs to hear your voice," his father appealed.

"Thanks, Dad. I'd like that." Horatio understood just how much his mother missed him. Within moments, his mother was on the phone.

"Hello," she answered.

"Mom." Horatio sighed.

"Ace, is that you?" She began to weep.

"It's me, Mom." He could hear his father, the personification of strength, quietly thanking God in the background. "Mom. Dad. I'm so sorry for the hurt that I've caused you," he continued. "I've prayed daily that God would give me the words to tell you how truly sorry I am. All I can say is I love you, so much. You deserve a better son than what I've been to you."

"Nonsense, Ace," his mother began, "you have brought more joy to our lives than words could ever express."

"And, Son," his father said, "it's your mother and I who question things that we might have done differently."

"Dad, you and Mom could not have done anything more or differently to let me know that you have always given me your best." He continued, "I never doubted that. I've picked up the phone more times than I can remember to call and apologize for allowing myself to be convinced otherwise."

"Can you come home for a visit anytime soon?" his mother pleaded.

"I want to so badly. I miss you both so much." He sniffled. Gathering himself, he continued, "I have some time off beginning January 15th. Maybe, if you have nothing else going on, I can come then."

"Son, short of our own funeral, nothing on Earth can stop us from being here for that," his dad promised.

"Thanks, Dad. Thanks, Mom" was all that Horatio could manage as he wiped tears from his eyes.

For the next two and a half hours mom, dad, and son enjoyed the best conversation they could have ever hoped for. Circumstances leading up to Horatio's move away from Virginia Beach were revisited and respectfully discussed. It was agreed with unanimous joy that Horatio would journey home during the week of January 15th for the first time in three years.

"Merry Christmas, Mom and Dad. Thank you."

"Merry Christmas, Son. We love you," his parents responded in unison.

The call ended at eleven eleven. It was no coincidence. Horatio understood that according to scripture, the number one represented unity. He chuckled. He remained seated in his chair for a while, pondering how precious the family is to God and Satan, albeit for different reasons. God established that families should remain together, while Satan seeks to cause division. The plan for separation that Satan had enacted against members of the Smiley family came to an end, tonight.

Day 23
December 25th - Tuesday (Christmas Day)

Horatio was slow to get up. Understandably, it took a while to fall asleep after his telephone reunion with his parents. Looking over at the clock, he noticed that it was eleven forty-five. "Wow. Almost noon. I must have been more tired than I thought," he said, rubbing his eyes.

He remembered the families that he intended to visit, today. As he shaved and showered, he was reminded of the commitment he made to Kelli and Rene to be at their home at two o'clock. "I guess I'll begin at the Brocks and play it by ear the rest of the day. Four families to visit. What was I thinking? Please don't let me disappoint anyone today. Lord, should I let my hosts-in-waiting know that I've bitten off more than I can handle and, I won't be able to make it?" The Lord was silent.

"I get it. I got myself into this so, you're going to let me get myself out. I know. I should have consulted you first." He laughed. "Don't worry, I'll learn, Lord. Sooner or later, I'll learn."

He made a grilled cheese sandwich and poured a glass of juice while he readied himself to leave. He didn't want to make a poor impression by appearing to be famished at his first opportunity to meet Kelli and Rene's parents. By one-thirty, he headed out the door for the first stop of what always proved to be a very busy day. He was enthusiastic about his visit with the Brock family. Something about being in the company of Kelli and Rene caused him to feel at ease.

During his time at Good Shepherd, he hadn't entered into many personal associations outside the circle of his church family. He understood the importance of being guarded when in the company of his church members. He sensed that he was still under surveillance by Bill Nelson's minions and, as a result, always had to be cautious. Careful of what he said, to whom he said it, etc. Horatio clearly understood that demonic spirits were capable of influencing people to become agents of confusion.

Using his GPS device, he arrived at the Brock residence exactly at two o'clock. Before he could open his car door, Kelli and Rene exited the house to retrieve him.

"Merry Christmas, ladies!" he hailed as they approached the car.

"Merry Christmas, Pastor!" they responded joyfully.

"Oh, just a minute. I almost forgot." He returned to open the rear door of the car and, reaching in, he produced a Christmas floral arrangement in one hand and a tray of Italian butter cookies in the other.

"Pastor, you didn't have to bring anything," Kelli began. "We just appreciate you being able to join us for dinner today."

"I hope you brought a healthy appetite, Pastor," Rene said. "Our mom worked all night to prepare her signature dish for you."

"That's so nice. What, may I ask, is her 'signature' dish?"

"She stayed up all night fixing escargot on a bed of fresh seaweed," Rene informed, enthusiastically.

"Isn't escargot snails?" Horatio asked sheepishly.

"Oh, yes," Rene replied. "Big, juicy snails. They kind of taste like pieces of undercooked liver. You do like liver, don't you?"

"To be honest, I'm not particularly big on liver," Horatio confessed.

"Well," Rene continued, "Mom likes to make it for us. We don't want to do anything to hurt her feelings. Is that okay with you, Pastor?"

Horatio didn't respond audibly but a look of *Man, what have I gotten myself into now* was all over his face. Inwardly, he thanked God for giving him the foresight to make the grilled cheese sandwich before leaving his house. So at a loss for words was he that he hadn't noticed Rene and Kelli struggling to maintain a serious look about them. Climbing the stairs to the front porch, Kelli opened the door and escorted Horatio into the house. Inside, Mr. and Mrs. Brock greeted him warmly.

"Pastor," Mr. Brock began, "we have heard so much about you."

"I can't remember Kelli or Rene speaking as glowingly of anyone as they have you," Mrs. Brock said.

"Wow," Horatio responded, "you're all making me blush," he confessed. Everyone laughed.

"Mother, can I have some time off for good behavior?" Mr. Brock asked his wife, jokingly, as he untied the apron from around his waist.

"Well, I guess you've earned it."

"Come on into the living room and have a seat," Mr. Brock said as he led Horatio into a nicely decorated, sun-filled sitting space. Kelli and Rene followed close behind as observers.

Horatio sat on a sofa with Rene and Kelli on either side of him, while Mr. Brock sat in a recliner that was unmistakably his favorite chair.

"So, you pastor the Church of the Good Shepherd?" Mr. Brock asked.

Kelli and Rene gave a look to each other as if to say, *Here goes Daddy, again.*

"Yes, sir," Horatio replied. "I've been the church's senior pastor for three years now. I'm also the associate pastor, pastor's assistant, maintenance director, and office secretary."

Everyone laughed, including Mrs. Brock who continued to work diligently in the kitchen.

"My wife can hear a pin drop from one hundred yards away," cautioned Mr. Brock.

"You can say that again," Kelli confirmed.

"I heard that," Mrs. Brock responded. Again, laughter erupted.

"So, Pastor, please tell me about yourself. Are you from the Scituate area?" Mr. Brock asked.

"No, I'm from Virginia Beach." He went on to discuss his ministerial and educational background, present undertakings, and future aspirations. He concluded by sharing the event of his telephone reunion with his parents a few hours earlier. The Brocks hung on his every word.

"Pastor, you are a good man," Mr. Brock continued. "I can understand why my daughters are so impressed with you."

"Thank you, Mr. Brock. You are very kind."

"Please, call me Deacon," Mr. Brock instucted.

"Deacon, huh?" Horatio asked, inquisitively.

"Yeah. For some reason, that's the name my mom and dad decided to tag me with when I was born." He continued, "My folks were good Catholics. They attended weekly Mass but never served in any official capacity within the parish. My mom told me that God had given her that name for me. I've always found that to be very curious, given that I've never held any desire to serve in the clergy. I guess I must have frustrated God's calling on my life."

"Yes. That is very interesting." Horatio continued, "Do you still attend your childhood church?"

"No, sir," Deacon continued. "I became frustrated with the foolishness that was going on in the church. The day that they closed our church for 'financial reasons,' I walked away and never looked back. Generations of faithful followers and families being told, 'You can't come back here because the church has bills to pay.' Nobody was fooled by that. Everybody knew what the truth of the matter was. To this day, I can't understand why the church would not acknowledge its wrongdoing. Those poor kids and their families. Unacceptable and unforgiveable."

At that moment, Mrs. Brock came into the room.

"Dinner is ready," she announced. "Everybody come along into the dining room before the food gets cold."

Once seated, Horatio began to scan the table in search of Mrs. Brock's favorite dish; escargot, on a bed of chilled seaweed. He noticed a delicious roasted turkey at the center of the table setting. A variety of covered chafing dishes encircled the turkey.

"Hope you're hungry, Pastor." Mrs. Brock continued, "I've prepared something special that I think you'll enjoy."

Lord, Jesus, Horatio thought to himself, *help me deal with these snails, gracefully.* "Well, I've heard that you are a wonderful cook and escargot is your signature dish," he replied. "I'm kind of a steak and potatoes guy, but I'm willing to give it a try."

"Escargot?" Mrs. Brock responded. "Aren't those snails? Who told you that? I've never cooked a snail in my kitchen and don't expect to begin any time soon."

Rene and Kelli broke into a belly laugh that soon overtook everyone.

"You girls didn't…" Mrs. Brock began, placing her hand over her mouth to contain her amusement.

"Guilty," Rene confessed.

Horatio's face reflected a look of great relief.

"Rene, you haven't lost your touch." Deacon laughed, and then explained, "Pastor, Rene has always been the family comedian. It's so wonderful to see her laugh, again. You know, after all she has been through…." He got up from his chair and went over and gave her a hug. "Pastor," Deacon continued, "I believe that you have helped Rene and our family in a way that you can't begin to understand."

"You're right, Deacon," Horatio acknowledged. "I'm not sure what it is that I'm being credited with, but I'll do it again so long as Mrs. Brock holds to her promise not to prepare any escargot."

"Don't give it a second thought, Pastor," Mrs. Brock assured him.

Rene and Kelli continued to enjoy his reaction to their practical joke. The next two hours passed as if it were only a few minutes. The food was excellent. Horatio continued to compliment Mrs. Brock with every bite of food that he ate. Joy and laughter filled the dining room. It was four o'clock and Horatio, admittedly having overeaten, wasn't too excited about going out to visit with other families where he would be expected to dine. He didn't want to run the risk of hurting his subsequent hosts' feelings because he had eaten elsewhere.

"Do you have to go, now, Pastor?" the Brock family asked.

"I'm afraid so."

"Maybe you can come to dinner on Sunday," Deacon suggested.

It was obvious that he was very impressed with Horatio.

"I'd love to, but I've been invited to dinner with a dear elderly couple next Sunday. Maybe the Sunday after."

"Done!" Kelli was quick to respond. "It's a date, I mean a deal!" Kelli was embarrassed. She knew that she'd be hearing about her slipup as soon as Horatio left.

As Rene handed him his coat, she asked, "Pastor, do you have a busy week ahead?"

"Usually, the week after Christmas is quiet," he began. "In anticipation of that, I made a commitment to attend a Foster Parenting information meeting at Mercy Ministries Home for Children."

"Really?" Rene was surprised. "But you're a pastor. Why ever would you be going to a Foster Parenting class?"

"To be honest," Horatio began, "I stopped in Mercy Ministries' office the day I waited in the parking lot for you. I was curious to learn more about the organization, so I went inside to pick up some program literature. Actually, the elderly couple that I am having dinner with next Sunday worked in the foster care system. They had remarkable experiences with eighty-six children that were entrusted to them. They have a five-bedroom house that, with minimal repairs, can be available to move some of the children into a less transient environment. Then, there's another family who I believe could be an awesome blessing in helping to reestablish their property as a loving foster home. And, by the way, I'm a pastor, not a priest. I can marry, father children, and live life as God established that I, as a man, should. Believe me, I thank God, every day, for that ." He chuckled.

"Sorry, Pastor. My mistake. Would you mind if I tag along?" Rene asked. "Maybe I'll get to see Daniel."

"Thank you, God," Mrs. Brock blurted out, unable to contain her enthusiasm. "I'm sorry," she began. "I've been praying for this moment for a long time." Tears welled up in her and Deacon's eyes.

"I'd like that very much, Rene." Horatio continued, "The meeting begins at six o'clock. Let's meet at five forty-five in our usual place," he said in a joking manner. With that, he thanked everyone for a Christmas Day that he would always remember. After exchanging hugs with each of the Brocks, he bounded out the door and headed for his car. Before pulling out of the driveway, he waved good bye to his hosts, who continued to wave from the front porch.

Horatio managed to visit with three other church families before returning home for the evening. He continued to think about the time that he spent with the Brock family. At ten thirty, he retired for the evening.

Day 24
December 26th - Wednesday

Horatio awoke to the sound of fire engines racing past his house at seven forty-five. The odor of smoke filtered into his bedroom. *Oh, Lord*, he thought aloud. *I hope that's not someone's house burning.* He quickly got up and made his way to the bedroom window. He watched another fire truck head down the street until it turned a corner and disappeared from view. Looking above the tree line, he noticed a plume of smoke hovering over the area near the town dump. There were no homes in that section of town. "Thank you, Lord."

Now, wide awake, he pours himself a glass of juice and spends the morning studying scripture and praying. As he prayed, a tangible presence of God manifested. The still voice whispered, "I am with you." It was the same voice that had visited him two weeks before, in his office. As quickly as the voice came, it departed. "Don't leave. Come back, please. I have so many questions," Horatio pleaded, to no avail.

After a few minutes more of reading scripture, he decided to take advantage of the post-holiday lull in activity and return to bed for a catnap. Dozing off, he began to dream.

In his dream, Rene Brock, a little boy, and he were picnicking in a green pasture. The sun shone brightly and birds sang from nearby treetops. Horatio reached into his pocket, pulled out a small box and, on bended knee, presented Rene with, what he recalled to be, a ring. "Rene, I love you," he continued, "Please, be my wife?"

Before Rene could react, Horatio's mother and father, Mr. and Mrs. Brock, Kelli and several Good Shepherd church members appeared. They gathered around to witness his proposal. Rene attempted to respond but couldn't open her mouth to answer him. An invisible, supernatural hindrance had manifested and locked down her ability to speak. She tried, again and again, to answer without success. Frustrated, she wept. Wiping away her tears, she located a twig nearby, picked it up, and began to scratch some letters in the dirt. "NO."

A look of devastation registered on his face. The spectators began to point and laugh at him. His Father laughed and said, "We told him he would never rate as marriage material." The crowd joined in the laughter. Horatio looked around in disbelief. Humiliated and hurt, he began to weep. His tears flowed unceasingly. He took a red and white checkered napkin from the picnic basket and began to wipe his eyes. Drawing the napkin away from his face, he was able to witness the faces, previously recognizable as family members and friends, being transformed into demonic images, resembling those that were present in his recurring school gymnasium nightmare. Contorted faces in the crowd increased in number and became angrier as they advanced aggressively toward him. He stood to his feet and began taking backward steps to keep distance between them and him. Entities previously recognized as his father and Deacon Brock leaped on him and began choking him. Shaken and perspiring, he awoke from the dream. "Lord, what was that about? Why does this nightmarish situation continue to haunt me?"

Looking over at the clock, he noticed that it was twenty minutes before noon. He shaved, showered, and got dressed. As he microwaved a frozen meatloaf dinner, he remembered the delicious meal that he enjoyed at the Brock home the day before. Sitting at the kitchen table, his attention returned to the dream about Rene. Horatio didn't dream often. He believed that each dream was given for a reason. God wanted his attention and he knew it. This was the third time that he had a dream with that theme in which a crowd of people, inclusive of church members, attempted to harm and humiliate him. Unable to make sense of his dream, he began to experience frustration. He remembered his friends, George and Mattie Heywood, were always discussing their dreams with each other. *I wonder if they can help me understand any of this?*

Picking up the phone, he called the Heywoods to ask if he could stop by for a few minutes. George answered and was happy to hear Horatio's voice.

"Pastor, it's so good to hear from you. How was your Christmas?"

"George, it was very nice. How was yours?"

"Quiet, but nice."

"George, would it be okay if I stopped by? I had a dream and I'd like to get your take on it."

"Sure, come right over. Mattie and I don't plan on going anywhere today."

"Great. I'm on my way."

"See you soon," George said as he hung up the phone.

Twenty minutes later, Horatio was knocking at the Heywood's door. George ushered him into the kitchen, where Mattie had a pot of hot coffee brewing. Over a cup of coffee, Horatio shared his dream.

When he was finished, George and Mattie asked if this was the first occasion he had this dream. Reluctantly, he acknowledged that this was his third dream with the hurt and humiliation theme. At that, George and Mattie began comparing notes. Common denominators were discussed in detail. As George and Mattie dissected every aspect of what Horatio remembered, he began to inwardly question his decision to bring this situation to the Heywoods. While Mattie and George focused on his issues of persecution and rejection, Horatio began to experience a headache in his stomach and indigestion in his head. It was as though God had granted the Heywoods full access to his innermost insecurities.

The afternoon's discussion yielded some interesting aspects about Horatio. Namely, in times of adversity, he was a "runner" who was intimidated by outward appearances. To make matters worse, he, too often, trusts in himself more than he does in the Lord. Horatio was uncomfortable, but appreciative of the sensitivity and sincerity in the way that the Heywoods availed themselves.

The discussion graciously transitioned to his plans for the evening. He explained how, in his attempt to help someone, he had committed to attend a Foster Parenting information session. Having been involved in foster care programs before, the Heywoods asked if they could accompany him. They were curious to learn about the program's evolution since the time they closed their home to foster children.

"Are you considering re-entering the foster care provider system?" Horatio asked.

"Well, Pastor," George began, "ever since you introduced us to Ted and Ellen Willis, we've spoken almost every day. Seems Ted's employment situation hasn't improved much. In fact," George continued, "it's gotten worse."

"They're such sweet people. They could sure use some help." Mattie said, nodding her head. "Ellen is very interested in becoming a foster parent." She continued, "We've spoken at length about working together in resurrecting the program that we had here, before."

"That's great to hear," Horatio began. "I agree. They are good people and I appreciate your willingness to help them. Let me know if there is anything that I can do to help."

"So, can we go with you to the meeting tonight?" George asked.

"That shouldn't be a problem," Horatio replied. "I'll say you're my guests. Do you want to travel together or meet there?" he asked.

"George and I can find our way there," Mattie said. "Maybe I can get in touch with Ted and Ellen. What time does the meeting begin?"

"Six o'clock." Horatio continued, "We should plan to meet in the lobby at five forty-five. That way we'll be sure to get seats together."

"Wonderful. Five forty-five it is. This is exciting." Mattie was animated.

"I'm going to head back to my place to get ready," Horatio said. "See you then, the good Lord willing."

He was home by five o'clock to prepare for the meeting. He began to feel better about his commitment to attend the meeting and his decision to bring Rene. He remembered his conversation with the Brocks about his hoping that the Heywoods and Willises would join forces to become foster parents. "Lord," he thought aloud, "what are you up to?"

At five forty, he pulled onto Mercy Ministries' parking lot. He noticed Rene's car, immediately. He intended to keep her history confidential during his conversation with the Heywoods. He chose not to reveal that it was Rene who was in his dream.

Exiting his car, he walked over to Rene and escorted her into the administration building. She attempted, unsuccessfully, to conceal her nervousness. She had never before been inside the walls of the place Daniel knew as home. Moreover, if any member of Mercy Ministries' staff recognized her, it was their responsibility to call 911 and have her arrested for criminal trespass. Police records could easily confirm that a restraining order had been issued against her. Horatio tried to put her at ease. "Rene, will you pray with me?"

"I'd like that, Pastor."

He took her by the hand and prayed, "Father, we come before your throne of Grace, in the name of Jesus, our Lord, asking You to move so mightily in this evening's event that the spirit of anxiety that is afflicting Rene will be bound. Let her experience Your perfect peace. Also, we ask that You would cause reunification to come to Rene and her son Daniel. This we pray in Jesus' name. Amen."

"Wow," Rene responded. "I feel calmer already. This is amazing."

"Prayer works," Horatio said, "that's why scripture instructs us to be anxious about nothing, prayerful about everything."

Just then, the Heywoods walked into the lobby. Ted and Ellen Willis were with them. Horatio rushed over and gave them a hug. "Ted. Ellen. So good to see you. How have you been? And how are Becky and Noah?"

"Well, Pastor," Ted began, "the fact that we're here should tell you that you were right, I was wrong. And I remember my promise to you that I would sit with you for a day, a week, a month or however long it took for you to teach me why my situation remains a mess." Ted hesitated, "Pastor, be gentle with me, okay."

Ellen, George, and Mattie couldn't contain their composure as Ted resembled a young child who was just instructed to go get a switch and bring it to their parent for a "woodshed session."

"Ted," George said, chuckling, "Pastor isn't all that harsh."

Ted took little consolation in George's words of comfort. "You know," Ted offered, "I believe that I can honestly say that God has my attention."

"Good, but not good enough, Ted." Horatio laughed.

Rene continued to stand quietly off to the side. "Oh, my," Horatio said, motioning to Rene, "Everyone, this is Michelle." He knew that "Michelle" was Rene's middle name and he used that in order not to draw attention to her in the presence of any Mercy Ministries' staff members within listening range. Rene caught on and responded accordingly, shaking hands with the Heywoods and the Willises. At that point, they went into the conference room and sat together.

The foster parent prequalification and program policy portions of the meeting began and concluded on schedule. The Question & Answer session began with general inquiries from prospective care providers, as to common behavioral issues that "clients" would, likely, expect to experience.

"Let me be clear," emphasized Mrs. Monahan, the event coordinator, "Mercy Ministries does not entrust 'clients' to our care providers, we entrust 'children' to you." She continued, "Our children are no different from other children. They deserve to be loved, nurtured, and protected. Judy…," Mrs. Monahan spoke, motioning to her assistant, "please check to see if the children I invited to join us, tonight, are ready. If so, please bring them back as quickly as you can." Judy exited through a side door.

"As I was saying," Mrs. Monahan continued, "our children are like any other children their age. I am hopeful that before tonight's meeting is adjourned, you will be introduced to some of the children that, hopefully, you will have the privilege of caring for. Please understand that the children will simply enter in, say 'Good evening,' turn around, and exit.

This process may appear to be somewhat callous, but I do this to protect the children. You must understand," she emphasized, "the worst thing that can take place in these young lives is another disappointment. A glance, a smile, a question that can be experienced in the briefest exchange can result in a hope, an expectation, a 'feeling' that a child may hold tightly onto that goes unmet. So, when my assistant, Judy, returns with the children, please respond to their greeting with 'Good evening.' After they have exited the room, I will ask if you are interested in being a foster parent. If anyone has made the decision to withdraw from this opportunity, I would ask that you remain in your seat until this meeting has concluded. Is everyone okay with that?" she asked. All in attendance agreed. As questions were asked and answered, Rene prayed deep within her heart that Daniel would be included in the children who Mrs. Monahan had requested.

"Lord, if only I could see Daniel, even for only a moment...," she prayed in a whisper.

Just then, the same door through which Judy had departed opened wide and she returned with nine children in tow. Four boys and five girls who were of varied ages and ethnicities. They were polite and well-cared for. Rene searched their faces, looking for Daniel, but he was not among them. Horatio watched her from the corner of his eye, making sure she was all right. The children, in unison, recited "Good evening." They turned to leave, walking toward the same door they entered through when unexpectedly, the door was pushed open by an unseen force. A little boy, about five years old with strawberry blonde hair, blue eyes, and freckles came running into the room.

"Good evening," he said, trying to press through the exiting children. He moved toward the front of the room as if he were a fish swimming against the tide.

"Daniel! Oh, my God. It's Daniel." Rene clutched Horatio's arm while doing all within her ability to control her emotions. She fought to hold back tears. Horatio reached for her hand to steady her. By the Grace of God, it was only the Heywoods and Willises who noticed the exchange between them. They turned in their seats to check on Rene and Horatio but said nothing. Applications were handed out and contact information was exchanged. The meeting concluded within twenty minutes of Daniel's departure.

It was seven-thirty and very clear that Rene, the Willises, Heywoods, and Horatio needed to talk. The Willises children, Noah and Becky, were staying with Ellen's mother, so they were in good hands. After a quick call to Ellen's mother, the decision was made to meet at the Heywoods' home for coffee. Rene followed Horatio in her car.

Concerned for Rene, Horatio wanted to make sure that she was all right with the invitation to join the others. They were the first to arrive at the Heywoods. The night air was cold, so Horatio positioned the driver's side of his vehicle to come alongside the driver's side of Rene's car. Rolling his window down, he motioned to Rene to do the same. Complying, Rene, no longer obscured behind the glass, looked over at him. He could see that she had been crying. Interestingly, Rene saw the same thing taking place with him. His eyes, watered. His voice, unsteady.

"Pastor, are you okay?"

"Rene, I'm not sure."

"What's the matter, Pastor? Please, tell me." Rene, no longer focused on her hurt, sought to bring comfort to him.

"Rene," he began, "God has been speaking to me for a long time, but I chose to hear only what I wanted. My choice to rebel against him has resulted in years of frustration, self-deception, and isolation. Because of my arrogance, he had to bring me to a place so low that I couldn't see anything but up. In that time, I came to know and love him as my Heavenly Father. Something in my soul was forever changed. I repented, prayed, and recommitted my life to Him. Thankfully, he has allowed me to know His voice again."

"Pastor, I'm not sure that I understand," Rene responded. "You are one of the nicest people I've ever known. You give of yourself freely and work tirelessly for the benefit of others. Look at how you've helped me. Because of the time and help you've given me, I feel so much better about myself, my life, and God."

"Thanks, Rene. I appreciate that. I'm saying all of this to say that I need to speak with you candidly about a personal matter. About something God has shown me…," he paused, searching for a way to explain.

Rene was flattered. She didn't consider herself a confidante to Horatio. She was comfortable with him, but she didn't understand that his feelings were reciprocal. "Pastor, I am a very private person. Maybe that's something that I need to work at. But, what I'm trying to say is you can trust me not to share anything with anyone."

"Rene, I believe that. I, too, am a very private person. When I experience things that I don't understand, I usually try to sort things out on my own. Which brings me to my need to speak with you."

Rene was confused. "Pastor, what are you trying to say?"

At that, from behind the steering wheel of his car, Horatio told Rene everything he could remember about his, most recent, dream. He concluded with a profound confession. "Rene," he began, "the little boy in my dream was Daniel. I recognized him immediately as he walked into the meeting room tonight."

Rene was in disbelief. "Oh, my God. Oh, my God…. Pastor. I had a dream amazingly similar to yours."

"You did?" Horatio asked. "Why didn't you say anything?"

"I didn't understand it, either. I wanted to mention it, but I didn't know how," she explained.

"Wow, Lord. What are you showing us?" Horatio wondered aloud. Just then, the headlights of two vehicles turned into the Heywoods' driveway. Horatio and Rene exited their cars and met the Heywoods and Willises as they emerged from theirs. They moved quickly into the house to escape the cold night air.

Once inside, Horatio and Rene could detect a sense of giddiness by the interaction between George, Mattie, Ted and Ellen. "Okay, guys. What's going' on?" he asked.

"Pastor, we girls need a moment alone. Michelle, will you join us in the kitchen?" Mattie asked with a wink.

"Well, sure," Michelle responded.

"That works fine for us," George said. Ted nodded in agreement. "Pastor, let's go into the living room." George escorted them into the other room.

****

In the kitchen, Mattie sat at the table and motioned Ellen and Michelle to do likewise. "Michelle," she began, "I've known Pastor Smiley for a number of years. He's been like a son to George and me. I noticed something different about him this evening. Please, don't misunderstand, but he seems a bit love-struck."

"It was actually quite cute." Ellen giggled.

"So, woman to woman," Mattie continued, "what in the world has come over him?"

"Mrs. Heywood," Michelle began.

"Hold on a minute," Mattie explained, "My mother-in-law was Mrs. Heywood. Please, call me Mattie,"

"Thank you, Mattie," Michelle said. She continued, "Since we're making introductions, you can call me Rene." Mattie's eyes grew wide. Ellen was stunned.

"Why did Pastor introduce you as 'Michelle'?" Ellen asked.

For the next hour and forty-five minutes, Rene recalled events in her life that resulted in her being present at the Mercy Ministries meeting that evening. She began by telling them that "Michelle" was her middle name. As Rene continued to share her experiences with them, Mattie and Ellen, at times, were moved to tears. She appreciated the genuine concern that they had for Horatio's well-being. The ladies' session ended with a pact that was formed to "not rest until Daniel was returned home with Rene." They were in the middle of a group hug when the footsteps of George, Ted, and Horatio were heard coming down the hallway.

****

Prior to their return to the kitchen, George, Ted, and Horatio sat in the living room, positioned around the coffee table.

"Pastor, Michelle seems like a real sweet girl," George began. "Is she from around here?"

"She and her family are from Marshfield." Anticipating what George, as a man, was inwardly pondering but uncomfortable to ask, Horatio cut him to the quick, "And George, we haven't experienced intimacy at any level." He intended the latter part of his response to coincide with George's knocking back a bottle of water. "Wooosh!" was the sound of the water exiting George's mouth and nostrils in reaction to Horatio's perfectly timed delivery of his very personal relationship update. Ted roared with laughter at George's explosion.

"Whew!" Ted said while holding his stomach. "George, I haven't laughed this hard in years. Wow! Pastor, I've said it before and I say it again, your timing is amazing!" Ted continued to laugh.

"Is everybody okay in there?" Mattie's voice was heard from the kitchen.

"Everyone's fine," Horatio replied. "George might need another bottle of water, though."

"George, do you need me to bring you a bottle of water?" Mattie called out.

"No. I'm fine," George said as he, hurriedly, tried to wipe the water from his pants, his shirt, and the coffee table.

"Look, guys," Horatio began, "Rene, I mean Michelle, is someone who I have a healthy platonic relationship with. Nothing more, nothing less."

"Pastor, I didn't mean to pry into your personal affairs," George said. "I apologize if I offended you."

"George, I assure you no offense taken." Horatio laughed. "We're family here. It's not unusual to want to know what's going on in each other's life. So, ask away. What else do you want to know?"

From that point forward, the men discussed topics regarding family issues, challenges, and, finally, Michelle. The three so appreciated their time together that they agreed to do it more often. Further, they made a list of other men who they would enjoy being a part of future discussion groups. With that, they adjourned to the kitchen.

With Rene's permission, Mattie and Ellen brought George and Ted up to speed on her situation. Ted and George would occasionally experience the something-in-my-eye problem as details were revealed about the physical and emotional abuse she endured while trying to protect Daniel.

"This isn't right. Rene, you're quite a young lady. You've got my support. How can I help?" George offered, shaking his head.

The Heywoods and Willises agreed to work together in pursuing opportunity through the Mercy Ministries foster care program. Work would begin immediately to renovate and license the living space that would become home to the Willis family and the foster children. They agreed to stand in prayer that through this opportunity, somehow, someway God would bring reunification to Rene and her son, Daniel. It was after midnight when the group disbanded.

Day 25
December 27th - Thursday

Back in his office at nine thirty, Horatio continued to prepare for the New Year's Eve Watch Meeting service. He wanted no part in limiting God's ability to move freely during the service, so he decided to abandon the traditional template for the Watch Meeting program. He wanted the flow of the program to allow for flexibility.

Since Christmas day, weather forecasters were charting a significant New Year's Eve snow event. Initially, the storm track was projected to move well north of Scituate and would have no impact on the New Year's eve program. Today's forecast, however, was warning of an intensified low pressure system on a course that will move directly over Scituate. Hearing this, Horatio contemplated modifying the schedule for the New Year's Eve celebration.

"I wonder if I should move the start time from ten o'clock to six o'clock," he pondered. "Maybe the program needs to be rescheduled to January 1st. Maybe I should cancel the program altogether. After all," asking of himself, "what difference could missing one service make?"

Considering that it was four days before New Year's Eve arrived, any change concerning the time or date on such short notice would not be well received. The last thing he needed was another issue for the trustee board to be agitated about. He could already hear Bill Nelson going on and on about "Pastor Rice wouldn't have broken with tradition. He was a real Man of God…." Or, "Who does he think he is, rescheduling anything without checking with me first?"

"Besides," Horatio processed, "those who come will come, and those who won't, won't. That's between them and the Lord," he continued, "Lord, the ball is in Your court."

Immediately, he sensed a shift in his spirit. A peaceful, calming presence flooded his office. The sensation was not new to him, but he couldn't remember ever experiencing this feeling in such a powerful way. He knelt and began to pray. Within a matter of what seemed to be seconds, he heard the still, quiet voice saying, "Trust in Me. I am with you." The voice was clearer than it had ever been before. It departed as quickly as it appeared.

****

At ten thirty the phone rang. "Church of the Good Shepherd," Horatio announced.

"Pastor?" It was a man's voice.

"Yes. This is Pastor Smiley. Who am I speaking with?"

"This is Deacon. Rene and Kelli's dad."

"Deacon. How are you, my friend? I apologize for not recognizing your voice." Horatio continued, "I must have been distracted. Is everything all right?"

"Pastor, my wife and I just want you to know that we appreciate all that you're doing for Rene and our family." Deacon explained, "I'm not a man who easily cries, but just seeing the presence of life returning to my daughter … well, it brings tears to my eyes every time I think about all that she went through. I was angry at God. I was angry with my church for shutting its doors. I was angry with people who hadn't done anything to me, at all. I only knew that as protector and provider for my family, even though I gave it my best, my family was in trouble and I didn't know what to do. I was out of answers. Pastor, do you have time to chat?"

"Well, sure," Horatio responded. "When are you available?"

"How about now?" Deacon asked.

"That's fine. How soon can you be here?"

"I'm here, now. I'm in the church parking lot."

"Deacon, I'm coming out to get you." He hung up the phone and hurried to retrieve Deacon.

Walking to the parking lot, he could see Deacon emerging from his car with a big childlike smile on his chubby, Irish face. It was clear that Deacon genuinely appreciated his newfound friend. They embraced like a father and son long separated. They made their way back to the church. Inside Horatio's office, they began their time with prayer. Deacon wept as the Spirit of God descended upon him. They spent the better of three hours together that afternoon, continuing the conversation they had begun Christmas day. As the meeting concluded, they prayed again. Deacon was so grateful for the healing and understanding that God had imparted to him through Horatio that he danced a jig all the way back to his car. Horatio laughed as he observed Deacon's actions through a window overlooking the parking lot.

During his time with Deacon, the church phone had rung but Horatio chose to let the call go into voice mail. Retrieving the message, he recognized that the call was coming in from Rene's cell phone.

"Hi, Pastor. This is Rene Brock," the message began. "I just wanted to thank you for all you've done for me. I don't mean to be a bother, but I'd like to speak with you about a few things. I'm beginning to feel that I'm taking up too much of your time. In any event, if your schedule permits, would you call me after four o'clock? Thanks so much. Bye." The call ended.

Horatio looked at his watch. "One fifty-five. I hope Rene's all right." He sensed something taking place deep within him that he hadn't experienced in years. *What is this, Lord?* he pondered. *How can this be?* It was clear that Rene had found a place in his heart. A place that he had promised himself to never again allow anyone to enter. For it was there, in that place, that joy always turned to a hurt worse than death. "Get a hold of yourself. Slow down," he cautioned. Despite all of this, he looked at his watch again. Four o'clock seemed a long time off. "I hope she's okay." In his mind, he revisited everything that he and Rene had discussed. "Lord, I hope I didn't say or do anything to make her uncomfortable. If I did, please make it known to me and show me, please, how to correct it." He remained in prayer until five minutes after four. He had not heard the Lord speak to him during this time, so he concluded his prayer and picked up the phone to call her.

"Hi, Rene," he said, as she answered the call.

"Oh, hi, Pastor." She appeared to be in good spirits.

"Am I catching you at a bad time?" he asked.

"No. Not at all. Thanks for returning my call, so quickly. I didn't expect to hear back from you, so soon, with your busy schedule and all."

"Not a problem, Rene. So, tell me, what's going on?"

"Well, we started talking last night and I wanted to continue our conversation."

"I'd like that. When are you available?"

"I'm more flexible than you, so just let me know what works for you," she suggested.

Horatio didn't want to appear obvious in his enthusiasm to see her, so he tried to take it slow. "How about tomorrow evening?"

"That's fine."

"We can do dinner, if that's all right with you?".

"That will be fun. Who should we invite to join us?"

"Oh, right." In his enthusiasm, Horatio momentarily forgot about rule number one in ministry: people of the opposite sex should always meet in the company of others to guard against the wiles of Satan.

"Maybe, Kelli will be able to join us," Rene suggested.

"Kelli would be awesome," Horatio agreed. "What's your favorite food?"

"Well, I guess it would be a toss-up between seafood and Mexican food. How about you?" she asked.

"That's an easy one. Mexican food is at the top of my list." He chuckled.

"Great. Have you been to that new Mexican restaurant in Plymouth? It's amazing. Definitely worth the trip."

"No, I haven't heard about that one. Sounds excellent." Horatio was excited. "Shall we ride together?"

"That would be great."

"I'll pick you and Kelli up at your parent's home at, let's say, six o'clock?"

"Great. See you then." The call ended.

Horatio remained at the church until seven fifteen. He went home and prepared some pasta and sauce for dinner. For the remainder of the evening, he watched a basketball game. The game ended at eleven o'clock.

Day 26
December 28th - Friday

Walking to his office, Horatio noticed a delivery truck pulling out of the driveway. On the front porch of the church were two boxes. He expected that the boxes contained the church calendars. Bringing the boxes inside, he opened them up. It was the calendars, indeed.

"Thank you, Lord."

A sample calendar rested atop those to be distributed to the church's members. Interestingly, each calendar was packed in a clear plastic tube and labeled with the recipient's name.

"Nice touch."

He unwrapped and inspected the sample calendar. This was his first opportunity to evaluate the finished product, as he had not been required to sign off on the proof before the project went to print.

The images, print, and design appeared to be of excellent quality. Thumbing through the pages of the calendar, he smiled. The first box he opened contained one hundred calendars. The second box, of equal size, contained another one hundred pieces. Recognizing an error in count, he deduced that the extra calendars were probably the result of an overrun, a common occurrence in the commercial printing process. He placed the boxes in the corner of his office, where they were to remain until time for distribution. The final piece of the New Year's Eve service had come together nicely.

For the remainder of the morning he hunkered down, attending to a variety of year-end administrative matters that required his attention.

At two thirty, he went outside for some fresh air and a cup of clam chowder. He was back at his office twenty minutes later. While sitting at his desk, he noticed the portable compact disc player sitting atop a file cabinet in a corner of his office. He had purchased the player two years ago but never opened it. Horatio enjoyed contemporary Christian music but didn't dare to play it in the church. According to Good Shepherd's Trustee Board, if the worship music or the individual(s) who sang it wasn't, at least, eighty years old, it was not of God.

He remembered that he had, recently, purchased a disc that was produced by the Joy James Project, a gifted husband-and-wife worship team from the Boston area. He removed the player from the box and slipped the disc in. As the music played, he experienced a strong presence of the Holy Spirit. Reminded of the way King David danced before the Lord in the book of Psalms, Horatio was moved to do likewise. He took the music into the church sanctuary and, with hands raised and his face lifted to the Lord, he worshipped. Never before had he experienced anything like this. He sensed a powerful shift in the sanctuary's atmosphere. The presence of God's Holy Spirit was tangible.

Unaware that Mrs. Munsey, the youth choir director, had entered the sanctuary, he continued his song and dance. She watched in silence until he noticed her.

"Oh, my goodness. Mrs. Munsey, I didn't hear you come in," he said, apologetically.

"Pastor, that was awesome," she began. "That music. Who is it?"

"The Joy James Project," he replied. "They're a group out of Boston. This music is so anointed."

"You can say that again." Mrs. Munsey continued, "I could feel God's presence in here as soon as I walked in." She was animated. "I didn't mean to interrupt," she began. "I came to see if I left my reading glasses behind after last Sunday's service."

"No problem," Horatio replied. "I'm not even sure how long I've been at this. Do you know what time it is?"

"It's five fifteen," she replied.

"Five fifteen. Are you sure?"

"My mistake," Mrs. Munsey apologized, "Its five twenty-eight."

"Mrs. Munsey, I've got to go." He excused himself. As he hurried out the door, he asked her to lock up on her way out. He told her that he would be back later to turn the lights off.

He rushed home, shaved, showered, got dressed, and was out the door a few minutes before six o'clock. "Man, oh man. I hate being late," he mumbled. "Rene's going to think that I'm flaky. Tardiness makes for a lousy first impression. I'd better call her and apologize."

He didn't have Rene's cell phone number with him, but he did have Kelli's. In the midst of punching up her number, his phone rang. The incoming number was not familiar to him.

"Pastor Smiley," he answered.

"Hi, Pastor. It's Rene." She sounded deflated. He braced for disappointment.

"Is everything all right?" he asked, sensing she was calling to cancel their plans for the evening.

"Not really," she continued. "Pastor, I have a problem at work and…." Horatio held his breath. "I'm not going to be able to…."

He interrupted, "Now, now. Rene, it's not a problem. We can reschedule."

"Oh. Are you sure?"

"I'm sure. I'm sure," he said, as if trying to convince himself. "Call me tomorrow. We can coordinate our schedules. Okay?"

"Okay," she replied.

"Have a good evening," Horatio said as he hung up the phone. At that point, he was only a few minutes from the church so, he decided to return and close the building down. The joy that he had experienced earlier that afternoon had departed. Recognizing that a spirit of heaviness was attempting to overtake him, he chose to war against it.

"I rebuke you, spirit of heaviness, in the name of Jesus!" he declared. "Get thee behind me!" he commanded. The spirit lifted as quickly as it had descended. "Try to steal my joy, will you? Not today. Not ever." *Now, what was the name of that restaurant in Plymouth that Rene spoke of?* Unable to remember, he decided to try to locate it on his own. He recalled that Rene mentioned that it was in Plymouth Center. He expected that he could ask the locals for help in finding it. He did exactly that.

Thirty minutes later, he was at the traffic circle in Plymouth Center. His second inquiry resulted in a hit. The name of the restaurant was Baha Bob's. Easy to find, he was there in no time. The restaurant was packed. Entering in, he registered at the reception desk. "Table for one, please."

The restaurant hostess informed him that it would be a forty-minute wait to be seated. Choosing to wait, he found a seat in the karaoke lounge and enjoyed the floor show. The customers were varied, fun-loving, and well-behaved. As he occasionally engaged in conversation with other patrons, the forty-minute wait passed quickly. A buzzer device that he was given to indicate that his table was ready lit up.

A waitress greeted him at the hostess desk.

"Sir, at this time all we have is a table for four situated by the window looking out over the harbor," she informed him. "My manager instructed me to ask if you would object to sharing your table with another customer?"

"No. That will be fine," he replied.

"Thank you so much, sir." She continued, "My manager says he will gladly discount your bill. I suppose I should have mentioned that earlier." The waitress disappeared and returned with not one but two customers close behind.

Horatio was so busy looking at the menu that he didn't notice that his tablemates for the evening had arrived. It was Rene and Kelli. As Rene approached the table, she noticed that the man resembled Horatio but never in her mind did it register that it could actually be him.

"Pastor?" she asked, not yet certain from ten feet away.

Looking up, he thought that his imagination had gotten the better of him.

"Rene, Kelli. How did you know I'd be here?"

"We didn't," Kelli replied. "Rene was, I mean we were, so disappointed about not connecting with you tonight that coming anyway, was her, I mean our, only consolation."

Horatio quickly stood up and seated his company. Rene was embarrassed. She thought that Kelli's misspeaks were intentional. She elbowed Kelli while Horatio was looking the other way. At that moment, the restaurant's public address system alerted that a car's headlights, parked in the lot, were left on. When the vehicle's tag number was announced, Kelli realized that it was her car. She excused herself and returned to her car. Rene appeared a little bit uncomfortable as she sought to initiate conversation. Horatio chose to remain silent, if only for a moment, to allow her to explain why she stood him up. Graciously, he thought better of his strategy.

"Did everything work out okay at your job?"

"Oh, yes." Rene explained, "The person who is on the next shift had car trouble and asked me to cover for her. I was calling to let you know that I was going to be a little late and ask you to wait for me at my parent's house. When you told me that we could reschedule, I took that to mean that you had something else going on."

Horatio felt like a heel. "Rene, can you forgive me?"

"Forgive you for what? I was the one who was late," she replied.

"Rene, I overreacted. I honestly thought that you had changed your mind but you didn't know how to let me know without hurting my feelings."

"Pastor," she countered, "Six o'clock tonight couldn't get here quickly enough for me. It's true what Kelli said. I was so disappointed when you suggested rescheduling. I really wanted to discuss further the dream that we seem to have shared. The only way that Kelli could console me was to bring me here so that I could ponder 'what if.' I thought that you had changed your mind."

They both laughed. At that moment, Kelli returned to the table.

"What did I miss?"

"Nothing much. Just going over the menu," Horatio responded, giving a wink to Rene, while Kelli perused the menu.

Everything about the evening was perfect. The food, the conversation, and the company. Horatio and Rene chose to discuss their dream privately over the phone the following day. To make the experience even sweeter, the restaurant manager discounted Horatio's tab by fifty percent. He increased the waitress' gratuity to include the amount of the discount. They left the restaurant together and bade adieu. They ventured northbound on Route 3 in their respective cars. It was after eleven o'clock.

****

Wife and mother Mary Scott of Goose Creek, South Carolina, was at a place in her life where all she knew was heartache. Each day she experienced emotional abuse and marital infidelity at the hands of her trifling, husband, while being disrespected and deceived by her emancipated children. Christmas day came and went without a single "Thank you," "Merry Christmas," or "I love you" in appreciation for the time and effort she expended in a seemingly futile attempt to bless her family with gifts, purchased with her hard-earned, Christmas fund savings. Having grown up in a highly dysfunctional home, Mary dreamed of one day having a loving, healthy, happy family. Now, in her third marriage, she experiences severe bouts of depression. Her children accused her of causing them to play the role of 'second fiddle to Mommy's husbands.' They were quick to blame her for all that was wrong in their lives, and there's plenty wrong. Through it all, Mary continued to give her children, friends, and strangers her heartfelt love and encouragement. Years of giving, but not receiving, has left her in a state of being fully depleted of the strength to continue on.

The final straw came at her job yesterday: she was given notice that her position was being eliminated after sixteen years of dedicated service to her employer.

Now, having no job, a self-centered, unfaithful husband and failed relationships with her children, Mary plummets into a state of deep depression. Deciding that she has had enough of life, she establishes her exit plan. She decides to pack a bag the next morning and begin a one-way, twenty-hour trek to Cape Cod, Massachusetts. Since a child, she dreamed of visiting the beautiful, sandy beaches of Cape Cod. Suitors would promise Mary a Cape Cod wedding if only she'd say "Yes." It was never a secret that Cape Cod was the place she longed to be, if given the opportunity to choose.

Through the failed marriages and broken promises, Mary never became bitter or unforgiving. She has given her best in life, but life hasn't given her its best. Brokenhearted, alone and diminished, she cannot face the agony of living another day. Having cried to a point of having no tears left to shed, she just wants to go her perfect place and die, quietly.

Day 27
December 29th - Saturday

Mary had her bags packed and was pulling out of her driveway at ten o'clock. She had written letters to her husband and children the night before, apologizing for not being a better wife and mother. Unsure of her husband's present whereabouts, or for that matter whether or not he had come home the night before, she taped his letter to the refrigerator door. Her daughters lived nearby but, not wanting to experience another episode of disrespect, she chose to mail them their letters. Driving through town, Mary was reminded of the people she had known. Just before turning on to the interstate, she fueled up her car and checked the fluids and tires. Once back inside the car, Mary prayed to God for protection. Her prayer lasted long enough for the person in the car behind her to begin sounding their horn, to move her away from the gasoline pumps. She waved apologetically and drove off.

****

Horatio arrived at the nursing home at one o'clock. It was the first time he had visited with his "extended family" since the Christmas holiday. He was pleased to see them again. The residents and staff presented him with their "Person of the Year" award for the third time. He gave the gift of a video exercising system to the nursing home. It was hilarious watching the staff members and residents attempt to keep up with the exercise and Indy 500 race car games. Everyone had such a wonderful time that the staff delayed serving dinner.

At six o'clock, Horatio made his way home. He had a taste for some Chinese takeout, so he stopped by the Pho Ho Ho restaurant. After dinner while drinking a cup of peach tea, he reviewed his sermon notes for the Sunday morning church service. He was in bed by ten o'clock.

****

Mary was traveling along Route 95 northbound at seven thirty when steam and the smell of anti-freeze began to enter the passenger compartment of her vehicle.

Great! she thought to herself. Having experienced broken radiator hoses before, she understood exactly what was happening beneath the hood of her car. She exited at the next ramp at Dale City, Virginia, and drove slowly in search of a motel. It was obvious that no service station would be able to help with her problem at that time of night. Within ten minutes, she located a quaint motel where she remained, praying and reading her bible until Monday morning.

Day 28
December 30th - Sunday

It was the last Sunday morning of the year. The temperature outside was twenty-eight degrees and sunny with a steady northwest breeze. Scituans count it a great day to share with family. Unfortunately, the majority of Good Shepherd's members chose to spend their family time, today, in venues other than in church. On his way to morning service, Horatio noticed significantly fewer vehicles in the parking lot than usual. Sensing a bit of a letdown, he endeavored to maintain an attitude of joy. Understanding that joy is a weapon that yields great power in battling against spirits of depression and frustration, he pressed on. The church members looked to Horatio for encouragement, and he didn't want to let them down.

Entering with his usual smile, he greeted several people as he made his way to his office. Closing the door behind him, he dropped to his knees and prayed for strength.

"Lord," he pleaded, "Your people have come to receive Your Word this morning. Please send it, I pray, in the name of Jesus. Amen."

With his notepad and Bible in hand, he made his way to the church sanctuary. The morning service was poorly attended and uneventful. Holding to the usual service protocol, he closed down the building at twelve thirty.

After church, he stopped at the grocery store before his visit with the Heywoods for Sunday dinner. George and Mattie didn't attend church service because George's arthritis had flared up. Mattie alerted Horatio of the likelihood of their absence the evening before. Inside the Village Mart, he went directly to the pain reliever section and placed a large bottle of George's preferred pain reliever into his basket. Next, he made his way to the produce aisle. He loaded the basket with bags of sweet potatoes, baking potatoes, red bliss potatoes, onions, peppers, carrots, beets, apples, oranges, bananas, tomatoes, and romaine lettuce. Then he went up and down other aisles in the store. A Virginia ham, a roasting chicken, 3 pounds of Boston Scrod, rice, beans, pasta, bread, pie crust, a cake, eggs, and ice cream all were placed in the shopping cart. Leaving from the checkout counter, he smiled and thought to himself, *This ought to get George and Mattie off to a good start for the New Year.* Arriving at the Heywoods, it took three trips back and forth to the car before all the bags were inside.

"My goodness." He could hear Mattie speaking to George as she opened the first two bags, unaware that several more were on their way in. By the time the last of the bags were inside, George had made his way to the door to hold it open for Horatio.

"George, you shouldn't be standing by the open door in this cold air," Horatio insisted. "You go and sit down. Mattie and I have the situation well in hand." George reached out and hugged Horatio. Mattie was off to the side with teary eyes.

"Now, Mattie," George began, "what's all that about?"

"George, I can't help but thank God for our pastor." She continued, "Pastor, in the years we've known you, you've never brought pain medication to us. I don't want to seem ungrateful, but why now?"

Horatio appeared stumped. "That's a very good question," he began. "To be perfectly honest, I'm not sure. I can remember walking into the store and going directly to the medicine aisle. Why? Is something wrong?"

"George had a terrible time last night," she replied. "At one thirty, I gave him the last two tablets of the very same pain medicine that you brought today. He finally fell asleep around two o'clock. I intended to call you this morning and ask if you would be so kind as to stop along the way and pick up another bottle for us. I didn't wake up until ten thirty and my call went directly into your answering machine. I didn't leave a message because I had second thoughts about asking you to go out of your way like that. I prayed that God would touch someone's heart to bring George something to ease his discomfort. Now, here you show up with the only brand of pain medication that he'll use."

Horatio could only respond, "Wow."

"You said a mouthful, Pastor," George chimed in. "You are truly connected to us by the Holy Spirit. Mattie and I agree that God is about to do something powerful around here. And, we believe that you are a very significant part of what is about to happen. Call it wisdom or a just some old people talking, but it's gonna happen and its gonna happen soon. Mark our word."

Mattie fixed George a peanut butter and jelly sandwich to eat before taking his medication. When Mattie and George asked Horatio why he brought so much food, he reminded them that he may not get the opportunity to see them again before leaving for sabbatical.

****

That afternoon, Mattie cooked, George continued to heal, and Horatio thanked God for using him, as He did. They had a wonderful time together. Horatio left for home at seven thirty. The stars were hidden behind thick clouds and the wind blew aggressively from the northwest.

"Boy, it's getting ready to storm." By eight o'clock, he was safely home. He called Rene, but the call went directly to her voice mail. He left his name and number on her service with a "Just calling to see how you're doing" message. He was disappointed that he wasn't able to connect with her. Understanding that New Year's Eve would be a long, busy day, he went to bed early.

Day 29
December 31st - Monday (New Year's Eve)

At seven fifteen, Mary Scott was on the phone arranging for her car to be repaired. A local mechanic recommended by the front desk clerk instructed her to bring her car to him as soon as was possible. She did and, her car was in the service bay before eight o'clock. Within minutes of her radiator being fixed, she was back on the highway, expecting to be on Cape Cod by ten o'clock that evening. The weather in Virginia was cloudy with occasional showers. She paid close attention to the weather forecast for New England. It showed that the storm system that was bringing rain to Virginia was headed north. The rain was predicted to change to snow along the Connecticut and Rhode Island border, later that afternoon. Mary didn't let that affect her travel plans. She was convinced that she could stay well enough ahead of the storm.

****

At seven thirty, Horatio moved his pillow aside to check the time, yet again. All night long he tossed and turned in search of a comfortable sleeping position. His mattress felt like it was stuffed with an equal measure of coarse gravel and dried leaves. His slightest movement resulted in a noisy, prickly feeling.

"Lord, let me rest," he prayed.

He drifted off into a deep, restful sleep. Understanding that it would be a very long day, he remained in bed until one-thirty that afternoon. He spent the remainder of the afternoon and the earlier part of that evening reading scripture. Experiencing a strong presence of God's Spirit, he prayed that it would remain with him through Watch Meeting.

****

By four o'clock, Mary Scott was on the George Washington Bridge in New York City. Traffic moved along at a snail's pace. Inclement weather resulted in wet roadways and numerous fender benders that only served to make the long trip longer. Staying the course, traveling via Route 95, she stopped for coffee and a sandwich at a rest area in Connecticut. Wanting not to lose time, she filled her gas tank at the service station adjacent to the restaurant and continued north. Mary had not received a single phone call or message from any of her family members since leaving Goose Creek.

"Oh, Lord, hasn't anyone even noticed that I've left home? Don't they care?" she pondered. Experiencing bouts of crying, loneliness, and desperation, she held to her plan. Mary was determined to be on Cape Cod before the end of the day.

Travel conditions quickly took a turn for the worse as she approached the Massachusetts state border. Gusts of wind blew curtains of snow and freezing rain onto the windshield, limiting her visability. Mary's car was not equipped with snow tires and adequate wiper blades, so she slowed her pace to a crawl. Turning on to Route 93 North up ahead, she saw a road sign, "Braintree/Cape Cod." It was eight forty-five. Excited at the thought of being so close to her destination, Mary's spirit lifted. The snowfall continued to intensify. The tops of trees, vehicles, and the roadway were covered with snow.

The glaze on the poorly treated roadway was all that it took for a car to spin out and roll over just before Exit 14 southbound. The State Police established a detour at Exit 13 via Route 3A. Mary's car went into a spin that scared her half to death as she turned onto the Route 3A leg of the detour. She had never before driven in snow this deep. With no sign of cars ahead of her and no indication of any behind, she spotted a sign that read "Scituate Harbor." The arrow on the sign pointed "East," so east she drove. Visibility improved as she headed further along the road.

The Watch Meeting Service

Horatio made his way to the church sanctuary by eight thirty. He planned to be there early to welcome and thank the members who braved the storm. The snow had begun to fall a few hours earlier, but road and pedestrian travel was manageable. Not long after he had switched on the lights and turned up the heat, people began to arrive. In addition to the familiar faces that came through the door, he noticed a surprising number of visitors. Perhaps, he thought, they're friends and relatives of the regulars. Nevertheless, he was pleased with the turnout. During the next ninety minutes, Horatio encouraged those in attendance to pray as the Spirit of God led them.

"Pray for someone tonight," he encouraged. Pray for a family member, a neighbor, a friend. Pray from your heart. After all," he continued, "that's what the Lord commands us to do." There was a meager response to his appeal, but that didn't deter him from praying any less passionately, as he sat in his chair at the center of the Sanctuary platform.

****

Tired, lost, and hungry, Mary decided to seek lodging for the night. Up ahead, she noticed increased street lighting and pedestrian traffic. Approaching a well-lit parking lot filling in with cars, her curiosity was piqued. She parked her car and followed behind others entering a church. Inside, Mary sat in a pew at the rear of the sanctuary. As she warmed her hands and feet while listening to music playing, she experienced a sense of peace that had been absent from her life for a very long time.

****

At ten o'clock, Horatio stood and opened the service with prayer. His message was prefaced with an urgent appeal that those in attendance would endeavor to live for the Lord, not for themselves. Included in the body of his sermon was the profound statement, "God is not obligated to bless you with one day of life more than He has chosen to give you." Lifting his eyes to look beyond the lectern, he could see that he had struck a chord with the audience. He continued to speak words that, at times, found him inquiring of the Lord, *Where did that come from?* Pressing on, he noticed that the sanctuary was filling up. *This is interesting*, he thought to himself, *we haven't had this many people here on days with perfect weather*.

As he continued to minister, more people continued to come. Eventually, the sanctuary had filled in to the point of standing-room only. *Lord, what in the name of Jesus, are you doing?* he remembered asking. He concluded the evening service with a prayer of gratitude to God for bringing all in attendance through the year just completed. He prayed for God's continued blessing for the New Year. Horatio withheld the announcement regarding the passing out of calendars because he didn't want the visitors to feel left out. He expected that there would be some extra calendars, but certainly not enough to give to each adult, present.

"Lord, I'm going to need your help with this," he whispered.

Eventually he came and stood at the front of the pulpit where he instructed individuals to come forward and receive their calendar as their name was called.

"Anyone remaining who has not received a calendar at the end of the distribution process but would like one, please remain seated and I will do what I can to get one to you."

Two church elders were summoned to assist him. The first box was opened and Horatio began calling names.

"Mary Scott, please come forward," he requested.

"Oh, my goodness," he muttered. "There's nobody in our church with that name. This isn't starting out very well."

He called out again, "Is Mary Scott with us tonight?" He paused, uncertain of what to do.

From the back of the sanctuary, a woman called out, "Here!"

He had absolutely no recollection of ever having met Ms. Scott, but he breathed a sigh of relief at the sound of her acknowledgement.

Looking around, Mary hesitated for a moment before walking to the front of the church to claim the calendar.

"That can't be for me. There has to be another Mary Scott that they're calling for," she processed aloud. In that moment of hesitation, no one else responded to the call to come forward. She knew that her presence at Good Shepherd was not planned or expected. How could it be that she would be called to receive a church calendar? It became clear to her that God intended for her to be at Good Shepherd, tonight.

"Thank you, Lord, for remembering me," she whispered as she made her way to the front of the church.

As Horatio handed her the calendar, she hugged him. Mary clutched it as though God had handed it to her personally. She returned to her seat giddy as a schoolgirl.

"Henry Williams, please come forward."

Henry was one of the church regulars. After the twelfth calendar was handed off, something very curious began to unfold: the names imprinted on the outer packaging of the next group of calendars were unfamiliar to Horatio or the elders assisting him. Without exception as the names were called, someone would make their way to the front to claim their calendar.

"Lord, what's going on?" he asked, looking Heavenward.

The exercise concluded with every adult in the audience receiving their personalized calendar. There was not one calendar that remained unclaimed.

In years prior as the calendars were distributed, recipients would leave immediately thereafter. This year was different. Everyone returned to their seat. It was clear that they had witnessed a mighty move of God. People who had never been to the church before provided a detailed account of how they came to be present. They, too, could see the handprint of God on their experience. Horatio, so moved by all that had taken place, knelt down and prayed.

"Thank you, Lord. You have answered my prayers. And you have answered as only you can. You are truly awesome! Have your way, Lord. Let your will be established in this Sanctuary and in all the earth. Thank you."

Voices in the audience shouted, "Halleluiah!" Others wept.

Most who attended the Watch Meeting remained in the sanctuary after one o'clock that morning. Horatio didn't want the experience to end. Fully exhausted after the last of the attendees had left, he closed down the church with the help of Rene and Kelli. After escorting them to their car, he went home.

In his bed, too excited to sleep, Horatio continued to recall the events of the evening. As he continued to marvel over the calendar distribution experience, he remembered that no calendar had been prepared for Bill Nelson. Thankfully, he didn't attend the Watch Meeting. Nevertheless, this posed a huge problem. Bill Nelson was an outspoken opponent of Horatio's attempts to move away from some of the traditional ways of the church. There was little that Horatio could do to correct the oversight at this hour. There were no calendars remaining, and it would be unreasonably expensive to have a single calendar printed by the calendar company. After a while, his anxiety left and he was able to drift off to sleep.

Day 30
January 1st – New Year's Day

At eight thirty, Horatio was awakened from a sound sleep by someone pounding on his door. Scrambling to his feet reaching for his robe, he made his way to find out what was going on. At the door was Captain Mel Askew of the Scituate Police Department. Opening the door, Horatio greeted the captain with a hearty "Happy New Year."

"And, a Happy New Year to you, Pastor," Mel responded. "Pastor, isn't Bill Nelson a member of your church?" the police captain asked.

"Yes, he's the chairman of our trustee board. Why do you ask?"

"Well, I hate to be the bearer of bad news," Mel continued, "Bill was found dead in his driveway last night. Apparently between the hours of eight thirty and ten thirty last night, from the information we have available, he slipped on some ice, sustained blunt trauma to his head, passed out, and succumbed from exposure to the elements. At eleven forty-five, he was pronounced dead at South Shore Hospital."

"Wow. Poor Bill," was all that Horatio could manage, shaking his head in disbelief. He continued, "I should have sensed that something was wrong when he didn't show up at the church service last night. Bill has never missed a New Year's Eve Watch Meeting."

"Well I'm sure he tried, but it just wasn't in the cards," Mel responded. "Anyway," he continued, "thought that you would want to know, as you'll probably be getting a call from the funeral director, seeing that Bill was a member of the church."

"Okay, Mel. Thank you for letting me know. I'll make sure I get word to our church members."

Closing the door and left with a moment to gather his thoughts, Horatio remembered the last time he saw Bill. There was contention between them because Bill was obvious in his disapproval of Horatio as the church's minister. Still, though grieved by Bill's death, he regretted the way that he responded to Bill's animosity.

****

It was New Year's Day and dinner commitments made were dinner commitments to be honored. After some time in prayer and preparation, Horatio headed out to his first invite.

His first stop would be at Shelly Story's home. She was a faithful member of the Good Shepherd and was front and center at the previous evening's service.

At her home in the company of eight guests, Shelly revisited the events of the New Year's Eve service.

"Pastor," she started, "who were all those visitors that were at the service last night? That lady, Mary Scott, the man in the red shirt and the college student from Harvard, I spoke with them all. I invited them to come visit us, again," she said. "They didn't seem to be connected with anyone in the church. Did you invite them?"

"Shelly, I was so blessed by all of the visitors that I could only thank God for sending them. I hadn't met any of them before, but they all seemed like very nice people. We did manage to get some contact information for most, if not all, of them, so I do expect to follow up with each of them."

"That's good," Shelly said. "Pastor, let me tell you I really love those calendars. I was thumbing through mine this morning looking at the beautiful scenes and reading the scriptures and I noticed a red blotch on one of the pages. Has anyone mentioned anything to you about a red blotch on theirs?"

"No, Shelly, this is the first I've heard about any problems. To be perfectly honest, I haven't even opened mine yet. May I take a look at yours, to see what you're referring to?"

While Shelly left to retrieve her calendar, he prayed that the problem with Shelly's calendar was unique to her. Within a few minutes, she returned with the calendar in hand. She opened it and presented the page with the blotch to Horatio.

"My, I see what you mean. You can't miss that," he acknowledged. "The blotch is in the shape of a red cross. Very interesting," he continued. "I haven't opened my calendar yet, so I'm not sure if mine has this issue or not."

Other guests at Shelly's dinner party had not attended the Church's New Year's Eve service, so they had nothing to add to the discussion. Horatio informed Shelly of Bill Nelson's death.

On hearing the news, Shelly said, "God, bless the dead."

After the dinner had concluded, Horatio thanked Shelly for the invitation and complimented her cooking. Excusing himself, he headed for the Burkes' home for coffee and dessert.

****

At the home of Suzy Burkes, four generations of her family were gathered together to welcome in the New Year. The year just ended had been difficult for the Burkes. Suzy, the matriarch of the family, was a prayer warrior who understood the power of prayer. Entering in, Horatio was the recipient of a chorus of "Happy New Year" greetings. Suzy's children and grandchildren were not churchgoers. While some had committed their lives to God in earlier years, worldly cares and influences had caused their commitment to waver and, eventually, fail. Nevertheless, they all had respect for a "man of the cloth." Almost immediately, Suzy began to speak about the New Year's Eve Watch Meeting.

"Pastor," Suzy continued, "that was the best service that I have ever attended. I felt goose bumps all up and down my arms. And the calendars were beautiful."

"Indeed, it was a wonderful service." Horatio chuckled. "I was truly blessed. Nobody wanted it to end."

"And, Pastor, I just can't stop talking about my calendar."

"Speaking of which, Suzy, let me ask you a question about your calendar: did you notice anything wrong with it?"

"Wrong?" Suzy inquired. "My calendar is fine. I didn't notice anything wrong with it. I have never seen a nicer one. In fact, let me go get it. I meant to show it off to my children." She went to her bedroom and quickly returned. "Look, everybody, at the gorgeous calendar the Church gave me," she announced. Everyone oohed and ahhed at the calendar's photography. As Suzy's family flipped through the pages, someone asked, "What does this red cross mean?"

Horatio's heart sank. "May I take a look at that?"

Perusing the calendar, he immediately recognized the blotch as being identical to the red cross-shaped blotch that appeared on Shelley's calendar.

This is not good, he thought to himself.

As he continued to analyze the red cross, he observed something very interesting; the blotch on Shelley's calendar appeared on the July page, while the cross on Suzy's calendar was on the April page. Horatio was at a loss for explanation or understanding as to how or what might have caused the blotch to occur randomly. He began to feel discouraged, having seen two out of two calendars with the blotch issue. *How many more?* he wondered. *How many more?*

Returning home from the Burkes, he intended to go immediately in search of his calendar. By now, his curiosity had the better of him. Would that too familiar red cross or blotch or whatever it was show up on his calendar, too?

Walking through the front door, his attention was drawn to the flashing red light of his messaging service. "I'd better get that." Any messages left on his home telephone would usually be of an urgent matter. Calls pertaining to regular church business would routinely go to his office phone.

Hitting the "Play" button, the device announced that there were four new messages. The first message was from a local funeral home informing him of the receipt of Bill Nelson's remains. The call was to request his help in scheduling the funeral service. The remaining messages were from church members calling to speak to him about red blotches appearing on their calendars. He was in no hurry to return any of those calls. After all, what could he tell the calendar recipients? He had no answer.

He retreated to his kitchen to find his calendar lying on the dining table. Pulling up a chair, he carefully examined each page one by one. January, okay. February, okay. March? April? May? June? July? August? September? October? All okay. November? There it was. *That darn blotchy red cross*, he thought to himself. *How about December?* he pondered. *Thank you, Lord. December's okay*. He sighed. Quickly, he turned back to the November page of the calendar. He recalled that on Shelly's calendar, the blotch appeared on the July page. On Suzy's, it was the April page. Looking closer at the blotch on his calendar, he observed some interesting characteristics:

First, the blotch was the color of crimson.

Second, the blotch was in the shape of the cross.

Third, the border of the image resembled flames.

And lastly, the cross was clearly inside the block on his calendar indicating the seventeenth day of November.

"What's going on? This makes absolutely no sense."

After he had asked of himself every question he could and was unable to come up with any logical answer, he went to bed.

"What a difference a day makes," he agonized as he lay in bed, staring at the bedroom ceiling. "Twenty-four hours ago, I couldn't sleep because I was on cloud nine. Now, I can't sleep because I'm in a haze over these blotches." Horatio was at a complete loss for answers. He accepted that there was nothing he could do to resolve the problem at this hour of night. "Happy New Year," he said sarcastically.

Day 31
January 2nd - Wednesday

Before he was ready for it, the new day had arrived. Moving a bit slowly due to emotional and physical fatigue, Horatio prepared for another day at the office. An oppressive spirit came upon him with such ferocity that he cried out to God to break it off him. As he prayed, the heaviness began to lift. Next, he launched into singing songs of praise that fully put any evidence of the oppressive, spiritual attack to rest.

"Devil, for you to try to come against me like this, I know that something good is about to happen." He finished dressing and picked up an apple on his way out the door.

In his office, the first order of business was to make arrangements for Bill Nelson's funeral. It had been requested by Bill's widow, Joan, that the service be scheduled for Saturday afternoon, to allow time for her son Billy to be present. At the time of his father's death, Billy was assigned aboard a naval vessel somewhere off the coast of North Africa. His leave had him scheduled to arrive home late Friday evening. Having completed calls to the church's music director, hospitality committee chairperson and trustees, it was agreed that the funeral service would begin at one o'clock. With that settled, Horatio worked on other matters before him.

****

Bill Nelson had established that Pastor Bell would stand in for Horatio during his sabbatical. Pastor Bell was the nephew of Horatio's predecessor. It was the responsibility of the trustees to provide the necessary support for Pastor Bell. Choosing to take the high road, Horatio contacted members of the trustee board to offer his assistance. Arthur Mutton, interim trustee board chair, made it clear that they didn't require his help.

Pastor Bell was no stranger to the Church of the Good Shepherd. Though a likeable man, he struggled with a distractive sinus condition that caused him to make snorting sounds when he spoke. This condition caused his sermons to become unpleasantly long. Church attendance usually dipped to less than half of what it would be on a regular Sunday when Pastor Bell was the guest speaker. Despite all of this, in the Church of the Good Shepherd, "politics is politics." Horatio prayed that the church's members would experience a smooth transition while he was away.

****

The next order of business for Horatio was to retrieve any messages from the church's voice mail system. Once connected, the service announced, "Seventy new messages."

No way, he processed. Did that machine say seventy messages? It must have said seventeen. He played the announcement again.

"Seventy new messages."

"Okay. Might as well get comfortable," he thought aloud as he sipped from a bottle of juice. He grabbed a notepad.

Programming the play sequence, the system began "First new message."

"Hi, Pastor Horatio." It was Katie White, an elderly church parishioner who called so frequently that she needed not introduce herself. "Pastor, did we have any extra calendars left from the other night?" she asked. "I need four more to give to my sons and daughter. They were so nice that I would like to give each of my children a calendar for their homes. I told them if they went to our church service, they'd have gotten their own. By the way," she continued, "has anyone mentioned red stains on their calendar? Thank goodness the pictures weren't affected. Please let me know when I'll be able to pick up the additional calendars. Thank you and God bless."

"End of message," the service announced.

"Next new message," the service continued to play the remaining sixty-nine messages as Horatio carefully jotted down the details of each call in the course of the next two hours.

Expectedly, the majority of the messages related to some aspect of the church calendars. While some calls applauded the calendar's design and photography, the overwhelming majority of messages questioned the presence of a distinguished red blotch appearing on their calendar. Initially, Horatio deduced that there was an organized effort to make clear the point that he should have remained with the previous calendar vendor.

"I'll bet the trustees have something to do with this fiasco," he muttered. "I can't believe that I just handed them another opportunity to take issue with me. Why couldn't I have left things as they were? Change was not required." He found himself praying to God for forgiveness for anything he had done that was outside of His will or instruction.

Obligated to place return calls to his parishioners, he referred to the notepad with each caller's name and phone number. Just before he dialed the first phone number, an idea, in fact, a strategy emerged from all of the confusion over the calendars. It was clear that most, if not all, calendars contained a red, cross-like blotch. That was a foregone conclusion. It was becoming increasingly clear that the blotches appeared randomly on the calendars. So the plan he crafted was this: call every calendar recipient and chart the month and day that the blotch appeared on their calendar. In so doing, there would be an ability to document the frequency and location(s) of the blotches that, perhaps, would motivate the calendar manufacturer to reprint the order.

****

One by one Horatio called each of the seventy people who had left a message. He managed to reach most callers on his first attempt. At the conclusion of the phone conversations, having charted specific information regarding the dates and frequency of the blotches, he could not identify a clear pattern of print error. "So much for that plan," he muttered. Continuing to review the list of names and corresponding blotch dates while trying to make heads or tails of it all, frustration began to set in. Deciding to put the calendar matter to the side, at least for the moment, he got busy with other church business.

Two hours later, the office phone rang. Before he could give a proper greeting, a voice on the other end announced frantically, "Pastor, Jonah Tye is dead." It was church member Sam Wooden, who went on to explain, "Seems Jonah was climbing the lighthouse stairs and, about halfway up, he lost his balance and fell. Broke his neck."

"Sam, you must be mistaken," Horatio responded, trying to calm the caller. "I spoke to Jonah just a short while ago. He was at home."

"Pastor, I'm telling you he's dead," Sam explained. "I spoke with Doc Taylor. He's been Jonah's doctor forever. Doc ought to know what Jonah looks like."

"Let me call you back, Sam," was all that Horatio could think to say. He sat slumped in his chair, staring at the list of names and numbers that he had returned just a short while ago. There, number twenty-seven on the list, was the name Jonah Tye. The notation associated with Jonah's calendar was: blotch location - Jan. 2.'

"Oh, my God!" Horatio blurted out. "January 2. Today is January 2. Jonah died on January 2. The blotch on his calendar was set on January 2." So many thoughts continued to rip through his mind. *Is this a fluke? It has to be…,* he processed. It was as though some unseen force had delivered a powerful gut punch to him. He felt sick to his stomach. He cried out, "What have I gotten our church into?" he agonized. "Poor Jonah. What have I done?" The questions continued. No answers were forthcoming.

Horatio was uncharacteristically shaken. This would be the second of two funerals to be scheduled in the church within two days. "What is going on?" he asked as he sat slumped in his chair.

He retrieved his list of names, numbers, and blotch dates from the center drawer of his desk. Only sixty-one of the two hundred calendar recipient names were included on his list. Working with the limited information he had available to him, Horatio was able to determine that the next reported blotch date was January 9. He prayed that the seven-day break in time would be sufficient to establish any relevancy between the blotch date and the death of Jonah Tye. Saddled with a migraine headache having an intensity that defied description, he headed home and retreated to his bed.

Oh, he thought to himself, *why couldn't today be January 15th? What is going on, Lord?* He stayed in his bed with a cool compress applied to his forehead for the remainder of the day. Tossing and turning, watching night transition into daybreak, he experienced yet another sleepless night.

Day 32
January 3rd - Thursday

The clock on the nightstand said seven eighteen. Using a pillow to shield his face from any hint of approaching daylight, Horatio wanted to spend one more hour in bed. That plan came to an abrupt end. Someone at his front door continued to press on the buzzer as if the house was on fire. Jumping up and putting on his robe, he ran to see what the commotion was about. Approaching the front door he gave the knob a yank. There, at the storm door, stood Sam Wooden.

"Sam, is everything all right? Is everyone okay at home?"

Horatio was deeply concerned that Sam may have done something terrible to someone while in a fit of anger. Sam was known as a 'hothead' and people generally steered clear of him when he was in one of his moods.

"Everybody's good."

"Well then, Sam," Horatio continued, breathing a sigh of relief, "what brings you here to my home so early this morning?"

"Pastor, Jonah Tye bought the farm yesterday," Sam replied. "I just found out that his calendar had a red blotch on yesterday's date and he died yesterday. My calendar has the same kind of blotch as Jonah's. I don't want to die. I am not ready to die. I might have an anger management issue, I might even be guilty of being a bully, but Pastor, I'm here to tell you I'm not stupid. I need to get into the church and pray for my sins right away. I figure if I start today, by the time my date gets here, maybe God will change His mind. I heard all about that grace stuff you keep talkin' about. I'm gonna pray for some of that grace. I'm gonna repent until I can't repent no more. Now, if you don't mind, I'll walk with you to the church." Sam stood there waiting.

"Hold on, Sam," Horatio said. "You'll at least allow me time enough to get washed and dressed, I hope."

"Oh, yeah. I'm sorry. Take your time," Sam replied. "I'll meet you over at the church. Take your time, Pastor."

Within the next few minutes, Horatio met Sam at the church. Entering the building ahead of Sam, he turned on the lights and turned up the heat in the sanctuary. "You all right, Sam?" he asked, as Sam hurried to the foot of the altar and knelt.

"Yeah. I mean no. I mean, I guess so." Sam continued, "I'm about to launch into a prayer now."

"Okay, send up a good one," Horatio responded as he started to walk away.

"Okay, here goes," Sam said, as if he were about to jerk a 300-pound set of barbells.

Horatio continued walking toward his office without looking back. His backside had just made contact with his seat cushion when there was a weak knock at his office door.

"Hello," he responded, uncertain of whether or not he was hearing things.

"Pastor, okay to come in?"

Sam opened the door and, with his head positioned just inside the door frame, said, "Can you please teach me how to pray?"

"Sam, nothing could please me more. Come on in and sit down."

In the hours that followed, Sam came to know the Lord. It was as much an awesome experience for Horatio as it was for Sam. Sam opened up to Horatio about hurtful childhood experiences that caused him to be held captive by spirits of hurt, anger, and unforgiveness as far back as he could remember. Sam confided that he had an eighth grade education and felt as though the whole world was smarter than him. He dreaded the occasions when his young children would ask him for help with their homework assignments. There was such an outpouring of pent-up self-criticism and sorrow that Sam's eyes began to tear up. The tears were full of so much pain that each one hit the floor with the weight of a sewer grate. He apologized, continually, for crying. Before long, Horatio was overcome with grief for Sam.

"Sam, I am so, so sorry for the hurt that you've experienced. God's Word tells us that we are to confess our sins, one to another. I need to confess and apologize to you. You see, I labeled you as someone who was beyond help. I was wrong. In fact, that was wicked of me to think that of you. Can you please forgive me?"

"Pastor, I can't say that I blame you. That morning you saw me and Theresa having words on Front Street…."

"Yes, I remember," Horatio recalled.

"Well," Sam continued, "I was about to come across the street and give you a piece of my mind. Lord knows it wouldn't have been my first time doing something like that.

Anyway, I went to turn my body toward you to come in your direction but my body, my feet, my mouth, I mean, not one part of me would do anything but stomp off in another direction, like a scolded child. I couldn't understand that one. So you don't owe me any apology. Your take on me was right."

"Thanks, Sam. I appreciate that." For a while longer, he mentored Sam in the how-to of prayer.

"That's it?" Sam asked.

"That's it, Sam."

"Wow. I wish someone had taught me this before. As soon as I get through praying and repenting for myself, I'm going to pray for everyone I can. Especially for my friends who need help but don't know how to pray for themselves. Thanks, Pastor. I've got to get out there now. No time to waste. I've got a lot of praying to do." Sam was gone just that fast.

For the rest of the morning, Horatio remained in his office reviewing the listing of names and corresponding blotch dates as reported on the calendars. He received a call from the funeral home, informing him that Bill Nelson's son, Bill Jr., was on route home from his military tour of duty. At twelve noon, Horatio decided to get some fresh air. On his way out of the building, he observed Sam at the front of the sanctuary, emphatically, launching prayers high into the spiritual atmosphere.

After stopping at the post office, Horatio headed to the sandwich shop. While standing at the service counter, he noticed a beehive of activity in the vicinity of the Town Wharf. Fire engines, two police cars, and an ambulance were visible. As he started across the street to check on the commotion, a car horn startled him from behind and he moved to the side. The horn belonged to the car driven by the county coroner's office. Someone was dead.

"Oh, Lord, no." He saw Mel Askew standing by his police car, so he walked over to speak with him. "What happened, Captain? Anybody we know?"

"Don't know yet," Mel replied. "I'm still waiting on a positive ID. Doesn't look like anyone from town."

"If I can be of any assistance to the bereaved, I'll be at the church," Horatio offered.

"Thanks, Pastor," Mel said as he continued jotting down some notes.

With sandwich in hand, Horatio returned to the church. Entering the vestibule, he could hear Sam still going strong in his prayer.

Hearing the door open and close, Sam looked up.

"Pastor, I heard a lot of sirens a little while ago. Is everything okay outside?"

"Seems like somebody just died while on a fishing trip."

"Was he one of ours?" Sam asked.

"Not sure, yet."

"Oh, God. I don't want to die," Sam pleaded as he quickly returned to his prayer position in front of the pulpit. "Pastor, please call my wife and ask her to put my dinner in the oven. I'm going to be home late tonight,"

"Will do, Sam," Horatio promised. He remained in his office for the rest of the day, intensely reviewing the list of calendar names and dates. In the course of his review, he noticed that November twenty-eighth was Sam's date. As he closed up his office for the evening, he could hear Sam still going at it. He asked Sam to pull up the exterior door when the time came for him to go home to his wife and family. Sam assured him that he would.

Day 33
January 4th - Friday

At seven fifteen, Horatio awakes to the sound of someone knocking at his door. Putting on his bathrobe, he makes his way to see who it is. Sam Wooden and a few of his friends are standing on his porch.

"Morning, Pastor. Mind if we wait for you at the church?"

"No problem, Sam."

"And, Pastor, can you teach the fellas to pray like you taught me? They're kind of worried about their eternity too, if you know what I mean."

"I'll be right with you, Sam. Just give me a minute to get some clothes on, okay?"

"That's fine." Sam continued, "We'll see you there."

As the men walked toward the church, Horatio could hear them speaking among themselves about learning to pray. *Lord*, he thought to himself, *what are you up to?*

After opening the church sanctuary for Sam and his friends, Horatio told the men that he was going home to shave and shower. He promised to return straight away and mentor them in the way of strategic prayer. Walking back to his house, he noticed Mel Askew's police car headed in his direction. He gave Mel a wave. Mel pulled over.

"Got a minute, Pastor?"

"Certainly, Mel. How are you doing this morning?"

"Well, I'd be a whole lot better if I could make some headway in piecing together the story behind that guy who died on the fishing boat yesterday. Pastor, you wouldn't, by chance, know anything about the man, would you?"

"Why do you ask?" Horatio inquired.

"Well, we've identified the deceased but we can't understand what business he had in town. He was staying at a bed and breakfast on Route 3A but a check of his room didn't reveal very much. The only thing that ties him to this area, in any way, was one of those calendars like your church gave away New Year's eve."

Oh, Lord, no, Horatio processed inwardly. Feeling somewhat uneasy, he had to ask, "The calendar. Can I see it?"

"All of the deceased's personal belongings are at the station." Mel continued, "I can tell you this, though: the calendar was in the original wrapper. Unopened."

"I'd like to take a look at it, if possible," Horatio requested.

"Why all the curiosity about the deceased's calendar? Is there something I should know?"

"I have a partial listing of the names of calendar recipients," Horatio explained. "I'm curious to see if his name is on that list."

"After it's released from the evidence lockup, you can make that request to the deceased's next of kin. I can tell you this," the police captain offered, "From what we've been able to determine, the name of the deceased is, or should I say was, Thomas Rhone."

"Hmmm. Thomas Rhone doesn't ring a bell. I'll check to see if any of our congregants knew him."

"Thanks, that'll be helpful, Pastor."

"Okay, then. I'll speak with you later, Captain. I've got people waiting on me." Horatio returned home to wash and shave. Soon after he returned to the church. Once there, he immediately went to his office in search of the list of calendar recipients. Locating it, he perused the list for the name Thomas Rhone. That name was not on the list. Understanding that his list included only one-third of the calendar recipients, he continued to feel uneasy. He decided not to share any of what he had learned from Captain Askew until he had a chance to inspect Thomas Rhone's calendar. He didn't want to cause any additional anxiety to be put upon his members. He left his office and went to the church sanctuary to give some time to Sam and his friends.

In the church sanctuary, the men were seated in the front pew, as if to get as close to the pulpit as possible. They had begun discussing the fate of Jonah Tye. Interestingly, four of the six men had attended the Watch Meeting service. The two who hadn't attended were there, today, out of sheer conviction for not living right. They had heard all about the calendar and deduced that if something bad were to happen to their friends and they happened to be with their friends at the time, they might unintentionally get caught up in or even mistaken for their friend. So, playing it safe, they came to pray for God's forgiveness and, if possible, reconsideration of their fate.

Entering the sanctuary, Horatio apologized for the delay in his return. Wanting not to distract the men from focusing on the purpose for being at the church today, he did not mention anything about the Thomas Rhone matter. Sam introduced Horatio as "My pastor" to the two men who hadn't been to Good Shepherd before. The men greeted Horatio with an enthusiastic, "Good morning, Pastor." For the rest of the morning, he sat with the men. He counseled them through scripture that spoke to their individual circumstance. The attention level of each man present, including Sam, was commendable.

"Now, that's what I'm talking about! What'd I tell you?" Sam said, jumping out of his seat. "Is this some powerful stuff or what?" Sam went on to tell his story of what had transpired in his life since he learned, from "My Pastor" how to pray. Unbeknownst to Horatio, the day that Sam spent praying in the church, he experienced an angelic presence. He told of how, while praying, a very tall man, not known to him, entered the sanctuary. At first hearing footsteps, Sam assumed that it was Horatio coming in. The man came and knelt down alongside Sam. As Sam lifted up his head and looked in the direction of the man, he noticed that the man was staring him. Before Sam could say anything, the man spoke, saying, "The Kingdom of our Lord rejoices at the return of his child." The man smiled, stood up, and walked out.

"I didn't hear his footsteps walking away or doors closing behind him. He just disappeared," Sam explained. The sanctuary was filled with absolute silence for about 30 seconds.

"Wow," said Mark. "I wish that would happen to me."

Sam explained, "That's why I wanted you guys to come here with me this morning."

Horatio was awestruck. "Sam, this is truly amazing. Why didn't you share this earlier?"

"Pastor, did you ever see something that no matter how much you try to explain it, nobody's gonna believe you?" Sam asked. "That's how I expected people would respond to that."

"Well, I'm telling each of you here: God is doing something in this place," Horatio explained. He went on to tell the men of how the Spirit of God ministers to him. "This same relationship is available to anyone who calls on the name of Jesus Christ as Lord and Savior," he assured the men. "And if you ask Him to, He will reveal himself to you. Just ask."

With that, questions of how, when, and why were asked. In the Sanctuary, as instruction and explanation was provided that morning and afternoon, each man's appreciation for God's grace changed forever.

Bidding the men good-bye as they left the church, Horatio returned to his office to close it down. It was four thirty and the sun had set. Sam and his friends walked out of the building aglow with the manifested presence of God in their hearts. They were animated and now they wanted to share it with others.

"Where do you think we should go?" Eddie asked.

They each seemed to be thinking of the same place, but no one wanted to be the first to make mention of it.

Finally, Alex asked, "Do you think God would want us to go to the Fishing Hole?" The Fishing Hole was a local pub that Sam and his friends frequented.

"Well," Sam responded, "we are called to be 'fishers of men.'" The others laughed at the irony of their choice of where they would "launch into the deep." In a matter of minutes, they were in the pub. Familiar faces greeted them. One of which was Chester, the bartender.

"What can I get for you, boys?" Chester inquired.

"Chester, my good man," Dan explained, "we no longer thirst for demon rum. No, we prefer to be filled with the Holy Spirit."

"Yeah," Sam chimed in. "We have tasted and seen that the Lord is good."

"Go on. Get real." Chester laughed, unconvinced.

"No, Chester. We've seen the error of our ways and the curses we've been a party to," Dan said.

"Sure, you have. Sure, you have." Chester still unconvinced, waited for 'April Fools' or 'Gotcha' to follow.

"Barkeep, is the karaoke machine working?" Scott asked.

"Now, I'm 'Barkeep.' Chester continued, "What's going on with you? If you want to turn on the machine, just flip that green switch on the wall, Renaissance man."

Scott walked over and flipped the switch. The karaoke machine began to play "Jesus loves me, this I know…." Immediately, others in the pub, about thirty strong, joined in song with Sam and friends. As the song went forward, people started replacing their adult beverages with juice, water, or soda. On some faces, a tear was present. The Spirit of God had entered in. After a few choruses of "Jesus loves me," Scott searched the menu of songs that the karaoke system offered. Next, they sang "Amazing Grace." Other songs of praise continued to fill the tavern.

Chester, scratching his head, was heard to say, "In all the years we've played that machine, I've never seen these songs listed on the karaoke menu. Where the heck did they come from?"

Sam called out, "Don't you know, Chester? God reprogrammed the machine." The pub crowd cheered and sang for the next hour. After that, the crowd began to thin out as the men went home to their families.

****

Horatio was at home continuing to review the list of names and blotch dates that he had prepared. According to the information available to him, it would be six days, more, before the next blotch date would arrive. He was about to enter into prayer when he heard a knock at the door. It was Sam Wooden.

"Good evening, Pastor. I know that you're not usually in the church on Saturday morning, but I was wondering…."

"What time would you like me to open up the church for you, Sam?" He saw where Sam was headed.

"Seven thirty would be perfect."

"It will be done, Sam."

"Thanks, Pastor. You have a good night, now. And Pastor, me and the fellas really appreciate what you did for us today." Sam walked away singing 'Jesus loves me, this I know, for the bible tells me so….'"

Horatio, returning to his prayer, began with, "Thank you, Father…."

Day 34
January 5th - Saturday

The new day brought with it sunshine and warmer temperatures. Horatio had set his alarm for seven fifteen, so that he could be sure to have the church open on time for Sam. Quickly getting dressed, he made the trek to the church and unlocked the front door. He didn't see any indication of anyone waiting to get in. He chose to give Sam the benefit of doubt and leave the building open. Returning home, he shaved and showered, as he saw no benefit in going back to bed. After cleaning up, he cooked scrambled eggs and sausage. It was eight ten. Looking out his window, in the direction of the church, he watched for evidence of people coming or going.

"Oh, Lord, I should have known that Sam was just talking last night. He's probably still at home in bed," he muttered. Concerned about leaving the building unlocked and unattended, Horatio made his way back to the church to lock it down. Opening the door, he could hear a woman's voice.

In the sanctuary, he saw Teresa Wooden standing in front of the pulpit. With tears in her eyes, she told twenty-seven people who were present, this Saturday morning, about the transformation her husband experienced. "Sam," she was saying, "was impossible to live with. So many times I convinced myself to take my babies and leave. Why? Because Sam never gave me a compliment. He would always treat me as his child rather than his wife. He would rather spend time and money with his friends than be at home with his family. I'm certain there were times that if I had not kept silent, he might have put his hands on me. Living with Sam was not easy. The only reason I stayed was because I knew that Sam never cheated on me with another woman. That was God's way of letting me know that Sam loved me the best he understood how. When times got heated, I made up my mind: 'NO MORE!' Every time I got to the door, I felt that God was telling me to stay. It was not unusual for me to cry myself to sleep nights. I believed that dreams of a happy marriage and family life were meant for others, not me. I felt that God was punishing me for something that I had done earlier in life. My children always looked sad and intimidated because they were by-products of the world that was my reality. Then, one day," she continued, "something changed. Sam went to the New Year's Eve watch meeting with me, here at this church. He wasn't a regular face in the Sunday morning service, but I pleaded with him to not let me go to the Watch Meeting service alone. At first he told me, "NO! I ain't interested." (Mimicking the way Sam spoke.) "But something in my spirit told me to ask him again. And if he said 'No,' then ask again. And keep on asking, until he agreed. Well, after asking Sam fifteen or twenty times, he said, 'Okay.'" Those in attendance began to laugh and cheer. Sam was red-faced but cheered right along with everyone else.

"And let me tell you, something," Teresa continued, "When Sam said, 'Okay,' I heard God say, 'Well done, Teresa. You get Sam to the service tonight and I'll take it from there.' Well, the children and I stood with Sam in the service and, before our very eyes, something moved in him." The audience cheered, again. "Sam hugged me and the kids, apologizing, crying, laughing, telling us how much he loves us and how we have blessed his life and…."

Unable to control her emotions any longer, Teresa wept with joy. The crowd still standing and cheering saw Sam stand up, walk to his wife, embrace her, and kiss her as though it would be a kiss that would make up for all those he should have given her through the years, but didn't. Now, it was Sam's turn to cry. He didn't care who saw him.

"Listen, please," Sam began, "If God can bring a change like this in me, he can do it in you, too. I think about all that time I lost being a mean, miserable, selfish, bullying man and I can only apologize to Teresa, my children, to God, and to you, my friends. I want to you to know that for anything and everything that I have done to hurt any of you, I am deeply, sorry. You know," he continued, noticing Horatio at the back of the sanctuary, "Pastor, would you please stand with Teresa and me up here? You know," he repeated, "God has blessed us, men, with the responsibility of representing Him in the way we provide for, protect, and love our families. And, we have a choice to make: are we going to obey or rebel? I choose, from this day forward, to obey."

Every man present stood in place and proclaimed, "I will obey. I will obey. I will obey." The chorus of affirmation was so powerful that some of the townspeople walking outside the church, hearing the commotion, entered in to see all of what was going on. "There's something good going on in this church," Sam continued, "Pastor Smiley spent his time teaching me how to pray. I never understood the 'how to,' when or why, but after a little while with him, I understood that when I pray, I'm talking with God. And, when I am in the presence of God, every little worry, every little fear that I have carried in my heart is no longer mine to deal with because I have given it to Him. And, when all that stuff has gone out of me, I am free to focus on being right and doing right in the eyes of the Lord. Now, if you tell Him you're gonna be right. Be right. If you tell Him you're gonna do right, you better do it. God don't favor no hypocrites." Everybody cheered. "One more thing," Sam continued, "If you don't know how to pray, don't feel bad. Pastor is an awesome teacher and I've learned he can't say no to anyone who wants to learn." Turning to Horatio, he said, "Pastor, is there anything that you would like to add?"

Horatio, touched by all that was said, took a step forward and spoke, "Well, first I want to thank you for the kind word and, second, to let you know that I guess prayer classes will be held each weekday morning at nine o'clock here in the sanctuary." The sanctuary erupted in laughter and applause.

After the meeting, Horatio was surrounded by many of those in attendance. Three couples had asked him to perform a ceremony for the renewal of their vows, four people signed on for the prayer instruction class, and one couple signed on for premarital counseling. All in all, it was an unforgettable experience for everyone there. At ten thirty, he locked down the church building and returned to his house.

****

Sitting in his kitchen having a cup of peach tea, Horatio considered all that had taken place in the church that morning. Of everything that he had witnessed, what stayed with him most was the statement that Sam spoke: "There's something good going on in this church." Horatio prayed that Sam was right. But, in his spirit, he wasn't so sure. Considering that two, possibly three, people connected to the church had died within the past week, how could 'something good' be taking place at Good Shepherd? It appeared that the calendars he ordered and distributed at the Watch Meeting service were tied to the deaths. True, Bill Nelson never received a calendar. But to have died on his way to the Watch Meeting service and not have a calendar there with his name on it appeared, as though, someone knew that he wouldn't be there to receive it.

"This can't be coincidence. Lord," he began to pray. "Was it wrong for me to accept the offer of free calendars for the church? Did I allow a spirit of death to come into the Body of Christ? What have I done? Lord, forgive me for making decisions without inquiring of you first. Please, have mercy on those who received a calendar. Bless them, oh Lord, with long life, I pray, in the name of Jesus."

Horatio sat at his kitchen table and prayed for Jenny Murray, the person who, according to his chart, would next arrive at the blotch date. Her date with destiny was January ninth, four days from today. She was a charming young woman and single parent. Her daughter, Mary, was the light of her life. Last year, Mary was diagnosed with lymphoid leukemia. Children afflicted with this condition experience anemia, bleeding, bruising, recurrent infections, abdominal pain, labored breathing and swollen lymph nodes. During this time, many days had been a challenge for Mary. Jenny's love for Mary took no backseat to any celebrated mother-daughter relationship. Jenny had excellent support from family and friends, but the physical and emotional demands that she bore in caring for Mary were reflected in her countenance. The natural luminescence that Jenny's smile used to bring into the dreariest of environments came now with noticeable effort. Her energy and ability to focus on matters not pertaining to Mary were understandably diminished. Mary had recently developed an infection in her blood system and was back in Children's hospital. Several prayer warriors invested countless hours praying for Jenny and Mary.

Now, Horatio sits contemplating what approach to take with regard to Jenny's blotch date. Jenny already has so much to be concerned about. Should he risk causing her additional anxiety about what he understood the blotch to represent; that being a visit from the DEATH angel? Or should he keep quiet and remain hopeful that she would be spared? After all, he could be wrong. He prayed to God that he was wrong. He couldn't decide what to do but, he knew that her blotch date was four days away. The sick feeling in his spirit escalated to a throbbing, migraine headache. He reached for a bottle of aspirin and chased four pills down with a cup of water. "Yech," was all he could manage to verbalize.

In his heart, he wasn't motivated to visit the nursing home later that afternoon, but he had given his word. He planned to go as soon as Bill Nelson's funeral service ended. *Put on a happy face for all to see*, he thought to himself. *After all, isn't that what pastors are called to do. Be cheerleaders to the discouraged, visitors to the shut-ins, and shepherds to the flock.* He sensed a cynical spirit trying to overtake him. "I rebuke you, foul spirit, in the name of Jesus!" After a while, the dark spirit retreated.

****

He returned to the church at twelve noon to open up for the funeral director and his staff. Floral arrangements and guests began arriving shortly thereafter. He returned to his office and remained there until time for the service to get underway. While in his office, he continued to pray that God would forgive him for not feeling a deeper sense of loss in the passing of Bill Nelson. Further, he prayed that the Spirit of God would deliver him of any ought that remained in his heart towards Bill, Arthur Mutton, and other members of the Church's trustee board.

Walking into the sanctuary, he recognized Bill's widow seated in the front pew with a young man he assumed to be Bill's son. Mrs. Nelson sobbed as her son attempted to bring her some measure of comfort. The service was well attended. Present were representatives from the local chapter of the Masonic Hall, the Lion's club, the Rotarians, and V.F.W. Post. The church's trustees served as pallbearers. Horatio had never before participated in a funeral service that was as ceremonial as was this. Bill's eulogy was likened to an informercial for his business, modified to include a resume of his educational credentials, military service, financial accomplishments and fraternal allegiances. At the conclusion of the ceremony, Horatio extended his condolences and offered his support to Mrs. Nelson.

As he spoke with her, he noticed that, off to one side of the sanctuary, her son, Billy, was speaking to the young man, Thad, from the hair salon. As he stood there observing their interaction, Thad looked over at him and waved. Waving back, Horatio smiled and headed over to meet Billy, as he had never before had the opportunity.

"Thad, my friend. How have you been?"

"Hi, Pastor. I'm good. Nice church."

"Hi, Billy. I'm glad to finally meet you," Horatio began. "I've heard your name mentioned often. Seems you have quite a following around here."

"Pastor, pleased to meet you, sir." Billy continued, "Thanks for the kind things you said about my father. God knows he wasn't the easiest person to get along with."

Horatio was taken aback. It was clear that Billy's relationship with his father was strained. "How long will you be in town?"

"Two weeks."

"Maybe we can break bread together before you leave," Horatio suggested.

"I'd like that, Pastor. I really would. Mind if I give you a call next week?"

"That would be great. Here's my cell number." He wrote it on the back of his business card and placed it firmly in Billy's hand.

Turning to Thad he said, "Thad, I'm reminding you of the standing invitation to come and visit with us. I hope you'll accept it, soon. As you can appreciate, 'Tomorrow is promised to no man.' I'm not giving up on you," Horatio said with a smile.

As Horatio turned to walk away, Thad called out to him, "Pastor, I'll walk out with you."

There was no graveside burial service, as Bill Nelson had made known his desire to be cremated. Exiting the building, he could sense the eyes of many there watching and wondering what was said in his conversation with Billy. Horatio noticed Arthur's obvious attempt to surveil his exchange with Billy.

"So, Thad, how is it that you know Billy?"

"Billy and I traveled in the same circle of friends since we were fifteen. We didn't go to the same school or live in the same town," he continued. "We were 'mall rats,'" he said, with a chuckle.

"What's a 'mall rat'?"

"I guess you'd say we were kids with no wheels, no money, no plan and, absolutely no desire to be at home," Thad explained with a sense of 'those were the days.' "Billy and I joined the 'mall community' at about the same time, so we were the newbies. Billy was a cool kid who couldn't get far enough away from his father," Thad continued. "He did everything he could to rebel against his father's plans for his life. He wanted no part of being successor to the family business. He rejected opportunities to attend some really good schools, even though he was highly recruited by several collegiate baseball programs. I think what really sank his relationship with his father was when Billy invited Harvey to the senior prom as his date."

"Is Billy gay?" Horatio asked in his best matter-of-fact voice.

"Pastor, I'm going to plead D.A.D.T. to that one," Thad replied.

"D.A.D.T. What's D.A.D.T.?" Horatio asked.

"You know," Thad continued, "Don't ask, don't tell."

At that point, the walk to Thad's car had come to an end. He reminded Thad once again of the standing invitation to invest a Sunday morning of his time at Good Shepherd. Thad promised to do so, soon. Horatio went home to prepare for his trip to the nursing home.

****

Walking through the doors of the nursing home, Horatio experienced the presence of heaviness. Staff members, friends, and family of some residents were already gathered together in the community room.

"Good afternoon, everyone," he said with enthusiasm.

A somber, "Good afternoon, Pastor," was the scattered response.

"My, my. Why the sad faces?" he asked.

"Widow Taylor passed on this morning," Floyd said. A few of the residents began to cry.

"Oh, no. What happened?"

"She went to bed last night, like she always did," Floyd began. "Came time to wake up this morning and she didn't. The nurses tried their best but, she was gone. Gone. Just like that."

"Pastor, I'm afraid of what's going to come of me when it's my time," Willie Greene confessed. "How can I be sure that I'll end up in Heaven and not hell? I know Widow Taylor is in Heaven, because that's all she ever talked about. That's where I want to be, too."

"Willie," Horatio explained, "God wants us all to be with him. He doesn't want a single one of us to miss out on our inheritance."

"Inheritance. What inheritance?" Chip Sampson perked up.

"Chip," Horatio began, "Jesus tells us in the gospel John chapter 14 that 'In My Father's house, there are many dwelling places (homes) …I am going away to prepare a place for you…. And when I go and make ready a place for you, I will come back again, and will take you to Myself, that where I am you may also be.' Now, and for eternity, Widow Taylor is in the loving care of Jesus. She is in her Heavenly home," he concluded.

At that point, some hands were raised as if those in attendance were children in a classroom. "Pastor," Margie, one of the older residents, asked, "What do I have to do to be sure that I will go to Heaven when my time comes?"

"Yeah," Willie joined in, "what do we all have to do?"

"It's very simple," Horatio explained. "It's as simple as believing in your heart and confessing with your mouth that Jesus Christ is the risen Lord. Has everyone here acknowledged Jesus Christ as Lord?"

Some hands went up with certainty. Others were raised tentatively. Some remained down. Several people in the room acknowledged that they had never before read a bible.

"Pastor," Nurse Carla asked, "I was baptized as an infant and go for confession. Is that good enough?"

"No," Horatio responded. "You must confess with your whole heart that Jesus Christ, the Lamb of God and risen Savior, is Lord. Hard to do as an infant, wouldn't you say?"

"I'm not taking any chances," Cindy Gibson began. "Pastor, tell me what I need to say."

For the next ninety minutes, he conducted a bible study on the why and how of making ready for a life everlasting with God. Eight people accepted Jesus Christ as Lord that afternoon. An enthusiastic request was made for a weekly Bible study by the residents. Horatio agreed without a moment's hesitation. For the remainder of his stay, he fielded a broad range of questions concerning death, Jesus, sin, redemption, repentance, and much more. He recalled his time there as being his best visit, yet. After the study session had concluded, he returned home.

At his kitchen table, his attention returned to the decision he had to make regarding Jenny Murray. Should he alert her to his concerns or remain silent? During dinner and afterward, he continued to weigh the benefits versus the consequences of fully disclosing his concern to her. Unable to decide, he went to bed praying for God's guidance in the matter.

Day 35
January 6th - Sunday

Walking into the church, Horatio noticed Jenny Murray sitting in the front row. She was there with only a few other church members, as it was early. She sat there motionless. Her eyes stared straight ahead. Her gaze shifted ever so slightly to be in perfect alignment with Horatio as he took his position at the lectern. Jenny's presence in the front row was so distracting to him that he refused to look up as he fumbled through his sermon notes and bible. Unable to remain seated any longer, she rose to her feet.

"Is it me or my baby who's going to die?" she demanded. "Tell me, you coward! Tell me! What kind of evil person are you?" she continued. "Why have you brought such wickedness into our church?" She ran up the aisle and out the door.

The parishioners who witnessed the anguish that Jenny experienced could no longer remain silent.

"You're a wicked man, Pastor," a voice called from the crowd.

Another voice added, "We never should have allowed you to bring your evil ways into this community. Get out! Leave. Now! Go on!"

Horatio felt so guilty about the consequence associated with the calendars that he was unable to respond to the attack. He picked up his notes and bible and quickly exited the church. He found himself walking aimlessly along the Driftway, the road that led out of Scituate. The pain that he felt was so deep that all he could do was cry out, "Father, forgive me."

At that point, his alarm clock buzzed. His face and pillow were wet with tears. "Whew. I was dreaming?" he asked with uncertainty. "Thank you, Lord."

As he lay there, he realized that his heart was beating quickly and his mouth dry. In that moment, he decided to have the discussion with Jenny. At the very least, he figured, she would know as much as he did. Now, wide awake, he got up and prepared for church.

****

Going directly to his office, Horatio could hear the organist warming up in the sanctuary. He had hoped that this morning's service would be a continuation of the New Year's Watch Meeting event. He prayed that the presence of the Holy Spirit would return as powerfully as it had manifested that unforgettable night. While many who attended the Watch Meeting service were in church this morning, there appeared to be distraction that was rooted in the matter of the calendar blotches. It was clear that people were caught up in the mystery and, possibly, the consequence indicated via the crimson cross on their calendar. A local newspaper reporter is present at today's church service.

As the Praise and Worship portion of the service concluded, Horatio positioned himself behind the lectern with Bible and sermon notes in hand. In the twenty minutes that followed, he labored to stay the course with the message, to no avail. It was clear the members wanted to discuss the calendars. Everyone present was respectful of church protocol, so they did nothing to disrupt the service.

Finally, setting aside his notes and bible, he commenced a 'town meeting' style of conversation to discuss the matter of the calendars. Taking the position of listening rather than speaking, he fielded questions from those in attendance.

Glen Morris was the first to speak. "Pastor, is there any truth to the talk going around that the red cross on my calendar is indicating the day I'm supposed to die?"

"No, Glen. I believe that you're referring to Jonah Tye's passing. While it's true that Jonah's calendar did have a blotch date of January 2nd, which coincided with the date he died, the coroner hasn't yet disclosed the cause of death. There have been no other such instances that have taken place relative to the calendars, that I'm aware of."

There were several others who participated in the "question and answer" session and, through it all, Horatio was honest in his answers. The church members appreciated his candor. Any evidence of anxiety that existed prior to the discussion was abated. In closing, Horatio reminded everyone that he would always be available to anybody needing to talk about the calendars or any other matter.

After the Church meeting had ended, Horatio drove to his favorite seafood restaurant to ponder what next he should do for the benefit of the church. Should he tender his resignation? Should he postpone going on sabbatical for the sake of damage control? And what should he do about Jenny Murray? She didn't attend church service today. Was it because she had already heard the talk going around town about the calendar and decided to leave the church? Should he hold to his decision to share his concerns with her? He had so many questions and not a single answer. Horatio cared deeply for the members of his church family and would do anything to demonstrate the sincerity of his heart. His seafood platter wasn't as satisfying as he had come to expect. A spirit of fatigue came upon him so aggressively, as he attempted to finish his meal, that he began yawning. He returned home and climbed into bed. There he stayed for the remainder of the day.

Day 36
January 7th - Monday

After fifteen hours of seeking consolation in his bed but finding none, Horatio realized that the best thing to do was to get up and go to work. The spirit of depression was working aggressively to shut him down. He prayed, diligently, until that spirit lifted. He was back at his desk before eight o'clock. Uncertain of how many people, if any, would show up for the morning prayer class, he wanted to be there on time.

As he waited for the nine o'clock hour to arrive, he searched the church's files for Jenny Murray's contact information. Locating her phone number, he called her with the intention of scheduling a meeting to discuss the calendar situation. His call went into her voice mail, so he left a message asking that she call him at his office. It was twenty minutes before nine o'clock, so he walked across the street to get a cup of peach tea and a Boston crème donut.

On his way back to the Church, he saw a Crown Victoria parked out in front. *This can't be good.* Sure enough it was Mel Askew, Scituate's police chief, waiting for him to return. "Good morning, Chief," he greeted with his usual cheerful demeanor.

"Morning, Pastor. We finally wrapped up the Thomas Rhone matter."

"Really. What was the cause of death?"

"The jury's still out on that. It's the coroner's issue, now," the chief sighed. "I can offer you this, though: I asked Rhone's widow for the calendar that was found in his room and she handed it over. Here you go," he said, reaching into the front seat of his car. There it was. The calendar that tied Mr. Rhone to the church's Watch Meeting event. "So, Pastor," Mel asked, "what's so important about this calendar?"

Horatio had to think quickly. Not wanting to lie, he responded, "Katie White had called to request additional calendars for members of her family. I told her I'd see what I could do."

"That's nice," Mel continued. "If I hear anything more about our friend, Mr. Rhone, I'll let you know."

"Thanks, Chief. I'd appreciate that." He watched as the chief got into his car and drove away. There on the sidewalk, in front of the church, he stood. In his hand the key to knowing the role that this calendar played, if any, in Mr. Rhone's date with the Death angel. He went directly to his office.

Once inside, he closed his door and inspected the calendar. Yes, it was definitely one of the calendars given out at the Watch Meeting service. Interestingly, the calendar had not been opened. Packed in the original cellophane wrapping, he had a choice to make: open it or leave it alone. Better to know, or not? And what about Jenny Murray?

If by opening the calendar he was able to confirm that the blotch shown therein coincided with the day Thomas Rhone died, he'd be obligated to tell her the whole truth. On the other hand, if the blotch date didn't correspond with the date that he died, that would bring great relief to all who had received a calendar. He remembered praying, "Lord, please tell me what to do."

Just then, the phone rang. The call screen displayed Jenny Murray's number. "Good morning, Jenny. Thanks for returning my call."

"Hi, Pastor." She sounded exhausted. "Sorry, I wasn't here when you called. I was at the hospital with Mary."

"How's Mary doing?"

"She's not doing well, at all. She has a blood infection again. A bad one. The specialists are doing everything they can to get a handle on it, but Mary's little body is so weak. They're telling me that if the infection isn't sufficiently managed within the next two days, her condition could become critical. So, to answer your question, I'll know better within the next forty-eight hours," she responded.

Two days? Horatio processed inwardly. That's Jenny's blotch date. "I'll be praying for Mary?"

"Pastor, I appreciate that." Jenny continued, "In fact, the reason I'm here at home is to shower, get some clean clothes, and return to her bedside."

"Mind if I follow you there?"

"Nothing would please me more. Can you meet me at the Friendly's restaurant by exit 13? Say one hour?" she asked.

"Done. See you there," he promised. With all that was going on, Horatio had lost track of his commitment to be available for prayer instruction. Fortunately, no one had, as yet, shown up. He wrote a note and placed it on the church's front door, apologizing for any inconvenience that the class postponement had caused.

During the next thirty minutes, he prepared for what might well become a prayer vigil that could go all night. He shut down his office, returned to his house, packed a toiletry bag, and grabbed two bottles of water. Within the next thirty minutes, he was on his way to meet Jenny.

He arrived at the restaurant parking lot before her. Within minutes he saw Jenny's car pulling into a parking space on the other side of the lot. He started his car and pulled alongside of her vehicle, motioning for her to take the lead. She acknowledged his signal and headed for the highway that would take them to Children's Hospital in Boston.

****

Forty-five minutes later, they were inside the hospital. Mary's immune system had weakened substantially, so only Jenny was allowed in her room. She led Horatio to the hospital's chapel where he began to pray. After a few minutes, she left him to visit with Mary. Horatio appreciated the power of prayer, so he prayed with expectation. He gave God thanks for healing Mary from any effects that the infection had caused her little body to experience. As he prayed, he felt the presence of the Holy Spirit fill the chapel. Alternate bouts of sweat and a tingling sensation is much of what he experienced during his time in prayer. Although he could hear the doors of the chapel open and close as people came and left, he remained vigilant in his prayer. At one point, he felt a touch on his right shoulder. Uncertain as to whether it was divine or human, he pressed deeper into prayer.

"Hi," he heard the voice of a child say. Looking over, he saw a little girl five or six years old standing to his right. "Will you please pray for my brother?" she asked.

"Hi, there. What is your name?" he whispered.

"Julia."

"Julia, I would be honored to pray for your brother. What's his name?"

"Joshua," she replied.

"Julia, do you know how to pray?"

"Yes," she said, nodding her head.

"Will you pray with me for Joshua?"

"Okay," she agreed.

They began slowly reciting the Lord's prayer. Not knowing how much Julia knew about prayer, Horatio wanted to begin with a prayer that might be familiar to her. As he prayed the words, "Our Father," Julia joined in.

She prayed, "Our Father, hello be the name, the kids will come, they should be fun, on earth and in heaven, Amen."

Tears began to well up in Horatio's eyes because he knew that Julia was giving her best effort. It was obvious that she was very concerned about her brother. After they finished praying, Horatio asked about her brother. "Julia, why is Joshua in the hospital, today?"

"He was riding on the sidewalk and then he went on the street," she explained. "My daddy told him never to do that, but he went on the street. He got runned over by a car. I'm not going to do that with my bike," she said with certainty. "Joshua's leg was bleeding but my Daddy's with him."

From all that Horatio could determine in speaking further with Julia, she had wandered away from the Emergency Room waiting area and ended up in the chapel, without her daddy's knowledge. Julia's father was a single parent, left to raise her and Joshua after their mom was killed in combat, two years ago. Julia told Horatio, "My daddy takes good care of me and Joshua. He works very hard."

Concerned that Julia's father would be worried, should he return to the waiting room to find her missing, Horatio escorted her back to the Emergency Room. He remained with Julia until her daddy returned. Within twenty minutes, Julia's father, a young, clean-cut man whose eyes were reddened, emerged from the Emergency Triage area.

"Daddy, Daddy!" Julia called out at the sight of her father. "I'm right here," she motioned her daddy over.

According to Julia's father, Joshua's prognosis was good but they had to admit him to monitor the extent of his bruising overnight. The doctors suggested that he take his daughter home and get some rest. As he reached down to pick up Julia in his arms, she said, "Daddy, this is my friend. We prayed for Joshua." Her daddy was appreciative.

"Thank you, sir. My name is Danny Ryan. Thank you for your prayers."

"Hi, Mr. Ryan. My name is Horatio Smiley. Pleased to meet you," he said, as he extended his hand to shake the hand of Julia's daddy. "How is your son doing?"

"Joshua's doing better than they first thought. He's a lucky kid." Danny continued, "He came out of it with a slight concussion, a deep bone bruise in his arm and some internal bleeding that showed up on an initial scan, but miraculously stopped. The doctors can't understand what caused it to stop so quickly. They want to keep him overnight for observation. That boy of mine must have an angel watching over him."

"Indeed, he does," Horatio agreed. "Here she is, right here," he said, pointing to Julia. "She's quite a prayer warrior. You should be proud of her."

"God knows I am," Danny said as he gave her a kiss and a hug. "Take care, sir." Danny and Julia went home.

****

Horatio quickly returned to the chapel in case Jenny stopped in. He didn't want her to think he left the hospital without checking further on Mary's condition. He picked up with his prayer for Mary right where he had left off, at the time Julia came in. He labored to return to the level of intensity he experienced earlier in his prayer. It was as though a dark force was hindering him. He stood firm on God's Word and declared, "I rebuke you, demon spirit, in the Name of Jesus!" Immediately the oppressive spirit lifted and was gone. The heated, tangible presence of the Holy Spirit returned. Horatio entered into deep, fervent prayer as if to make up for the time he spent praying with little Julia. Sometime later that evening, Jenny returned to the chapel. She was sobbing.

"Jenny, is Mary all right?"

"Pastor, Mary is responding to the medicine! God saved my Mary!" She wept.

He knew that there was a time for questions and a time to be silently thankful. This was not the time for questions. "Lord, Your mercy and grace endureth, forever." He gave thanks as he hugged Jenny. They understood that through God's grace, little Mary was being restored. Jenny decided to stay the night at the hospital, so Horatio remained for a while longer before returning home. It was eleven forty-five.

Day 37
January 8th - Tuesday

Horatio was back at his office at eight o'clock. He checked for messages in his voice mail. The system announced, "One new message. Message number one."

"Hi, Pastor. This Sam Wooden. Heard something came up yesterday, so you didn't have the prayer class. Hope everything is okay with you. Just want to let you know that if you need me to help with the class, I'm available. In fact, I'm kinda hoping to be your assistant or something. Let me know if you need anything in the meantime. I'll try you back later. Again, this is Sam. Sam Wooden. Bye."

"End of message," the system announced.

Horatio, looking upward asked, "Lord, what are You doing?" He couldn't help but laugh.

At nine o'clock, four people walked into the church. "Good morning, Pastor. My name is John Davis and this is my wife, Dawn. And these are the Taylors, Greg and Rose."

"Well, good morning all" Horatio welcomed. "Nice to see you."

"Pastor," Dawn began, "thank you so much for making yourself available to us. We noticed the change that had taken place in the Woodens' marriage and we're hoping that God can move like that in ours."

Her husband, John, explained, "Our marriage has been under some stress on and off, like a lot of other marriages these days. Dawn and I would separate over stupid little things that, in hindsight, weren't worth the energy or time that we gave them. And when I say 'separate,' it wasn't like I moved out or she went to stay with her folks. We would continue to live in the same house sharing the same space as though we were invisible to each other."

"We didn't talk to each other or even look at each other," Dawn confirmed.

"Same here," the Taylors acknowledged, nodding their heads in complete agreement.

Greg Taylor elaborated, "We often felt that there was something working against our marriage. We knew that neither one of us wanted our kids growing up in a single-parent household, like we did." He continued, "We wanted a better home life for our kids than we had growing up."

"Well, it sounds like we have some talking to do," Horatio said. "Is anyone familiar with the scripture Amos 3:3 that asks: 'How can two walk together, lest they be agreed?'"

Dawn and Rose recognized the scripture. John and Greg did not.

"I'd like to ask some general questions to better understand your experiences," Horatio explained. "I don't know how much time you have to spend with me today, but what we don't discuss this time around, we can work to set up a time that will be convenient to you later on. Also," he added, "do you prefer to meet as individual couples or together?"

A quick, unanimous "Individual couples" was the vote. For the next ninety minutes, Horatio instructed them on the purpose, process, and power of prayer. Then, he scheduled counseling times with each of the couples to begin after his return from sabbatical. Before adjourning, he prayed for their marriages and homes to be blessed. "Lord, I asked that you would send those who are ready. You never disappoint. Thank you," he prayed aloud.

****

Back at his desk, his attention returned to Mary and Jenny. Remembering that her blotch date was one day away, he needed to know Mary's condition. He understood that the status of a critical-care patient could turn for the worst at a moment's notice. Especially, a patient dealing with Mary's issues. He placed a call to the hospital and requested to speak with a patient information representative. His inquiry was directed to a nurse who provided a generic update that continued to list Mary's condition as 'guarded.' "Guarded?" he questioned. "What the heck is that supposed to mean?" He sensed a spirit of anxiety trying to overtake him. "Spirit of anxiety, I rebuke you in the name of Jesus," he declared, "Get thee behind me! I'll have nothing to do with you, today!"

In his time with Jenny, the day before, he hadn't remembered to get her cell phone number. His attempt to reach her at home resulted in his call going unanswered. He had no other way to contact her. Looking to his left, as he returned the phone handset to its cradle, he could see the calendar that once belonged to Thomas Rhone. It was within reach. Staring at it, it seemed to be taunting him.

Here I am. The answer to your question lies just inside my cellophane wrapper. Don't be a coward. If the answer I possess isn't what you hoped for, then it can remain a secret between us. No one but you and I will know.

"I need some fresh air," Horatio muttered. Picking up his coat, on the way out the door, he eyed the calendar with contempt.

The weather in Scituate was clear and cold. A brisk ocean breeze caused Horatio's eyes to water as he made his way to the nearest sandwich shop. Opting to eat his sandwich there, he found a seat by the window looking out to the sidewalk. From his vantage point, he could see Sam Wooden across the street talking with a group of teenagers. The body language that the teens displayed moved from disconnect to near disbelief. Deciding to wait and watch, Horatio noticed that the group was drawing closer to Sam as he continued to speak with them. Eventually, they all went inside the bowling alley. Curious as to what was going on, he wrapped up his sandwich and walked across the street to the bowling alley. Once inside, he observed Sam in deep discussion with the teens. Curious, he waved to Sam as he walked in their direction.

"Pastor," Sam called out, motioning him over. "You guys, this my pastor. Pastor Smiley, meet our town's next generation of movers and shakers. I've been discussing God's Word for the past hour and the Holy Spirit has been moving, mightily."

"Really? How so?" Horatio asked.

"Well," Sam explained, "I was walking along Front Street and, as I approached the group, the Spirit of God instructed me to ask Tony if he would let me pray for him. I said to Tony, by the way, this is Tony," Sam made the introduction. "As I was saying, I said to Tony, 'The Spirit of God is instructing me to pray with you.' Tony said, 'Fine.' I asked if there was anything, specifically, that I could pray with him about. He said that his mother was dealing with some health issues. We prayed while, I guess, his buddies looked on. The next thing I know, his friends were standing with us in prayer. After we finished praying, I tried to impress upon him the importance of fully trusting the Lord to deal with his mom's stomach condition. I opened up my pocket Bible and recited II Timothy 1:7."

"The Lord did not give us a spirit of fear but, rather a spirit of power and of love and of soundness of mind," Horatio recited.

"Exactly." Sam was animated. "I told Tony that his spiritual enemy, the devil, wants him and his mother to stress out and be discouraged. Tony said, after the prayer, he felt a heaviness lift up off of him. He called his mother, right then, to share the scripture with his mother. He dropped to his knees when his mother told him that she had just returned from the hospital for a follow-up and the doctors sent her home because the x-ray equipment was apparently malfunctioning. The tumor that was clearly visible the last time they checked, only a few weeks ago, was not showing up in the scan today. Tony's mom told him that she continued to hear the voice of God telling her, 'I'm with you' when she prayed, but she didn't understand that He was dissolving the tumor. She was crying. As Tony explained the situation to his friends, tears welled up in their eyes. Man, it was beautiful."

Tony confided, "I thought this whole God thing was some kind of joke. This guy starts praying for my mother. Next thing I know, I'm starting to feel something take hold of me, like I've never experienced before."

"Pastor, I've got to admit," Sam confessed, "I didn't know where the words were coming from, as I prayed. They just kept coming. I asked the Holy Spirit to help me pray, but … wow!"

"Isn't God awesome?" Horatio explained. "What you all witnessed was God's love for us." Everybody nodded in agreement.

"I want to see more," Dennis said. "I want to know God, like you and Mr. Wooden," he said to Horatio.

Sam was beaming. It was as though someone had just paid him the highest compliment he had ever received. "Man, I love the Lord," Sam declared. "I'd give anything just to be able to teach people about how good He is."

"You know, Sam, God works in mysterious ways," Horatio reminded him. He continued, "We never know what God has in store for our future." Everybody chuckled at Sam's enthusiasm.

"Pastor," Tony began, "can you show me how to pray like you and Mr. Wooden?"

"I'd love to, Tony, but I'm scheduled to be away for a few weeks on sabbatical. Would it be okay with you, Sam, if I assigned this opportunity to you?"

Sam was speechless. "Really? Are you serious, Pastor?"

"Sam, I'm very serious. Your prayers have power because of your faith." Horatio continued, "I've noticed the transformation that your life has undergone because of your faith in God. I believe that you are ready. So I ask you again, Sam Wooden, will you do it?"

"YES! YES! Absolutely," Sam replied. "Oh, my Lord," he continued, "Pastor, you're the best. I mean, Lord, You're the best. I've got to go tell my wife." Sam ran off in the direction of his house. All that could be seen of Sam, as he quickly disappeared in the distance, was the back of his head and the soles of his shoes.

Horatio invited Tony, Dennis, and the others to be at the church Saturday morning at twelve noon. He assured them that he and Mr. Wooden would be there to receive them. He bade them good-bye and returned to his office.

In his office, Horatio's eyes immediately went to Thomas Rhone's calendar. He wanted so badly to rip the cellophane wrapping off it and be done with the mystery, for better or worse. The Lord hadn't, yet, responded to his prayer for instruction, so he chose to wait. Checking his phone for messages, the service announced, "One new message." With pen in hand, he prepared to write down the message details.

"Pastor, my name is Joyce Rhone, Thomas Rhone's widow."

Horatio's stomach became queasy. He sensed in her voice that the woman had been crying. Her message continued, "Police Captain Askew suggested that I give you a call. He seems to think you knew my Thomas. I have a question to ask you about a calendar. Will you please call me at 7775515?"

"Man, oh, man. What am I supposed to do with this, Lord?" he asked. He prayed for divine instruction. *Slow to speak, quick to listen,* he heard the Spirit of God minister to him. Taking a deep breath, he picked up the handset and dialed the number. Mrs. Rhone answered her phone on the second ring.

"Hello."

"Good afternoon, Mrs. Rhone. My name is Pastor Horatio Smiley. Am I calling at a bad time?"

"No, Pastor. Thank you for returning my call." She continued, "Pastor, I understand that you are aware of my husband's passing. Strangest thing, I must say," she paused. "He was an expert fisherman. Each year, he'd treat himself to a few days of fishing. Sometimes deep sea, other times freshwater. He loved fishing more than most anything else in the world. He was healthy as a horse but, the autopsy showed that he had a massive heart attack. I don't understand what happened. Forgive my going on and on."

"Mrs. Rhone, please don't apologize," Horatio said, trying to comfort her. "How can I be of help to you in this difficult time?"

"My husband attended church much of his life." Mrs. Rhone continued, "Twelve years ago, the church we were members of began, as my husband put it, 'compromising its focus.' Apparently, the religious doctrine that was being taught shifted from 'inspiring' to 'entertaining' the church members. At the conclusion of each Sunday morning service, he came away feeling less equipped then he was going in. The church's focus of emphasizing ritual over relationship and sensitivity over sin caused him to become discouraged. Eventually, he renounced his membership and walked out, mad at the church, mad at God. He couldn't understand how God could allow such perversion to go unpunished." She concluded, "He died, never having made peace with God."

"Unfortunately, what your husband experienced is not uncommon in churches today, Mrs. Rhone." Horatio explained. "People are lulled into believing that 'if they mean well and don't commit some heinous crime, they'll go to heaven. It's a shame. Worse than that, it's a lie from the pit of hell."

"That's the reason I called you," Mrs. Rhone explained. "My son, Chip, told me the Spirit of God is in your church. I would like my husband's funeral service to take place there. It would bring great comfort to this old woman."

"Mrs. Rhone, I would be pleased."

"Oh, thank you, Pastor. I don't mean to be unreasonable, but can the service be held on Saturday, the twelfth?"

"I'll make the request to our Board of Trustees, as soon as I get off the phone. They may require that a service fee be remitted with the application."

"That's fine. Will you let me know as soon as you hear of their decision?"

"You have my promise, Mrs. Rhone."

"Thank you so much. God bless you." She hung up the phone.

Horatio took a deep breath. "Lord, did Mr. Rhone die as the result of his calendar? I'm so sorry and I repent for bringing the spirit of death into your house. Please forgive me," he continued. "Thank you for bringing him to Good Shepherd before he passed on. I pray that he was blessed at the Watch Meeting."

****

Horatio placed a call to Trustee Board Acting Chairman Arthur Mutton to get approval for the Rhone funeral. As luck would have it, Arthur answered the phone.

"Hello, Mutton residence."

"Arthur, Horatio Smiley. How are you doing this afternoon?"

"Afternoon? It's more like evening, Pastor. I'm doing okay, I guess. Is everything all right at the church?" he asked in his usual monotone voice.

"Yes, yes. Everything is just fine." Horatio continued, "Arthur, I just received a request from Mrs. Thomas Rhone, the widow of the gentleman who died last week while on a fishing trip. She asked if his funeral service could be held at the church."

"Why at our church?" Arthur sounded offended. "Why does every 'Johnnie come lately' expect us to open up the doors of the church to them?" He huffed, "I don't feel good about this. I don't … I mean we don't know anything about the deceased or his family." For the next few minutes Arthur continued on, giving reasons for his apprehension.

"Arthur," Horatio interrupted at the first opportunity, "will you please present the request to the board? Mrs. Rhone has agreed to pay whatever cost the board assesses. Besides," he continued, "Mr. Rhone was present at the Watch Meeting service, so you might say Good Shepherd was the last church he attended prior to his death."

"Well, I can't make any promises. I'll talk with the board and get back to you with our decision. I'm not promising anything, you understand?" Arthur was emphatic.

"Thanks, Arthur. I know the Lord will be pleased if we can bring some measure of comfort to Mr. Rhone's widow. Have a good evening."

"It's not about 'comfort,' it's about what's right…." Arthur was still talking when Horatio hung up the phone.

Sitting in his chair, he glanced in the direction of Thomas Rhone's calendar. Holding fast to his decision to wait on God's instruction on whether or not to open it, he was moved to call the hospital, yet again. He hoped to get a more informative update on Mary Murray's status.

****

Once connected to the Patient Services representative, he inquired about Mary's condition. "I'm sorry, sir," the representative responded, "I have no record of Mary Murray being listed as a patient in this hospital."

"Has she been discharged?"

"I'm sorry, sir. I am not authorized to disclose any additional information, at this time," the representative stated.

"I don't understand what you're telling me. Are you telling me that Mary has been moved to another hospital?"

"I'm sorry, sir," the representative responded with frustration.

"Excuse me, please. Is there a supervisor that I can speak with?" he asked.

"Just one moment, sir." His call was placed on hold, momentarily.

"Hello, this is Julie Martin. How may I assist you?"

"Hi. My name is Horatio Smiley. I'm Pastor to Mary Murray's family and I am simply trying to understand her condition and where she has been moved to."

"Pastor, Mary passed away at three thirty-five this afternoon." The voice continued to provide additional information but, he wasn't listening. In fact, he didn't remember hanging up the phone.

"Oh, my God. I knew I should have called Jenny and told her about the calendar," he agonized. "Why did I wait? If she had known, at least, she could have been better prepared for Mary's death. I chickened out. Why didn't I tell her? Poor, poor, Jenny."

His stomach was knotted up. He leaped up from his chair and ran to the toilet just in time. As he hung his head over the rim of the toilet, he began to wish that he could thrust his entire body into the commode and disappear, forever. Eventually managing to raise his head, he washed his face with cool water and made his way back into his desk chair. "I've got to call Jenny. I've got to call her and beg her forgiveness. Lord, God, I need your help. Please, give me the courage and the words to let Jenny know how truly sorry I am for all that I have caused to happen to her and her daughter. Lord, I have failed you. I repent for this wicked thing I've caused to come upon Jenny, Jonah Tye, the Rhone family, and the people of Good Shepherd."

He was grieved to the depths of his soul. He understood that he had no choice but to tender his resignation as pastor of Good Shepherd, immediately. With pen in hand, he began to put to paper the words that would, prayerfully, cause the curse to be canceled off the lives of everyone who had received a church calendar. His letter began, 'It is with….' The pen stopped writing. Attempting to shake the pen free of clotting ink, he shook it and shook it, to no avail. Locating another pen, he continued writing the letter. Again, the ink clotted. Frustrated, he threw the pen across the room and pushed the paper aside.

"Lord," he shouted, "why are You doing this, to me? You want me to go? I'll go. You want me to stay? I'll stay. Throw me a bone here. Tell me what you want. Please!"

He buried his face in his hands. "I need to call Jenny," he thought aloud, as he reached for the phone. He called her at home. The phone continued to ring until the call was directed to her voice mail. "Jenny, this is Pastor Smiley. Please call me on my cell phone as soon as you get this message. It's very important."

He considered calling her parents' home to ask if they had knowledge of her whereabouts, but thought better of it. He remained in his office for another hour. Before going home, he walked to the Village Mart and purchased a bottle of wine.

"Maybe this will help to relieve my stress," he muttered as he reached for a brand of wine that he remembered from what seemed to be happier days, a long time ago.

Entering his house, he took off his coat, grabbed a box of cookies, and adjourned to his living room with a glass of wine. He was not much of the fireplace type of man, but this evening he felt a chill in his body that wouldn't go away. Lighting a fire, he pulled a chair as close to the heat source, as he was safely able to do.

There in the dimly lit room, he wept. A floodgate of tears opened, pouring out all of the hurt, loneliness, disappointment, and regret that this man of God recalled in this moment of agonizing self-appraisal. His lips never touched the glass of wine. His heart never stopped believing that the Spirit of God was there in the room with him. He pleaded with God to speak to him. "Speak, Lord, speak," he beckoned over and over again. God was silent.

In the quiet, stillness, he hears his cell phone ringing. He left it in his coat pocket in the kitchen. Rising up from the chair, he goes to retrieve his phone. *It must be Jenny*, he processes.

Reaching into the pocket of his coat, he answers the cell phone just after the incoming call disconnects. Caller ID displays Jenny's number. Immediately, he returns her call.

"Jenny," he asks before she can say a word. "Is Mary all right? Jenny, I'm so sorry for not telling you about the calendars. Please forgive me."

Jenny interrupted, "Pastor. Mary is fine. What about the calendars?"

"Mary's fine?" he pauses. "Are you all right?"

"Mary's fine. I'm fine," she assured.

"But the people at the hospital told me Mary was no longer there," he said. "I assumed the worst."

"Oh, my goodness, no," Jenny said. "Mary responded unusually well to the antibiotics and her condition has been upgraded to 'good.' She is going to be back home with me tomorrow. Now, please. What were you saying about the church calendars?"

Horatio told her some of what had happened since the time that the calendars were distributed. As a result, he had come to fear the worst happening to everybody who received one.

"Well," Jenny responded after Horatio had finished his explanation, "My blotch date, as you describe it, is tomorrow and it looks like tomorrow is going to be the best day of my life. I can't speak for anyone else, but I can tell you that something wonderful is going to happen in my life, on January 9th. My baby's going to be back home with me."

"Jenny, thank you so much for all you've shared with me tonight," he replied, with great relief.

"You know, Pastor," Jenny continued, "I almost held off on calling you tonight because of the time. I'm so glad that I did. And, by the way, I don't know what you prayed when you were in the chapel praying for Mary, but God responded in a way so amazing that Mary's doctors said that they've never witnessed anyone, child or adult, experience such a quick recovery from the type of infection that she had contracted. Pastor, you're the best. Good night and thanks again."

"Get some rest and God bless you, too, Jenny." The call ended.

"Thank you, Lord Jesus. Hallelujah. Glory. Glory. Glory."

Horatio went to the kitchen, emptied out the contents of the wine bottle and glass into the sink, turned off the house lights, and went to bed.

Day 38
January 9th - Wednesday

Horatio awoke from a good night's rest, his first in a week. He was in the kitchen pouring a glass of orange juice when he glanced over at the letter of resignation he attempted to write the evening before. Picking up the paper, he started to ball it up and throw it away, but reconsidered. "Don't be too sure of yourself, Horatio. There's still another 197 calendars out there."

****

Back in his office at eight fifteen, his eyes went immediately to Thomas Rhone's calendar. The temptation to open it was not as intense as it was before he spoke with Jenny. Retrieving the list of blotch dates from his desk drawer, he began to peruse it to identify who next would meet their date with destiny. Just then, the phone rang.

"Pastor, this is Arthur Mutton."

"Hello, Arthur. And, how are you doing this fine morning?"

"Fine, thank you," Arthur continued. "I've spoken to the board and, as acting chairman, persuaded them to approve the Rhone application. We are requiring that a five hundred dollar service fee be received prior to our reserving the sanctuary for the funeral."

"Five hundred dollars? The church usually charges two hundred fifty. Why so much?" Horatio asked.

"New year, new pricing structure," Arthur replied. "If the widow doesn't want to pay it, well…, Pastor, she can have her husband's homegoing service someplace else."

"I don't agree with the five hundred dollar assessment, but I'll inform her of the board's position. I'll call you with her decision. What is the best time to reach you?" Horatio asked.

"I have a nine-thirty doctor's appointment. I should be home by one o'clock."

"Fair enough. I'll speak with you then, Arthur. I'll let you know of Mrs. Rhone's decision."

"Thank you. We'll speak, then." Arthur confirmed, as the call ended.

****

195

Horatio prayed, "Lord, I will to pray for Arthur and not judge him. Help him to understand that Good Shepherd does not belong to the board, it belongs to You." Convinced that he had shared some part in Thomas Rhone's death, Horatio decided to pay the five hundred dollar application fee that the board required. He called the Rhone residence and was connected to Mrs. Rhone.

"Hi, Mrs. Rhone. This is Pastor Smiley."

"Hello, Pastor. Any news?"

"Well, we're all set for Saturday at nine o'clock," he confirmed.

"Oh, thank you so much, Pastor." Mrs. Rhone said, relieved.

"Do you need any help in preparing the service program?" he asked.

"No, thank you, Pastor." She explained, "The funeral home seems to have everything in place. They just needed the time and location information. My son Chip is here with me now. My daughter-in-law, Susan, is flying in tonight from San Diego. They'll be here to help me with any loose ends for the next couple of weeks."

"That's wonderful, Mrs. Rhone. If anything should come up that you need help with, you have my number," he offered. "Lord willing, I'll see you Saturday morning." The phone call ended.

He continued to replay in his mind the way that Arthur Mutton had responded to Mrs. Rhone's request.

"Lord," he prayed, "Help me to understand what is taking place with Arthur and the church's trustees. Are these men as wicked as they appear to be? Am I not understanding what I, as a follower of Christ, must do to be excellent in my stewardship of this church?" At that moment the phone rang. It was Billy Nelson.

"Hi, Pastor. This is Billy Nelson. I met you the other day at the funeral," thinking that Horatio might not have remembered him.

"Billy, how are you, my friend? And how's your mother doing?"

"She's doing okay, I guess. I mean, you know, everything considered. Anyway, Pastor, I was wondering if I could stop by and 'break bread' like you said?"

"I'd like that, Billy. What's your schedule looking like?"

"Wide open," Billy said.

"How about doing lunch today?" Horatio asked.

"That would be great. Say, twelve o'clock?" Billy was appreciative.

"I'll order some subs. What kind can I get for you?" Horatio asked.

"Italian with everything, extra hot for me," Billy said.

"Done. See you at twelve." The call ended.

Horatio worked to clear his desk of a few files before Billy's arrival. He ordered the sandwiches to be delivered. They arrived the same time as Billy. He ushered Billy back to the church kitchen.

"What can I get you to drink?" he asked, before taking a seat at the table.

"Water is fine." Billy continued, "Pastor, I've got to tell you that I have great respect for you."

"Thanks, Billy," Horatio responded reflexively. "I'm flattered, but given that we've never met before, what have I done to deserve such respect?"

"Maybe more than you understand."

"I haven't a clue. Can you explain?"

"Pastor, my father was a difficult, controlling, self-righteous man." Billy explained, "Everyone who he interacted with was subjected to his bullying. Men, women, children, anyone and everyone who didn't do as he instructed or fell short of his expectation bore the full measure of his wrath."

"Your dad had some issues but…."

Billy interrupted, "Pastor, my father turned friend against friend, husband against wife and parent against child. He was a wicked man." Billy's face reddened with disgust, recalling his father's ways. Taking a moment to regain his composure, he continued, "Pastor, you are the only person I know who has been able to stand up to my father. I mean, you not only stood toe to toe with him, you beat him."

"Billy, I don't understand what you're talking about."

"Pastor, ever since you came to town, my father tried to run you out. He instructed the church's trustees to vote down anything that you proposed, to frustrate you and make you quit. Point is, you're still here and he's not. You notice that you haven't received a pay raise in the three years that you've been here? In fact, I understand that there have been 'payless paydays' to 'offset increased costs to your benefits package.' That's crap! Pardon my language. The trustees are supposed to adjust your salary every year to reflect a 'cost of living' increase, no matter what." Billy had Horatio's full attention. "And, then there's the matter of the Heywoods…"

"What about the Heywoods?" Horatio interrupted, while perched on the edge of his seat.

"My father has been trying to squeeze them off their land for years. Forty-seven years ago, that land belonged to my grandfather. When the town foreclosed on the property for unpaid taxes, it was auctioned off. Mr. Heywood was the successful bidder. He won it fair and square, but my father was determined to take it back. Not buy it or barter for it, mind you, take it back. Mr. Heywood was always a real nice man. Made no difference to my father, though.

"The Heywoods used to be foster care providers. My father used his influence at Mercy Ministries to have the worst kids, they could find, sent to the Heywoods. The strategy was, 'If the Heywoods didn't hurt the kids, the kids would hurt the Heywoods.' The orphanage sent kids who were pyromaniacs, 'cutters,' thieves, and worse.

"To make matters worse, the orphanage was always sending investigators to perform unscheduled visits and inspections. Word was that a kid with a history of starting fires was found with a book of matches in his pocket. No fire was ever set, but they blamed the Heywoods for not keeping close enough watch on the children. The kid said somebody set him up. The orphanage removed every child from the Heywoods' home, 'for safety reasons,' less than an hour later. Coincidence, Pastor? I don't think so." Horatio sat stoically, listening in disbelief. Billy continued, "To make the Heywoods' life even more miserable, my father warned that if he heard of anyone helping them in any way, they'd be next."

"That's sheer wickedness," Horatio heard himself respond aloud.

"No," Billy responded, "there's 'wicked' and then there's 'the wrath of Bill Nelson.' That was the wrath of Bill Nelson. When you befriended the Heywoods, it was like God sent you to save them just before they went down for the third time. You were a thorn in my father's big toe and he couldn't do anything to make you go away." Billy chuckled.

Horatio's mouth was wide open. He could sense it but, he wasn't able to do anything about it. Billy continued, "About three years ago, I received 'instructions' from my father to sign on as the ship's assistant to the Chaplin. He told me to get my credentials together because he had a position waiting for me at Good Shepherd as pastor. I led him to believe that I was onboard, but I couldn't have cared any less about his proposition. In fact, I'm moving to the West Coast as soon as my hitch is up. I was told that after the Watch Meeting last week, the trustees couldn't run you out of town if they strapped you to a missile and lit the fuse."

"Billy, how did you find out all of this?" Horatio asked.

"My mom. She's my best friend. She thinks very highly of you, Pastor. She stopped attending Good Shepherd years ago, when my father was appointed as trustee board chair. She said she wanted no part of any church that would look up to a man like him. She says she only remained married to my father out of fear of what he was capable of doing to us."

A flurry of thoughts and images went through Horatio's mind. He pushed his sandwich aside. His head felt as though it was about to explode. He struggled to maintain his composure. Billy remained there for another half hour speaking about other misdeeds of his father, but Horatio had become numb to Billy's revelations. His mind had reached the point of overload. "Oh, wow, Billy," Horatio interrupted. "I've got to be somewhere in ten minutes. You think we can continue this conversation, later?"

"Sure, I'd like that," Billy said.

Horatio could see that Billy needed someone to confide in but, why him? "How's Friday look for time?" he asked.

"I'm taking my mom to visit her brother in New Hampshire."

"Well, then. How about Monday?" Horatio asked out of conviction. "Monday will be the last day I'll be in town before I leave on sabbatical so, we may not have as much time as we'd like. I expect to be here in the office by nine o'clock."

"Monday works just fine, Pastor. I appreciate any time that you can spare. I'll plan to be here at nine thirty to give you a chance to have your coffee, in peace."

Horatio thanked Billy for his time as he walked him to the door. After his conversation with Billy, he needed some fresh air. The fact of the matter was that he had nowhere in particular to be in ten minutes. Horatio had lied; he knew that he lied and he repented. "Lord, please forgive me," he prayed. His brain, heart, and emotions felt like they had just gone through a meat grinder. With everything that Billy had revealed, the kitchen walls felt as though they were closing in on him. He needed some fresh air. He left the church, jumped in his car, and headed for Hummarock beach.

****

Sitting in his car, in the beach parking lot, he cried out to God, "Is this your idea of love? Why are you doing this to me? Haven't I suffered enough already?" Questions and tears. Tears and more questions. "Lord, I believe in Your Word. I will always believe. Show me, please, what to do with all of this. Please, show me."

At that moment, his attention went to the dreams that haunted him wherein masked, demonic figures chased him out of town. "My God," he exclaimed. "That's it. You were showing me what you wanted me to know. You were letting me see the source and the extent of wickedness that was coming against me. Lord, you were speaking to me. You didn't leave me alone, after all. You were right there with me."

Horatio was so comforted in that moment of understanding that his frustration turned to joy. He could better appreciate how God had trusted him to take on the battle for the members of Good Shepherd. He called Rene. He shared with her some of what God had revealed to him through Billy Nelson. Rene asked if he needed her to come to him so they could talk further. He asked, instead, that she would meet him at prayer meeting that night.

"I'll be there, Horatio. I mean Pastor," she assured. They giggled like two giddy schoolchildren.

****

Prayer meeting was exceptional. More than seventy members of Good Shepherd came to participate in prayer with Horatio, one last time before he left for sabbatical. The Woodens, Deacon and Mrs. Brock, the Willises, the Heywoods, Jenny Murray, and a handful of teenagers were among those in attendance. A tangible presence of the Holy Spirit filled the sanctuary. Prayer continued until seven-thirty. No one wanted to leave, so Horatio ordered pizzas and soda. The impromptu fellowship moved to the church kitchen. The building didn't empty out until ten fifteen. Rene, Mr. and Mrs. Brock, and Horatio closed up the church building. He was happy to see Rene at the prayer meeting. She was the first to arrive. Afterward, he walked Rene to her car. They agreed to call each other the following afternoon.

He returned home and continued to revisit all that he learned from his conversation with Billy Nelson. *Was his father capable of such far-reaching intimidation and manipulation?*

he pondered. He was deeply grieved about all that the Heywoods had endured. *They never once mentioned any of this to me. Were they even aware of all that had been going on?* A lot of questions but no answers. He drifted off to sleep praying about whether or not he should share with the Heywoods what he had learned.

Day 39
January 10th – Thursday

Mary Scott was awakened by a knock at the door of her motel room. She was beginning her ninth day on Cape Cod. For anyone to be outside her door at seven o'clock in the morning was very unusual, as it was the off-season for tourism. Then came another knock at the door.

"Hello. Who's there?" Mary inquired as she hastened to put on her robe.

"Mommy, it's us. Sissy and Dee," a voice outside said. "Are you all right? Please. Can we come in?"

Opening the door, Mary saw her daughters standing there. "How did you find me?"

"Your phone's GPS," Sissy explained. "After we found out that you were gone, we filed a missing person report with the Goose Creek police department. They tracked your phone to this location, yesterday." Sissy continued, "Mommy, we are so sorry for the way we treated you. Can you forgive us?"

"Come in." Mary stepped back and invited her daughters inside. "Of course, I forgive you. You're my daughters. I love you. What kind of mother would I be if I didn't?" She explained, "All I ever wanted was to love and be loved. You are more precious to me than anyone could ever be, yet, it was as if you couldn't care one whit less about me."

Sissy and Dee were convicted. "Mom," Sissy began, "you're right. Ever since we got in the car to come check on you, Dee and I have revisited all the mean and selfish things we've done to you."

"That's right," Dee agreed. "Mommy, you know that it's always been difficult for me to express myself. I mean, ever since I can remember, I've had a problem speaking my heart without making bad situations worse." She continued, "So, instead of speaking about the things that are going wrong in my life, I found it easier to talk about things that are messed up in the lives of others. I know that's wrong and prideful. I apologize. Mommy, my situation at home is so bad that it makes me sick to think about it, less talk about it." Dee's eyes began to fill with tears. "Mommy, it hurts and without you being there to encourage me, I'm afraid I won't be able to make it." Mary pulled Dee close to her and gave her a mother's hug.

"Mommy, I understand that a lot of the things I've done to you cannot be forgotten, but I'm asking you to forgive me." Sissy continued, "Ever since Dee was born, I allowed a spirit of 'second fiddle' to convince me that you didn't love me like you used to. I wanted all of your attention and no matter how much you did for me, I wanted more. Mommy, I'm so sorry for the hurt that I caused you. You deserved better than that. Please, come home," Sissy pleaded.

At that moment, there was a knock at the door. "Boy, this is a busy place this morning. Come in," Mary called out, still embracing her daughters.

The door swung open wide and there stood Roy, Mary's husband. Wearing his prized three-piece sharkskin suit, his hair slicked back and holding a bouquet of gas station flowers in his hand. He threw Mary a wink that, in times before, would draw her into his embrace.

"Roy, what on earth are you doing here?" Mary demanded. "Seriously, Roy, why are you even here?"

"Mary, I messed up. I messed up real bad, baby." he explained. "When I got your note saying that you were leaving me, something inside me changed." The annoying sound of a car's horn blasting from the motel parking lot appeared to interrupt Roy's plea for forgiveness. Just for a moment, he turned to stick his head outside the door, as if to give the person blowing the horn the evil eye. Regaining his focus, he continued with his apology. "No woman has ever loved me like you, Mary. I'm so sorry, baby. Please," Roy dropped to one knee, "forgive me. Come on home, please, baby. I'll do better."

Mary looked him square in his eye, "Roy, after all you put me through, I can still find it in my heart to forgive you. But," she continued, "my desire to be with you any longer is about as 'dead as disco.' Now, I'm going to say this once and only once, so I need you to focus. The house that you've been telling everyone that you paid for, I'm listing with my realtor. I'm selling it. You've got five days to get every last piece of your clothing, every one of your prized collectibles and anything else out of my house, before I hire someone to change the locks. And...." The car horn outside continued to disrupt any semblance of tranquility.

"Hold on one minute. Five days?" Roy hollered, "How the heck am I supposed to get my stuff out of there in five days? And where am I supposed to go? Woman, you can't do that to me. That ain't right!"

"Roy," Mary interrupted, "you wouldn't know 'right' if it bit you on your nose. But, letting bygones be bygones, I'll offer you this…."

Roy's demeanor changed dramatically. *Finally. I've got her now*, he celebrated inwardly. *I knew she'd come to her senses. This old hound hasn't lost his touch after all. I've got her right where I need her to be. After all, what woman can say 'no' to all this?*

Caught up in his moment, Roy reflected back on the way that certain ladies in Goose Creek would tell him that he's a real good catch. To this day, he continues to believe it. Standing there patiently waiting for Mary to offer up her apology for the foolish decision she made to distance herself from him, he didn't interrupt. Again, the annoying car horn outside began to honk.

"Roy, what's taking you so long?" a woman's voice called out from his car. "I need to pee."

Having come to the revelation that Roy had not traveled to Cape Cod alone, Mary continued with her 'offer' without missing a beat.

"Roy, I've got a little something for you," Mary paused as she turned to retrieve something from the chair beside the front door. "This is a road map. You'll save yourself about ninety minutes on your return trip if you go by way of the Massachusetts Turnpike to Route 84 south. That should give you a good four days to get your stuff out of my house. Thanks for stopping by." She slammed the door shut. Roy mumbled something or other, as he walked back to his car.

****

Mary, Sissy, and Dee celebrated Roy's dismissal. Sissy and Dee never liked him and were now able to freely discuss their disdain for him. The cleansing was appreciated by all, and long overdue. They continued talking, laughing, and hugging the rest of the morning. By noontime, they were hungry. They decided to go for a sandwich. Mary promised her daughters a brief tour of the surrounding area. On the way to her car, she heard the motel manager call to her from across the parking lot.

"Morning, Mary. How are you doing today?"

"I'm doing fine. Mr. Turner," Mary said, as she walked in his direction, "These are my daughters, Sissy and Dee. They drove up from South Carolina to visit with me."

"Well, hello, young ladies. So nice to meet you." Mr. Turner continued, "Mary, I've decided to sell the motel and take some time to enjoy my children and their families. They live in California and, well, since my wife died a few years back, the kids have been after me to come out there and live with them. I'm not getting any younger, so I'm packing it in. I don't expect anything to change over the next couple of months, but I didn't want you to be caught off guard if you notice unfamiliar faces poking around."

"Well, congratulations, Mr. Turner. That is so considerate of you to let me know what's going on and all. You certainly have a wonderful place here. I'm sure it will sell quickly." Mary continued, "Years ago, I thought about operating a bed and breakfast but I never pursued it. Mr. Turner, what would a business like this sell for, if you don't mind me asking?"

"You know, Mary, I haven't the slightest idea. This place has been bought and paid for so long that I really can't say off the top of my head. I would have to ask a realtor, I guess. Thankfully, I can be a bit more flexible in setting my selling price."

"Mr. Turner, how would you like to join my daughters and me for lunch? I just may be interested in buying this property myself."

Mr. Turner was taken aback, "Really, Mary. That would be wonderful," he continued. "Right off the top, that would save me from having to pay the realtor's fee. I could sell the motel quickly before this year's tourist season gets underway. Very interesting, indeed. What say you let me introduce you ladies to my favorite restaurant. I'm sure you'll like it. My treat."

"Sounds like fun," Mary agreed.

The food and the ocean view well represented everything that Mary expected of Cape Cod. Mr. Turner was a very nice, older man who introduced Mary to the restaurant staff as the new owner of his motel.

During lunch, Mary called her realtor about the sale of her house in Goose Creek. She negotiated the terms of sale with Mr. Turner that would allow her purchase of the motel to be stress free. Her realtor offered to buy her house for more money than she expected. Mary's dream of living on Cape Cod had become a reality. Sissy and Dee committed to relocate to the area so they could help Mary operate the business.

Back at the motel, as Mary and her daughters continued to plan for the new family venture, they began to coordinate closing dates and relocation arrangements.

"I've got a calendar sitting on top of the dresser," Mary remembered.

Sissy retrieved it and returned to the table where Mary and Dee were sitting. Removing the cellophane wrapper and unrolling the calendar to spread it on the table, Mary and her daughters remarked about the beautiful photography included on the January page.

"Oh, Mommy, you've already began marking the dates, I see," Dee observed.

"No, I haven't marked any dates. I honestly forgot that I even had that calendar." Mary explained, "That's the calendar I got when I visited that church on New Year's Eve.

"Well, somebody did," Sissy confirmed, pointing to a red blotch on the calendar. Clearly marked on the calendar within the January tenth square was the familiar red blotch that appeared on the other calendars distributed at the Watch Meeting service.

"Oh, my goodness," Mary said. "Look at that red cross. This is amazing. I wonder how this happened? This can't be coincidence." Mary and her daughters spent the rest of the day enjoying the best time, together, they could remember.

Day 40
January 11th - Friday

Henry Williams, a faithful, tenured member of Good Shepherd, began taking flying lessons last month. During the past thirty-two years, he has served as the CEO of the Williams Insurance Agency. His business had prospered and expanded sufficiently, enough, to require several satellite offices throughout New England. At sixty-two years of age, Henry is determined to work smarter, not harder. Unaware that today was his blotch date, he maintains his regular schedule. His objective, today, is to log additional flight time in his quest to qualify for a private pilot's license. With this license, he can fly to remote branch locations, instead of driving long distances every week.

Arriving at Norwood's municipal airport, twenty minutes before his instruction is scheduled to begin, Henry searches out his instructor. Within a few minutes, he locates the pilot inside the coffee shop. Ever since a young man, Henry was a comedian who could tell a funny story better than most. By the time he and the instructor had filed their flight plan, inspected the craft, were belted in and preparing to taxi to the runway, Henry had the instructor laughing so hard that the man had to wipe tears from his eyes.

As he positioned the plane for take-off, the instructor continued in his laughter. Within a minute or two they were airborne, headed northeast toward Boston. Five minutes after takeoff, the instructor experienced a severe asthma attack, as the result of his laughing bout. Henry thought the man's gasping for air was just the way he laughed. Suddenly, the pilot fell forward on the controls. The plane began to lose altitude. At that moment, everything became crystal clear to Henry. They were going down, and fast.

"Hey, guy," Henry hollered. "What are you doing?"

The pilot didn't respond. Immediately, he pulled the man away from the controls.

"Mayday! Mayday!" Henry shouted into the two-way radio. "Mayday! Mayday!"

A voice was heard through his headset, "Boston tower. This is Boston tower. What's your situation?" the voice asked.

"The pilot's dead! My flight instructor just dropped dead!"

"Are you able to land the plane, sir?" the voice asked.

"No! Negative. I'm a student. This is only my second time in this thing."

"I'm going to help you through this, but you have to do exactly as I say. Is that clear?" the voice insisted.

"Yes."

"What's your name, sir?" the voice asked.

"Henry. Henry Williams."

"Henry, I've got to get you on the ground quickly," the voice continued. "You have drifted into an extremely busy traffic pattern. You're about two minutes away from the Franklin Park municipal golf course. God is with you today. That's a perfect place to set your craft down," the voice said, reassuringly.

"This is an easy craft to land. Your landing gear is fixed and your wingspan is short. All you need to do is follow my instructions and you'll be safely down in no time at all. Sound good?" the voice asked.

"Just get me down. Please." Henry was scared.

"At two o'clock you'll see the golf course," the voice began.

"What? Two o'clock? I'm not staying up here for three and a half hours," Henry insisted. "You must be crazy!"

"Sir," the voice continued, "Two o'clock is the field position, not the time." The voice appeared to be amused by Henry's response.

"Oh. Okay. Got it." Henry calmed down.

"Descend to an altitude of sixteen hundred feet and maintain," the voice instructed. "Do you see the golf course at your two o'clock position?" the voice asked.

"Yes. I mean affirmative."

"Now, here's what I need you to do, Henry," the voice continued. "I've cleared the traffic pattern at your altitude. I need you to circle the course and identify the area where the least amount of activity is taking place. You got that? Repeat, do you copy my instruction?"

"Copy," Henry responded.

"Tell me what you see," the voice directed.

"I see a dead pilot in the seat beside me. He owes me a refund." Henry was becoming anxious.

"Henry. That's not helping us, now." The voice was firm. "Pay attention. Eyes on the field. Tell me what you see."

"Okay. The course is covered with snow. There are no visible bare spots except the roadway between the golf course and the animal exhibit at the zoo," he reported.

"Emergency response vehicles are on route to you. What is the condition of the road surface?" the voice asked.

"The road appears to be clear and dry. There are snow banks on either side."

"Excellent," the voice said. "Couldn't ask for a better situation. Hold on one moment," the voice said. "I just received word that emergency vehicles have closed the roadway at both ends of Franklin Field. They're telling me that you're cleared for landing. Let's bring this bird down. Are you ready?"

"As ready as I'm going be," he responded.

"All right, Henry," the voice instructed, "descend to eight hundred feet and stay within the perimeter of the park. Come around from the east at fifty knots so the wind will be at your back. Copy?"

"Got it," Henry responded. Henry was praying like he never prayed before.

"Altitude?" the voice inquired.

"Seven hundred eighty-eight feet. The wind is picking up." Henry was getting anxious.

"All right, let's make one more pass at three hundred-fifty feet," the voice instructed.

Within two minutes Henry was coming back around, with a southerly breeze at his back. He could see the emergency vehicles below.

"All right, Henry. Let's set this bird down," the voice said. "Come around one more time and as you approach the section of road adjacent to the course's parking area, keep your altitude at one hundred fifty feet. You will have a half mile of roadway ahead of you to set down on. At that altitude you'll be beneath our radar, so the emergency personnel will monitor you from the ground. Copy?"

"Copy," Henry responded.

Around the park for the last time, Henry went with the dead pilot at his side. He was feeling better about his ability to land the plane. *Going in*, Henry thought to himself. He brought the plane around perfectly aligned with the roadway ahead and began his descent. Nervous but determined, he continued on. At forty feet directly above the roadway, a sudden gust of wind took full control of the aircraft. It lifted the plane and caused it to roll to the right. Although he was off the tower radar, the tower staff could clearly hear him shout, "Oh, baby!!!" followed by a chorus of expletives.

Henry later acknowledged that he had no recollection of that moment. The only thing that he could remember was coming to, as the crew of firefighters extracted him from the plane wreckage. A powerful gust of wind had blown the airplane more than one hundred feet to the right and deposited it in the middle of the Franklin Park Zoo lion pit. Fortunately for Henry, the lions had been relocated to the indoor exhibit for the winter. The account of Henry's experience headlined the six o'clock evening news with the tagline: "Man Cheats Death."

Henry was admitted to Massachusetts General Hospital and released the following morning. The hospital staff managed to locate another pair of pants for him, as those he had worn during his ordeal had become so heavily soiled they could not be cleaned.

Day 41
January 12th - Saturday

Horatio was inside the church before seven-thirty to prepare for Thomas Rhone's nine o'clock homegoing service. While he had spoken with Mr. Doolan, the funeral service coordinator, he hadn't heard from Mrs. Rhone, since Wednesday. At eight o'clock, the hearse and a passenger car entered the church parking lot. Three men and a woman, dressed in black, moved the casket into the sanctuary. Shortly after, floral deliveries began to arrive. By eight thirty, everything was in place.

As mourners arrived, they were greeted and given service programs. Seated on the pulpit, Horatio perused the final version of the program to take note of any changes to the obituary, sequence of service, etc. By the number of mourners who came to pay their respect, it was clear that Mr. Rhone was highly regarded. Tears on the faces of elderly and young, alike, confirmed a heartfelt sense of loss because of his passing. Horatio's attention returned to the calendar that Thomas Rhone had received.

"Lord," he quietly prayed, "again, I repent for any part I played in causing Mr. Rhone's demise. Please bring healing and joy back to the Rhone family. Bless me with the right words to speak as I apologize to Mrs. Rhone for opening the door for the Death Angel to enter in and wreak havoc on her family."

His emotional discomfort transitioned to a physical affliction. His body began to sweat, his throat was dry, and his head started to throb with pain. He hurriedly excused himself and made his way to the men's room. Finding a place to sit, he remained there for ten minutes, doubting that he would recover in time to carry on with his participation in the service. The affliction that came upon him left him so disoriented that he forgot to apply the tried and proven antidote. *Prayer! It never fails,* he remembered. Quickly, he mustered enough energy and focus to repel the attack that he was under. Pressing through with prayer, he began to sense the illness lift away from him. Within minutes, he was restored. After splashing cool water on his face, combing his hair and straightening his tie, he returned to the church sanctuary.

Entering, his eyes went directly to Mrs. Rhone seated on the right side of the front pew. Her head was deeply planted in a handful of tissue as she wept. She was shouldered by a young man Horatio assumed was her son, Chip, as he was identified in the service program. Calling the service to order, he began with a prayer. In the span of forty-five minutes, guest vocalists sang, tribute from family members and friends was spoken and scriptures quoted. At the conclusion of his reading of the obituary, the Spirit of God prompted him to do something he had never done before. He extended the invitation for everlasting life. Asking and receiving approval from Mrs. Rhone, he spoke of the circumstance of Thomas Rhone's death:

"On January 3rd, Thomas Rhone went fishing," he began. "The sky was blue, no storms on the horizon, he set out with one thing on his mind: catching fish. Maybe a big fish or maybe a lot of fish; we'll never know, for sure. But we know that fishing was his favorite thing to do. Just ask Mrs. Rhone."

People in the audience nodded their head in agreement.

Horatio continued, "When Thomas set out that morning, little did he know that this would be his last time out doing what he loved to do. I can see him now, sitting in the boat hearing the waves lapping alongside, looking out on the horizon, thinking to himself: 'This is the life. It doesn't get any better than this.' Somewhere between the time he pondered that thought and the time he was scheduled to return to shore, God called Thomas home. He had a relationship with our Heavenly Father because he confessed Jesus Christ as his Savior. He knew that one day his time would come. And, he also knew that having made that confession, the promise of life everlasting on high with the Lord would be his to enjoy. No one or nothing could ever deprive Thomas of the promise that God made to him. God keeps His Word. So now, because of God's faithfulness and Thomas' confession of faith, we know that he is in a place where we can envision him looking out at the horizon saying: 'This is the life. It doesn't get any better than this.' The very promise that God gave to Thomas is the same promise that is available to you. If anyone here today has never confessed Jesus Christ as their Lord and Savior and, you want the benefit of everlasting life with God, please come forward."

People young, old, and in between, began making their way to the front of the church. Eyes of those who previously cried tears of sorrow were now crying tears of joy. Horatio could sense the manifestation of the same presence that was in the sanctuary the night of the Watch Meeting service.

In the presence of the earthly remains of Thomas Rhone, the Kingdom of God was increased by twenty-four souls. One of those who came forward was the funeral director's assistant. Some were Rhone family members and fellow fishing buddies. Prayer went forth and the confession of faith was offered. At the conclusion of it all, a chorus of Hallelujahs and "Thank You, Lord Jesus" filled the sanctuary.

Mrs. Rhone motioned to him. Instinctively, he deduced that she was upset with the direction the service had taken. Drawing closer to her, she reached out to him. Bracing himself, now well within her wheelhouse, he smiled to diffuse any anger that she might harbor.

"Now, I understand." She continued, "Now, I understand why my son insisted that Thomas' service had to take place here."

"Did you experience God's presence here tonight, Mrs. Rhone?" Horatio asked.

"Pastor, I absolutely did." She smiled. "When my son said, 'Go to Good Shepherd,' I told him 'No.' Unlike my husband, I was never a particularly religious person. I would have been satisfied with a simple service at the funeral home. Chip convinced me to contact you." She continued, "When I spoke with you the very first time, your spirit ushered in a calming, sincere presence in my time of grieving. By the way," she paused, "what's going on with the calendar?"

"Uhh, the calendar?" Horatio inquired, nervously. "I've been meaning to speak with you about that, but it never seemed to be the right time."

"Well, now's as good a time as any, I suppose." She continued, "So what can you tell me?"

Practically choking on his Adam's apple, he tried to speak the words to sufficiently apologize for his role in her husband's demise.

"Mrs. Rhone, I'm so...."

"Excuse me," Mrs. Rhone cut him short. "Pastor, you remember my son, Chip?" she asked, as he walked over and took her by the arm.

"Hi, Pastor. It's good to see you, again," Chip said.

"We've met before?" Horatio asked.

"Yes, but you might not remember me. I was at your church's Watch Meeting service. I'm still telling people about the amazing time I had that evening."

"So, you were at the Watch Meeting?" Horatio asked. "Your face seemed familiar to me but, I couldn't remember why. But, now I remember. It's good to see you, again. Refresh my memory, please, I seem to be having a senior moment. Did you attend the Watch Meeting with your dad?"

"Oh, no," Chip responded. "I came alone. Yeah, I came alone but I've never felt so much a part of anything as I did that night." He continued, "There was something going on in Good Shepherd that caused something to shift within me like I've never experienced before. I came away from that place a different person. It was awesome. It was as though God knew that I needed to be there." Chip explained, "I had left my parent's home to meet with a friend but, somehow, I ended up in your church that night."

"No doubt the events of that evening will be remembered by a lot of people for a long time," Horatio recalled.

"By the way, did my mother ask you about my calendar?"

"I was just about to mention that when you joined in the conversation," Mrs. Rhone explained. "Pastor, forgive me but, I made a terrible mistake in leaving Chip's calendar with Captain Askew. With all that was going on, well I'm sure you understand that I had no right to give Chip's calendar away without first asking if it was okay with him. I tried to retrieve it but the captain told me he had left it with you. Do you still have it?"

"I'm so sorry," Horatio began, "I have your husband's calendar but Chip, I never received any other calendar from Captain Askew. Perhaps yours was left behind at the motel or is still in police custody."

"Pastor, my father never received a calendar. He didn't attend the Watch Meeting service," Chip reiterated.

"This is all very strange. The only calendar that I received from Captain Askew was clearly labeled Thomas Rhone," he recalled.

"That's my calendar!" Chip exclaimed.

"But…," Horatio began.

"I'm Thomas Rhone," Chip declared. "On New Year's Eve, I planned to stop by a friend's house who had invited me to a party. Along the way, my car started acting as though it was running out of gas. I was looking for a gas station when my engine shut down. I left the car and started walking, having no idea where I was. I could see some streetlights and store fronts up ahead, so I made my way to the center of town but everything was closed, including the gas station. Cold and out of options, I began walking back, to my car. It was at that point that I noticed Good Shepherd. It was the first time that I had been to a church in years. I felt something taking place in me during the service. Afterward, I caught a ride back to my car. When I got back and tried to start it up, it turned over with no problem. I hadn't noticed that the gas tank wasn't as low on fuel as I thought. It was amazing," he concluded.

"So, you're a junior?" Horatio asked.

"Yes, sir. Thomas Rhone Jr. at your service."

"I've got to sit down. And, how is it that your dad ended up with your calendar?"

"My dad collected calendars," Chip explained. "When I was fourteen, I bought him a calendar for Christmas. He loved it. Every Christmas since that time, he looked forward to getting a calendar from me. In my job, I do a lot of traveling. Like any proud father, he wanted a souvenir calendar from everywhere I traveled, to show off to his friends. When my flight arrived behind schedule on New Year's Eve, I didn't have time to make my way to the mall, so I figured I would pick one up, later. After church service, I returned to my parent's home to share my experience at the Watch Meeting with them. I had the calendar in my hand as I walked in and, immediately, my dad reached for it. He saw the name Thomas Rhone printed on the outer wrapping and accepted it as his personalized calendar. I stayed the night and when I awoke the next morning, my dad had left to go fishing. He had taken the calendar with him."

"This is all starting to make sense." In the minutes that followed, Horatio explained the mystery and effect of the calendar situation to the Rhones. In the end, he was so relieved that he hugged both Mrs. Rhone and Chip for helping to put a large piece of the puzzle in place.

"By the way," Chip asked, "how did you know that I would be at the Watch Meeting? I mean, a calendar with my name printed on it, waiting for me in a place that I had never been before. How…?"

"Please, don't ask," Horatio cautioned. "That's an entirely different story for another day." He laughed, as if to say, *Lord, you got me.*

Horatio didn't continue on to the burial ceremony, as he had committed to be there to receive Sam Wooden and the teens for prayer instruction at noontime. After the remaining mourners had departed, he returned to the sanctuary and lifted hallelujahs to the Lord, until he, nearly, lost his voice.

****

Precisely at twelve o'clock, Horatio heard Sam Wooden speaking to someone in the sanctuary. It was the four teenage boys who had come to learn to pray.

"Good afternoon, gentlemen, Sam," Horatio announced as he entered the sanctuary. "It's great to see you all. Sam, don't let me interrupt. Carry on."

Sam didn't want to do anything to diminish Horatio's position as his pastor. "Are you sure about this, Pastor?"

"Sam, I couldn't be any more certain. My friend, you're ready. Teach these young men how to pray to their Heavenly Father."

Sam gushed. "Thanks, Pastor. Thank you so much." He asked, "Is it okay if I call home and share the news with my wife?"

"Of course, it's all right, Sam," Horatio encouraged. "Go make your call. I'll cover for you."

Sam returned quickly. Joining Horatio and the four young prayer students at the front of the church, Sam took charge and explained to the teenagers that prayer was a powerful weapon that only worked through strong faith and belief in God's word. By the end of their time together, the boys were versed in prayer as proficiently as some of the church elders. A strong, tangible anointing of God's Spirit had manifested in the sanctuary. What was scheduled to be a thirty-minute prayer instruction class turned into a one-hour worship experience.

****

After the first thirty minutes, Horatio excused himself from the group. He wanted to visit the nursing home one last time before his sabbatical began. He had remained in communication with Mrs. Lu Chang since the day he drove her home from the Village Mart. Earlier in the week, she agreed to accompany him to the nursing home, today. He called to alert her that he was on his way. Arriving at her home, he could see Mrs. Chang standing by her front door.

"Hello, Mrs. Chang," he called out from behind the steering wheel, motioning her into the car.

"Hi, Mister man of God," Lu Chang responded as she approached the car. Before he could exit the car to come around and open the passenger door for her, she was already seated and belted in. She appreciated Horatio's kindness and attention.

Ten minutes later, they were at the Driftway Nursing Home. Inside, Mrs. Chang observed closely the way that everyone responded to Horatio. Pulling on his sleeve to draw him closer, she whispered, "Mister Pastor, do you own this place?"

He chuckled. "No, Mrs. Chang. I am not the owner. This is my family. You see," he explained, "my biological family lives six hundred miles from here. God didn't want me to be alone, so he blessed me with the people here to be a family to me. May I introduce you as my friend?"

"No, thank you. Please introduce me as your family," she instructed with a smile. She held tighter onto his arm.

"I'd like that, Mrs. Chang."

"Not Mrs. Chang," she insisted. "I am Lu. My husband used to call me Lulu but I didn't like that name," she explained. "How would you like someone to always call you 'Mister Pastor, Mister Pastor?' Very annoying, my husband."

Horatio chuckled. "I can understand your point, Lu." Standing with Lu at the center of the community room, he spoke: "Everybody, can I please have your attention for a moment? I want you all to say hello to Lu. She's a member of my family and you know, if she's a member of my family, she's a member of our family. So please, give her a big Driftway Nursing Home welcome."

All who were able made their way over to give Lu a hug. Others smiled and waved from wheelchairs. Horatio announced the names of the greeters as they approached Lu. He delayed his usual departure time to allow Lu to have dinner with her newfound friends. At five thirty, he and Lu left the nursing home.

"Mister Pastor Smiley," Lu began, "I haven't had a fun day like this in a long time. Thank you so much for bringing me, today. Such nice people." She continued, "They said I can come back anytime."

"And, you should, Lu," Horatio encouraged. "Everyone really enjoyed your company. I'm going out of town for a month, but maybe we can think of another way to get you there while I'm away."

"Don't worry about me, Mister Pastor Smiley. I know what I can do," Lu explained. "I'll call the RIDE. They can take me there and bring me home. I'm already signed up for the service. I'll call them as soon as I get home."

He delivered Lu safely home and then proceeded to his house where he remained for the evening. In prayer, he asked God to speak mightily through him during the Sunday morning service. He thanked God for using him to bring joy and fellowship to Lu Chang's life.

Day 42
January 13th – Sunday

Horatio was greeted with a standing ovation by more than one hundred fifty church members as he made his way to his office before the start of worship service. He understood that this was God's way of confirming that his parishioners appreciated him. Every instance of doubt, criticism, and rejection that he had experienced during the past three years didn't matter anymore.

The morning service began with a time of praise and worship that was powerful. As hymns were sung and hallelujahs were shouted, people came forward for prayer. Prayers for healing. Prayers of gratitude. Prayers for provision. Prayers for strength to withstand difficult situations. Many wept. Many rejoiced. The Spirit of God filled the sanctuary.

Horatio folded up his sermon notes and followed God's lead. Without as much as a spoken word, God's covenant with Good Shepherd's members was made clear: "Believe on Me. Come and I will give you rest." He remained standing behind the podium with his hands lifted up. As the presence of God continued to manifest, spiritual afflictions that once held strong, fell away like chains and shackles that could no longer perform their function. The service concluded with communion and a prayer of dismissal.

At the main entrance of the church, well-wishers gathered around Horatio to extend prayers for safe travel during his sabbatical. Arthur Mutton and the other church trustees departed through a side door to avoid the appearance of sharing in any part of the celebration for him.

Lord, bless them anyway, Horatio prayed.

He spent the afternoon in Boston with Rene and Kelli, purchasing gifts for his mother and father. Unbeknownst to him, Rene slipped a handwritten note in the bag containing Mrs. Smiley's gift. The note made clear, with a woman's touch, the extent of sadness that Horatio expressed in his heart, as the result of being separated from her and Mr. Smiley. The letter went on to commend his parents for raising up a kind and Godly man.

After shopping, they enjoyed dinner at a Copley Square restaurant and then returned to the Brock family home. Horatio's visit was brief, as he anticipated that his last day in the office would be very demanding. He was back home by eight o'clock.

Day 43
January 14th - Monday

At nine fifteen, the church phone rang. Horatio answered. "Good morning, Church of the Good Shepherd."

"Hi, Pastor. This is Billy Nelson. Are you still able to meet with my mom and me for a few minutes today?"

"Your mom is coming?"

"Yes, sir. She said that she wanted to come along. After our meeting with you, she and I are going into Boston. Will it be a problem if she comes with me?"

"No. Not at all. I think we mentioned a noontime meet. Does that still work for you?"

"Twelve o'clock is perfect, Pastor Smiley. See you, then."

The phone call ended.

****

At ten thirty a voice called out from the church vestibule. "Pastor Smiley, good morning." It was Reverend Bell, Horatio's pastoral replacement.

"In here," he directed.

The Reverend found his way to Horatio's office just as he was finishing up a phone call.

"Good morning, Pastor Smiley," Reverend Bell greeted.

"Good morning, Reverend Bell. What brings you to Scituate?"

"I just met with Trustee Mutton. He requested that I come and sign some tax forms prior to Sunday's service," he explained.

"Every 'i' dotted. Every 't' crossed. That's Arthur, all right." Horatio chuckled. "Did you meet him at his home or office?"

"No, here in the church parking lot."

"The parking lot?" Horatio was curious. "Why didn't he come inside?"

"He said something about having to be somewhere in ten minutes," Reverend Bell responded matter-of-factly. "Anyway, I wanted to wish you bon voyage and assure you that the protocol you have established at Good Shepherd will be maintained."

"Thank you, Reverend Bell. I appreciate that more than words can express. I'm so sorry, but I am way behind schedule. I have a meeting to prepare for."

"No need to apologize. I completely understand." They shook hands and Reverend Bell departed.

Horatio sat stoically behind his desk. Arrows of suspicion pierced his peace. Fiery darts scorched his soul. He thought that any plan for derailing his pastoral leadership had passed on to the great beyond with Bill Nelson's demise. Clearly, he was mistaken. *Why would Arthur meet with Reverend Bell secretly? And what kind of tax forms did Reverend Bell fill out? Was it a W-9 or a W-4?* he pondered. "Lord, I'm so tired of this emotional roller coaster ride. I, truly, don't want to be here anymore."

****

At twelve o'clock, Billy Nelson and his mother arrived for their meeting. Horatio found the energy to get up from his desk chair and receive his guests in the vestibule. With a welcoming embrace, he walked them to the kitchen.

"Please, sit down," he began. "I picked up some sandwich fixings on my way in this morning. You never want to go to the big city hungry," he continued. "A sandwich there will cost you a fortune."

"Pastor, that is so nice," Mrs. Nelson began. "I told my son that I wanted to tag along, so I could have a moment to speak with you about my husband."

As far as Horatio was concerned, any attempt to minimize the damage that Bill Nelson had caused the Good Shepherd community required exceptional self-control. Understanding that Mrs. Nelson was still in a grieving mode, he purposed to do all within his ability to be compassionate in his response. Arthur's meeting with Reverend Bell didn't make the task, at hand, any easier. Retrieving the sandwich ingredients from the refrigerator, he engaged Mrs. Nelson.

"Mrs. Nelson, what is it about Bill that you would like to discuss?"

"Well," she began, "it's not so much what I want to discuss, it's more about what I want to apologize for."

Horatio's eyes darted from the table to Mrs. Nelson. A look of surprise registered on his face. "Apologize? Apologize for what, Mrs. Nelson?"

"For allowing my loyalty to overshadow my responsibility to Good Shepherd and God." She explained, "I was raised to believe that a woman's place was beside her husband, right or wrong. When I saw his wrong escalate to wickedness, I disconnected from Good Shepherd and, eventually, my husband. Pastor, I want you to know that although I was silent, I was never complicit. I never agreed with Bill's monomaniacal crusade to set right the wrong that he believed had been done to members of his family. He was obsessed with the need to restore his family's good name. I should have done more to expose Bill's agenda. I just didn't know what to do or who I could count on to stand up to him."

"Mrs. Nelson, I believe that God and He alone was the only one qualified to bring Bill around. Don't beat yourself up about this," he consoled. "Bill had some dedicated followers who continue to carry out his plan, even now."

"What do you mean?" Mrs. Nelson stood to her feet.

Over lunch, Horatio discussed Arthur's earlier actions. He also confided to Mrs. Nelson and Billy his frustration with the trustees and his prayer for God to move him away from Good Shepherd.

Mrs. Nelson was livid. "Those #@*%! Pastor, don't pack your bags just yet. I'll handle Arthur and the others," she promised. "I've been silent too long."

"That's kind of you, Mrs. Nelson, but I've already given this mess to God."

"Well, I understand, Pastor, but God speaks to me, too," she continued. "And, if I get a word from the Lord on how He wants me to proceed in this situation, well … I'll let you know. The very nerve of those meddling fools," she muttered.

"Boy, Mom. I haven't seen you this worked up in years." Billy chuckled.

"Well, Billy, it's time to stand up for what's right. Wouldn't you agree?"

Horatio and the Nelsons concluded their time together at one thirty. A friendship was cemented that obviously was of God. He agreed to meet again with Mrs. Nelson after he returned from sabbatical. At five thirty after clearing his desk of loose ends, he closed the office and went home.

Day 44
January 15th - Tuesday

At seven thirty, Horatio was awakened by the ringing of his doorbell. Quickly getting dressed, he made his way to the front door. The bell rang a second time, just before he was within reach of the doorknob. Opening the door, he was greeted to a chorus of "Good Morning, Pastor."

There on his front porch and spilling out onto the walkway were thirty-two bright and cheery faces that had come to bid him bon voyage. The smile on his face reflected both surprise and appreciation to the point of blushing. A familiar voice emerged from the center of the group, leading everyone in a chorus of "For He's a jolly good fellow." It was Sam Wooden.

"Pastor," Sam began, "I made sure that I stayed in the center of this group because the heart of anything is at its center. I want you to know that because of you, my heart will always be yielded to God and I love you, Pastor."

The gathering let out a collective sigh, "Awaaahhh." For the next ten minutes, everyone in the group received a "Thank you" and an appreciative embrace.

Horatio was more animated than usual this morning. He planned to quietly slip out of town and be on his way to Virginia Beach by eight-thirty. "So much for that plan," he chuckled, as he loaded his suitcase into the car. While excited about reuniting with his mother and father, he knew that he would miss the members of his church family. The six hundred-mile trip ahead would take eleven hours to complete but it didn't matter to him if it took eleven days. He missed his parents and he was looking forward to seeing them, again. At nine o'clock, he was behind the wheel headed down the Driftway toward Route 123.

****

In the neighboring town of Cohasset, behind the facade of a very affluent home, Aviana grieved the loss of a family member. For eleven years, Julep was her baby and best friend. Feeling sad and deprived of the most important relationship in her life, she has chosen to disconnect from her husband, Barry, and all social affiliations. Self-exiled to her master

227

bedroom suite for the past thirty-eight days, her depression and isolation was taking a toll on her marital relationship. As she lay in her bed this morning, there was a knock at her bedroom door.

"Ma'am, your breakfast is ready. May I bring it to you?"

"Leave it by the door, Marie," Aviana instructed.

The sound of the tray being set down and the maid's footsteps on the marble floor evaporated into silence. Eventually, she sat up to look out an oversized window to view her seasonally dormant garden. Soon after, there was another knock at the bedroom door.

"Aviana, I'm coming in." It was her husband, Barry. "Good morning, dear. Feeling any better, today?" He tried his best to indulge her need for consolation. Seeing no improvement in her physical or emotional disposition after five weeks, he decided to pursue a hands-on approach in bringing resolution to her grieving. "Come to work with me, today. Something I want to show you, at the office."

Barry and Aviana owned a car dealership that was very profitable. Years of hard work and long hours had resulted in substantial wealth and celebrity status in the business community.

"Not today. I'm not feeling well."

"Please, come with me. I think you'll be glad you did." After twenty minutes of his pleading, she acquiesced.

At ten thirty, Barry and Aviana were at the dealership. Before they had a chance to exit the car, several employees came out to greet her. With each well-intended expression of condolence received along the way to her office, she was reminded of Julep's demise. Managing to hold back her tears, she closed her office door and sank into her desk chair. The office walls were adorned with photos displaying happy times with Julep. Standing to her feet, she walked the perimeter of the room, moving from picture to picture, reminiscing. Before she could return to her seat, Barry knocked at the door.

"Okay to come in?"

"Yes," Aviana responded.

As the door opened wide, Barry walked in holding a picnic basket with a red and white checkered cloth covering the basket's contents. Eight employees stood behind him.

"Surprise!" Barry said, as he placed the basket on her desk.

The motion of the basket being set on the desktop caused the contents to become active. A puppy's head poked through the cloth's opening. The puppy was the same breed and coloring as Julep. Aviana was incredulous.

"What's this?" she demanded of Barry. "Is this your idea of some sick joke?" she fumed.

"I thought you'd like him," Barry explained. "He looks just like Julep."

"Get out of my office, you insensitive imbecile," she demanded. "And, close the damn door behind you."

It was no surprise to anyone that Aviana had a temper, but her reaction to the gift was, indeed, unexpected. Barry and all who stood with him during the presentation fled as though gun shots were being fired. She put on her coat and stormed out to Barry's car. Barry called her cell phone after receiving word that she was outside.

"Aviana, what's wrong with you? That was a lousy thing you did in there," he huffed.

"A lousy thing I did…?" she yelled back. "Get out here. Take me home now, Barry."

Immediately Barry emerged from the building, walking briskly to the car. A number of employees discreetly bore witness to the heated discussion that was taking place between their bosses. Understanding that this was neither the time nor place to discuss their differing points of view, they drove to a nearby restaurant.

Along the way, Barry conceded that he may not have adequately considered that Julep was an irreplaceable family member. He acknowledged that he, too, missed Julep. The acquisition of a Julep look-alike was meant to memorialize the good times that were shared with him. Aviana allowed Barry to fully complete his explanation before offering her response.

"Finished?" she asked.

"Yep. I'm finished."

"Barry, I'm going to ask you a question," Aviana positioned. "If you croaked tomorrow and I went out and married a follicly challenged man, fifteen years my senior with bad feet and bad breath, who bore a general resemblance to you, would you expect me continue with life as usual? Do you think that would diminish the pain of losing you after all we've been through together? Is that how you think, Barry?" she chastised.

"I guess not," he cowered.

"So, Barry, why would you expect anything less of my sense of loss over Julep?" Aviana scowled, "Is it because Julep was just another Pomeranian dog that you figured could be easily replaced?" She was becoming, increasingly, agitated.

"I get your point." Barry acknowledged his lapse of good judgement. Convicted, he asked, "What can I do to make it up to you?"

"I want a child," she was quick to respond.

"A child?" Barry was puzzled. "Isn't it a little late for that? I'm sixty-two and you're … well, you know. Having a baby is no easy undertaking for people our age, regardless of our resources."

"Barry, I have absolutely no interest in playing any part of the whole pregnancy thing," she emphasized. After a momentary pause, she asked, "You're still connected to that orphanage, right?"

"Yeah. We both are, actually." Barry chuckled. "Our business is the largest private financial supporter of Mercy Ministries, not to mention that I am on the board of directors. What are you thinking?"

"Let's talk further over a glass of cabernet." Aviana snickered.

Arriving at a nearby restaurant, they continued their discussion after ordering wine and appetizers.

"So, Aviana," Barry began, "what's going on inside that beautiful mind of yours?"

She looked directly into Barry's eyes and demanded, "You're going to get me a kid from that orphanage."

"You can't be serious."

"Not only am I serious, Barry, I'm drop-dead serious," she emphasized as she reached across the table and grabbed him by his necktie.

"But, I can't just walk into Mercy Ministries and walk out with a child," he reasoned. "There are rules and regulations that have to be satisfied…."

"Shut up and listen to me, you sniveling excuse for a man. I don't need to know about rules and regulations that aren't meant for people like us. You figure it out and let me know when it's time to begin my shopping spree at the orphanage. Who knows," she continued, "at the risk of losing all future financial support from us, they may even offer us a BOGO sale."

"A BOGO sale?" Barry asked. "What's that?"

"Oh, my dear, uninformed half," Aviana began, "BOGO means: buy one, get one free. It's what the lower income types might call a 'two-for-one sale.'" She snickered.

"Aviana, I'm not really comfortable with this."

"Barry. Earth to Barry," she continued as she repeatedly rapped her knuckles on the table. "I want to make this perfectly clear. I don't care one whit about what you're comfortable with. Just get it done. Set up a meeting today," she demanded. "Now, take me home. Waitress. Check!" she barked.

Barry waited for the bill while Aviana waited in the car.

****

At five twenty, Horatio turned on to Route 13, entering the Commonwealth of Virginia. He was less than two hours away from Baltic Avenue where he would once again be at home with his family and friends. Loaded down with gifts for his parents, he imagined how his mother's face would light up as she opened the case of her favorite brand of spiced apple cider. He knew his dad would parade around the house all week-long wearing the Red Sox team jacket and the Boston Celtics jersey that he bought. The half-gallon container of clam chowder and a substantial variety of North End pastries he brought with him would make certain for a successful reunion.

Places, faces, and experiences came to mind as he drove nearer to his family home. About five minutes from his parents' home, he was stopped at an intersection waiting for a red light to change, when Peg Tracy, Virginia Beach's gossip extraordinaire, pulled up alongside and looked over curiously at him. In the moment that it took for the light to turn green, she managed a halfhearted wave of her hand, while displaying an obligatory, "Nice to see you" smile. Horatio smiled and waved back.

Great, he thought to himself as Peg drove away, *I'll bet she's already on her phone alerting the troops*. Lord, bless her anyway. Soon after, he was turning into the driveway of his family home. His father and mother, with noses pressed against the glass of the storm door, were watching for him. Before he could put the car into park, they were holding open the door for him.

"Welcome home, Son," his father beamed while his mother cried. He embraced his parents, enjoying a long-awaited reunion in the darkness of their driveway.

"How long were you two waiting at the door?"

"Only a moment," his mom explained. "Peggy called and told us that she saw you stopped at 19th and Baltic."

"That woman hasn't changed a bit," Horatio said.

"Actually she has," his dad explained. "She's nosier now, than before." They all laughed.

"Lord, bless her anyway," Mrs. Smiley chuckled.

As they began to walk toward the house, Horatio remembered, "My bags. I'll be right in, Mom, Dad."

"Ace," as he was known to family and friends, his dad instructed, "We'll get the bags later. Come inside. We've got a lot to catch up on."

"Thanks, Dad. It will only take a minute."

With bags in hand, arm in arm, the three headed for the house. For the remainder of that evening and the duration of his return home, the Smiley family experienced understanding, healing, joy, and love as never before.

Day 45
January 16th – Wednesday

Arthur Mutton wasted no time in advancing the plan that his mentor and predecessor, Bill Nelson, crafted to rid the church of Horatio. At nine o'clock, he began placing calls to the other board members.

"Tommy. Arthur here," he began. "The board needs to meet tonight. It's urgent. The clock is ticking. We don't have much time."

"Geeze, Louise, Arthur. Are you on some kind of medication? You're talking jibberish."

"Listen, we've gotta move quickly if we're going to replace Smiley," Arthur explained. "He'll be back in thirty days."

"Okay already. Where's the meeting?" Tommy asked.

"Not sure, yet. I'm working out the details as we speak. I'll give you a call around noon and let you know," he promised.

After connecting with the other board members, Arthur set the meet time for six o'clock that night, at the lodge.

****

At the meeting, the board members were seated around their favorite table. Arthur called the meeting to order. Reflexively, Danny pulled out his notebook to begin recording the minutes of the meeting.

"Danny, are you kidding me? Put that away," Arthur demanded. "My God. Use your head. I want to be very clear: this meeting is off the record," he cautioned. "Anything that is discussed or decided here tonight is not to be shared with anyone, under any circumstance. Does everyone understand?" Every head nodded in agreement.

He continued, "On February third, we're going to hold a church meeting to expose Smiley as unfit to continue on as pastor of Good Shepherd. The evidence we've compiled against this guy over the last three years, when presented to the church membership, is guaranteed to cause his staunchest ally to withdraw their support of him."

"Are you sure about this, Arthur?" Tommy asked.

"Oh, yeah. I couldn't be more sure. I've received God's blessing on this."

"You've what…?" Tommy's eyes opened wide.

"You heard me. God has given our plan His seal of approval. No one can stop us now." Arthur chuckled.

"Arthur, exactly how did God express His approval?" Tommy asked, unconvinced.

Arthur sat back in his chair and motioned to the bartender to bring another round of adult beverages to the table. He began to share with his counterparts the source of his confidence about the undertaking.

"It's those calendars. Those calendars with that red spot," he said.

Tommy called out to the bartender, "Hey, Sid. Hold up on that round of drinks. Arthur doesn't need any more."

"Sid, bring the damn drinks," Arthur insisted. "Tommy's not paying, I am." Returning his attention to the discussion, he continued with his explanation. "Listen to what I'm telling you and you'll understand everything, as well as I do. You all know about the calendars that were handed out at the New Year's Watch Meeting, right?"

His question was responded to with a fifty-fifty split of nodding heads and blank stares.

"What calendars?" Sid asked as he stood over the table, handing out drinks.

"Sid, we need a moment here," Arthur barked. Sid walked away muttering something beneath his breath. "Can you believe that guy?" Arthur glared.

"So, what is it about the calendars that has you believing God endorses this plan?" Danny asked.

Becoming uncharacteristically animated, Arthur explained, "Listen, you've probably heard about what happened with Henry Williams, Jenny Murray, and a few others who received one of the calendars, right? Amazing things happened to each of them on the day that the red mark showed up on their calendar. Henry escaped a plane crash that should have killed him. Jenny's daughter was miraculously healed from a near-death situation. I heard that somebody landed their dream job after two years of being unemployed. Every one of these situations were verified by at least ten people. Now, here's where it gets good," Arthur let loose a sinister laugh. "Look at this," he said, as he removed his calendar from his briefcase. "Check out the date that the red mark falls on." He directed everyone's attention to the February page. "See it?"

"What do you know about that? February third," Tommy confirmed.

"That's right." Arthur was giddy. "Think about it: Smiley is out of town so there is no way that he can cause us a problem. His sheep are helpless without him telling them what to do. We can nominate and vote Reverend Bell in as Smiley's replacement without any opposition. I'm telling you we can't lose. The William J. Nelson Community Center will be built after all."

"You're right, Arthur," Tommy agreed. "We've got to do this for the sake of Bill's legacy."

The trustees bought into Arthur's plan hook, line, and sinker.

"We need to get together, again, to 'fine tune' our presentation," Arthur postured. "I'm thinking a week from Saturday, say eleven o'clock, right here. Anyone have a problem with that?"

Heads around the table indicated that there was no problem with the proposed meeting time.

"Good, it's settled." Arthur called out to the bartender, "Sid, refills, all around."

The meeting concluded after two additional rounds of drinks had been consumed.

Day 46
January 17th – Thursday

The distinctive sound of keys jingling in the hallway caused Aviana to call out, "Barry, is that you?"

"Yes, dear, it's me. I'm running late for a meeting at the office. I'll give you a call as soon as I can."

"Barry, come in here," she insisted. "Don't you dare leave out of this house without explaining yourself."

Barry sheepishly poked his head inside Aviana's bedroom. "Sorry, dear. I thought you were still sleeping."

"Barry, how am I expected to sleep without an update of the orphanage situation?"

"Yes. The orphanage situation," he repeated.

"You promised me that you would look into it. I'm sensing that you haven't done anything yet." Aviana was becoming frustrated.

"The fact of the matter is that I have very much begun the process of planning an effective strategy," he explained.

"Barry, don't insult my intelligence. 'Begun the process of planning an effective strategy?' What do you take me for?" she fumed. "Set up a meeting with whoever it is that you deal with at the orphanage or I'll take matters into my hands. Do you understand?"

"Perfectly, Pumpkin."

"I'll expect a favorable, progress report before noon, today. Barry, you can't be passive about this. Trust me. This is the only way to get things done with these nonprofits. Now, you may go to your precious meeting." She mouthed a kiss good-bye. Barry backed out of the room like a spanked puppy.

****

At eleven forty-five, Barry called Aviana with his update.

"Hi, Sweetie. Good news," he began, "I called my contact at the orphanage and we're scheduled to meet with her for lunch tomorrow."

"That's twenty-four hours from now. They can't meet with us today?"

"No. It has to be tomorrow," Barry responded firmly.

"Fine. I've decided that I want a boy. A cute little boy," Aviana continued. "I'm going to get in touch with the interior decorator and start setting up one of the bedrooms."

"That's fine, dear. I have to run." The phone call ended.

Day 47
January 18th - Friday

Barry and Aviana sat waiting inside the Mount Blue restaurant when they noticed a woman approaching their table. Barry stood to his feet and extended his right hand to greet her.

"Hello, Judy. This is my wife, Aviana." He continued, "Aviana, Judy is the assistant to the director of Mercy Ministries."

"So nice to meet you, Aviana."

"The pleasure is mine," Aviana responded.

After the exchange of pleasantries and small talk had concluded, Barry explained the reason behind his request for the meeting.

"Judy, Aviana and I have been very blessed through our hard work and clean living. In the hectic course of the life we pursued, the time for raising a family was never right. That was until now," he continued. "Judy, I'm not getting any younger, and Aviana and I believe that now is the right time. We have discussed, at length, the options that are available to us and nothing makes better sense than adoption through Mercy Ministries."

"That's wonderful," Judy responded. "I'll arrange for an adoptive parent qualification packet to be sent to you right away. The adoption process usually takes six to twelve months, so I recommend that you submit your application immediately. After that, you'll want to register for the first available series of parenting classes."

At that, Aviana abandoned her silent, patient demeanor.

"Thank you, Judy, for stating the protocol for those who come to adopt with hat in hand. Well done, indeed." She continued, "Take a very good look at my husband and me. Do we appear to be coming to you with hat in hand?"

Caught off guard about how she could, appropriately, respond to the question just posed, Judy didn't speak one word.

"Judy, my husband is a board member and a successful fund raiser. Our business contributes more than enough each year to pay for you and your boss's salary, not to mention that ungodly affair that you had with my husband four years ago. And, you consider yourself a Christian? You know, some people, like your employer perhaps, might not be as forgiving as I about your sordid, husband-baiting antics. Am I getting through to you, Judy?" Aviana glared.

Seeing no benefit in continuing to remain, Judy stood up to leave. Barry's mouth was agape.

"Barry, thank you for the invitation," Judy said as she extended her hand to Barry.

"Sit down, Judy," Aviana insisted. "Sit down or you'll be out of a job before the close of business, today."

Judy sat down. Barry remained silent.

"Judy, I didn't request this meeting for the sake of making friends. After all, how could any woman who sleeps with my husband be a friend to me? No, to be clear, I don't need a friend, I need an advocate. I believe that you can serve that function proficiently. So, we three are going to work together to accomplish my objective; that being the adoption of the child of my choice within the next thirty days. Can I count on you?"

"What choice do I have?" Judy muttered.

"Good. Now, explain the process to me so we can get this plan underway," Aviana instructed.

Judy took Barry and Aviana step by step through Mercy Ministries' adoption process. She agreed to hand-deliver an application to their dealership on her way home from work, later that evening. She counseled Barry and Aviana to limit their selection to a child whose parents had surrendered their right to reunification. After some additional arm-twisting, Judy scheduled a weekend tour of the orphanage so that Aviana could make her selection.

After the meeting, Judy returned to work. Tormented by mistakes of her past, she experienced bouts of crying. Despite her determination to live a respectable life since her affair with Barry, she accepted that Satan would never release her from past sin.

For the remainder of the meal, Aviana was, uncharacteristically, cordial to Barry. He appreciated that she had justifiably placed complete blame for his marital infidelity at the feet of Judy. After all, it was his position that Judy was a flirtatious woman who had undoubtedly engaged in this type of behavior before.

As they prepared to exit the restaurant, before their shadows cleared the building's entryway, Aviana lit into Barry in every way that he deserved. Assaulted with a barrage of legal and emotional threats, face slaps and public humiliation, Barry was reduced to something less than a grown man. Falling to his knees, crying and pleading, it appeared as though Barry was on the receiving end of a brutal mugging. Pitiful-looking as he was, the exchange concluded with Aviana leaving him in the parking lot to find his way home. Bloodied and sniveling, Barry knew that this was only the beginning of what awaited him at home.

****

Later that evening, with his face displaying evidence of a swollen lip and a blackened left eye, Barry tiptoed into the house at six thirty via a side door. Making his way to a guest bedroom, he paused at every turn along the way, expecting that Aviana was waiting in ambush. Successfully navigating his way through the house closing a bedroom door, he stretched out on the bed. Within thirty seconds of closing his eyes to rest, he could hear Aviana's footsteps coming down the hallway.

The bedroom door flew open wide. Clearly, she had not calmed down. He remained face down and reflexively clutched his pillow. Resigned to dealing, prudently, with the fallout from his extramarital frolicking, he accepted full responsibility and acquiesced to Aviana's conditions for reconciliation.

"Where is the application?" she demanded.

"Kitchen table," he whimpered.

"What time am I to be at the orphanage?"

"One o'clock, tomorrow."

She turned and left the room, slamming the door behind her.

Barry knew that he had deeply hurt her. *How did she find out about Judy? I wonder how much more she knows?* he pondered.

He, wisely, chose to remain holed-up in the guest room for the rest of the night.

Day 48
January 19th – Saturday

Aviana arrived at Mercy Ministries promptly at one o'clock. Judy intercepted her at the steps of the administration building. Ushering her through a locked gate at the side of another building and along a pathway, Judy led her to a playground area where sixty children of various ages enjoyed a seasonably, mild afternoon. Aviana studied the faces of the children and produced a camera from her pocket to snap a picture.

"Please, no pictures," Judy cautioned. "If word gets back to my boss that I was here with someone taking pictures, I'll be out of a job and you'll be minus one advocate."

"I wouldn't want you to lose your job, Judy," Aviana sneered, as she raised the camera to her face and took several pictures of the children. After returning the camera to her pocket, she pointed. "That child there. The red-headed boy wearing the brown coat. He's the one I want," she said. "What's his name?"

"That's Daniel," Judy responded.

"What's his situation?"

"There is no parental involvement in his case." Judy explained. "Word is his father is dead or in prison. His drug-addicted, emotionally disturbed mother chose crack over the boy. She signed off her parental rights. There's a restraining order against her to make sure she has no contact with the child or Mercy Ministries. This should be a slam dunk."

"He doesn't have any diseases or deficiencies, does he?" Aviana asked.

"No problems that I'm aware of. Seems to be fit as a fiddle."

"Good. Let's get the paperwork to your supervisor first thing Monday morning," Aviana instructed as she walked away.

Day 49
January 20th- Sunday

Reverend Bell's sermon was uninspiring. The presence of God was noticeably diminished in the message he sought to bring to the congregation. It was clear that Horatio's diligent, heartfelt prayer at the beginning of every worship service was necessary to come against any evil force that was assigned to neutralize the presence of God. The attendance was reduced by half and the after-service fellowship was canceled. The trustees, led by Arthur Mutton, showed little concern for the after-service fellowship protocol by quickly ushering the church's members out of the building, immediately, after the collection plates were retrieved.

****

Outside of Good Shepherd, Sam and Teresa extended an invitation for others to come and fellowship at their home, as they didn't live far from the church. They entertained twenty-eight guests. Teresa prepared sandwiches and coffee, while Sam and the children made sure that everyone was comfortable.

During that time, several church members discussed their struggles and requested prayer. As prayers went up, the presence of God entered in. The brotherly spirit of love and compassion that, expectedly, was found at Good Shepherd had migrated to meet those who had come to the Woodens' home, today. Those who chose to give over to God their cares and challenges received peace and encouragement in exchange. What Sam and Teresa considered 'a good thing to do' proved to be the God thing to do. They vowed to host the after-service fellowship until their pastor returned.

Day 50
January 21st - Monday

At six fifteen, the members of the Smiley family were sitting at the breakfast table. It was time for "Ace" to head back to Boston's Logan Airport where he would board the flight that would begin his Caribbean vacation. Excited to go, but not happy to leave, Horatio and his parents waited until the last possible moment to say good-bye. While drinking coffee and eating biscuits lathered with peach preserves, they cemented their travel arrangements for a May reunion in Boston.

"Mom, Dad, I know I've told you a thousand times, already, how sorry I am for disconnecting but...."

"It's been more like two thousand times," His father chuckled.

"Well, two thousand times, then," he continued. "I just want you to know that I love you both so much." A group hug followed and shortly thereafter he and his luggage were headed back to Boston.

The weather was clear and the traffic pattern light. The sun hadn't yet risen. His flight to Miami, Florida, was scheduled to depart at eight thirty. For the duration of his trip home, Horatio reflected fondly on the conversations, revelation and joy that he and his parents shared during his visit. He continued to thank God for bringing them together, again.

****

The return trip to Boston was problem-free and although tempted to stop by and check in on Good Shepherd, Horatio thought better of it. He continued, directly, to Boston's Logan International Airport. Arriving there at five twenty, he parked his car in the garage and found his way to the airline service counter. Positioned ninth in line, he took the opportunity to observe the exchanges between customers and ticket agents, as he waited to be called. All but one of the counter agents appeared to be pleasant and helpful. Passengers would be greeted with a smile and friendly repartee. Horatio prayed that he would not have to deal with the unpleasant agent at the end of the counter.

"Lord," he quietly prayed, "I've traveled six hundred miles over enough bad road for one day. I'm really, really tired. Please, spare me the need to interact with the ticket agent from Hades. This I pray in Jesus' name, Amen."

Immediately his prayer appeared to be working. Next to be served, he observed that the ticket agent with the bad attitude had signaled to another agent that she was taking her break. Placing a 'position closed' sign at her location, she began to make her way out. Before she could exit the counter area, a supervisor admonished her and directed her back to her position at the counter. The agent's demeanor elevated to a whole new level of ugly. With a smirk on her face that would stop rain, she bellowed, "NEXT!"

Horatio closed his eyes in disbelief. Stepping up to the counter and reading her name tag, reflexively he spoke, "Good evening, LaWanda. And how are you doing this fine evening?"

"Ticket, please," she instructed, opting not to make eye contact with him.

Handing her his ticket, he was moved to ask, "LaWanda, is everything all right?"

Somehow managing to stare up at Horatio without moving her head, she snarled, "Do I know you or something?"

"No, ma'am," Horatio acknowledged.

"Then, what's it to you how I'm doing?" she pressed.

"LaWanda, I don't know you but, I'd like to pray for you."

"Pray for me?" She drew back. "Mister, save your prayers for somebody else. My situation is beyond what your prayer or anyone else can do for me. I'm going through hell right about now. No one can help me and God doesn't seem to care, either."

Other customers and counter agents within listening range witnessed the exchange.

"What makes you think that God doesn't care?"

"My children and I are homeless," she spewed. "Our house burned up yesterday and we lost everything. If I miss any more time from work, I'll be fired. I have no family to call and no money to find another place to live. Now, you're telling me to pray?" She continued, "Mister, I've spent more time on my knees praying for the last day and a half than I ever have and things are getting worse for my family, not better."

"LaWanda, I'm so sorry to hear about all that you and your children are going through. Where are your children now?"

LaWanda was guarded in her response. She didn't know his motive for inquiring about her children. For all she knew, he could be an agent from Children's Protective Services. But, there was something about Horatio's demeanor that caused her to believe that he was genuinely concerned.

"They're in my car in the employee parking garage," she responded in a hushed tone. "If C.P.S. got wind of this, they'd accuse me of child endangerment. There's nothing else that I can do." Her eyes began to well up, seemingly conceding defeat.

"LaWanda," Horatio offered, "Solutions to our most difficult situations can be found in God. Trust Him. He'll carry you through." He didn't say anything more until LaWanda had finished processing his paperwork. As she handed him his boarding pass, he invited her to join him for prayer by departure Gate 25. He smiled and walked away.

He continued to lift LaWanda and her circumstance in prayer as he waited in the gate area. His attention went to his friend and co-laborer in Christ, Pastor Mona. He remembered that she owned rental property in Boston. At that very moment, his cell phone rang. It was her. Having not spoken with her in months, he could only laugh and confirm aloud, "God, you're amazing!" He shared the details of LaWanda's situation with her.

"Horatio, do you have a phone number that I can reach her at?" she asked.

"No, but I'm sure I can go and get it for you."

"Please. Do it now," she instructed. "In fact, give the young lady my number. Have her call me right away. Those children don't need to be spending the night in a car."

"I'll get right on it. I'll call you back in ten minutes," he promised.

Excited about a possible solution to LaWanda's dilemma, he quickly grabbed his carry-on and headed back to the ticketing area to give her the news. About a third of the way there, he could see LaWanda walking in his direction.

"LaWanda! I have great news," he called out from thirty feet away. "You need to call this number right away," he insisted. "I believe God is answering my prayer."

"You mean our prayers." She chuckled. "I was just on my way to thank you for your encouragement. You really helped me to pay attention to the things that I was speaking into my life. Imagine, me saying that God didn't care about me or my children. Those demons had me doubting the love of God. Can you believe that? They must have thought I was some kind of new fool to doubt the power of prayer. Mr. Smiley, can I use your phone to make the call? I don't have a phone." Her countenance transitioned from that of heaviness to one of excitement.

"LaWanda, take a deep breath." He laughed.

He called Pastor Mona and handed the phone to LaWanda before the call connected. After the second ring, Pastor Mona answered the phone, "Pastor Smiley, did you manage to connect with LaWanda?"

LaWanda's face registered a look of things beginning to make sense.

"This is LaWanda Peterson. Could you please hold for just a moment?" she asked. Turning to Horatio, the connection was made. "You're a pastor? I mean, you're a pastor!" she exclaimed. "I knew there was something going on with you."

"I hope that's not a problem," he responded as he motioned to remind her that she had Pastor Mona waiting on the phone. As LaWanda spoke with Pastor Mona, Horatio witnessed tears of joy and words of gratitude flow freely.

Returning his phone to him, LaWanda remarked, "God is too amazing!"

Horatio concluded his phone conversation with Pastor Mona while LaWanda stood before him mouthing the words: "Thank you, Lord. Thank you, so much."

"Well," Horatio began, "sounds like you and Pastor Mona hit it off."

"She's wonderful. She and her husband are on their way to sit with my kids until I get off from work tonight. She said that she'll work to locate some housing for us by the time my shift ends." Her eyes continued to well up. "What a difference twenty-four hours can make."

"You mean twenty-four hours of prayer," he emphasized.

"Right. Twenty-four hours of prayer." LaWanda couldn't agree more.

"I've got a plane to catch and you should go check on your children. I'll check in with Pastor Mona to see how you're settling in," he called out, waving good-bye as he made his way back to the boarding gate.

Within the next 30 minutes, he boarded his flight and was taxiing down the runway on route to the glamorous city of Miami, Florida. Upon his arrival, he retrieved his bags and hailed a shuttle to a nearby airport motel. He checked in and retired for the night at one fifteen.

Day 51
January 22nd - Tuesday

At eleven thirty-five, Horatio was awakened by a voice at his motel room door announcing, "Housekeeping." Somewhat disoriented, he sat up in his bed. Rubbing his eyes, he responded, "Just a minute, please." Looking over at the clock, he noticed the time. "Coming," he called out as he put on his robe. Opening the door, he saw a woman waiting with a fully outfitted cleaning cart.

"Buenos dias, senor," she greeted with a congenial smile.

"Hello and good day to you," he responded.

"Please, Mister. I clean your room now?"

"Twenty minutes more, please," Horatio requested. "I'll be out of your way. How's that?"

"I come back, later," the woman responded with a hint of frustration. The wheels of the maid's cleaning cart could be heard moving further down the corridor.

Twenty minutes later he was shaved, showered and, with suitcase in hand, headed to the motel office to check out. His travel itinerary required that all passengers board the cruise ship between two o'clock and six o'clock. It was twelve noon. He settled his bill and headed for the exit. Feeling like he was ready to take on a good, old fashioned breakfast, he decided to walk to a nearby Waffle House restaurant. While a meal of eggs, grits, pecan waffles and sausage was satisfying, his appreciation for the cook's culinary talent was tempered by all that he was witnessing from his seat by the window. Faces of men and women of various walks of life passed by, displaying heaviness, stress, and at times both. As beautifully as the sun shone outside, it was obvious that storms of anxiety and uncertainty were raging in the hearts and lives of so many people. "Lord, please send relief. Your people are perishing," he prayed. After finishing his meal, he paid his tab, left a generous tip, and went in search of a taxi to take him and his luggage to the cruise ship terminal.

Thirty minutes later, Horatio was standing at the base of an enclosed gangway that would take him on board the largest cruise ship he had ever seen. The smiling faces of well-outfitted cruise staff members greeted him as he stepped aboard. Directed to a registration table, he stood in a line with several hundred other passengers having a surname beginning with the letters R-T. The line moved quickly and before long, he had his welcome packet and cabin key in hand.

Stopping four times to ask for directions to his cabin, a childlike expression of euphoria was visible on his face. He marveled at the grandeur of the ship. His eyes darted from corner to corner, floor to ceiling, in area after area of the mammoth vessel. *How can this ship stay afloat?* he continued to ponder as he rode in a glass elevator to the ninth floor of the vessel. As he exited the elevator, a staff member was there to assist him to his cabin.

****

Entering his suite, Horatio was certain that a mistake had been made. The accommodations well exceeded what he had paid for at the travel agency. A large floral arrangement, a bottle of French wine, and a note sat atop a table in front of the balcony door.

"Do they do this for every passenger?" he asked the cabin steward.

"Actually, sir," the steward explained, "the wine, flowers, and note are for you from the captain." He continued, "It is my understanding that the captain has need of your service. I'm certain that it is all explained in the note. You should call him right away. He's a very good man. In the meantime, my name is Albie and if there is anything, at all, that you require, please ring me up at extension 1100."

"Thank you, Albie. I'll call the captain as soon as I read the note."

"Thank you, sir. Have a wonderful vacation." The steward left.

"I wonder why the captain would send me a note?"

Taking the note from the envelope, he opened it and read, 'Pastor Smiley, please be my guest for dinner this evening at the six o'clock seating. Kind regards, Captain Philippe Gervais.'

"This is interesting."

He left a message for Captain Gervais, thanking him for the gifts and confirming that he would see him at dinner.

It was two-thirty so, he decided to change into vacation-appropriate clothing and tour the ship. Dressed in Bermuda shorts, a 'Born to Worship' tank top and flip flops, he ventured out. On his way to the pool deck, he shared the elevator with five women of various ages. They were so scantily clad that there was little left to his imagination. He was so taken aback that he exited the elevator at the first opportunity. Finding himself in a corridor lined with passengers carrying adult beverages agonizing over results of a Keno game, he cringed.

"Lord, your people are going straight to hell wearing bikinis, drinking liquor, and playing Keno. Help them, Lord. Please," he prayed.

Choosing to board the elevator, yet, again, he pushed the button that was marked Shuffleboard Deck. Stepping out of the elevator, he observed, through a glass partition, several shuffleboard courts with mature men and women engaged in highly competitive matches. Seemingly, it was their children and grandchildren who cheered them on. Emerging from behind the glass enclosure, he was met with a flurry of profanities. Apparently, a miscue from one of the players caused a match to be lost. Without concern for young, innocent ears, a grandfather unloaded his repertoire of expletives in frustration.

Quickly back onto the elevator, Horatio went to seek refuge in his cabin. He was grieved by the thought of being trapped in this environment for the next seven days. There he remained in prayer mode until five thirty. Having lost interest in dining with Captain Gervais, he experienced second thoughts in his acceptance of the invitation. Yielding to his conscience, he was appropriately dressed and ready by five-fifty for dinner.

He found his way to the dining room where he was met by a member of the wait staff. Explaining that he was there as an invited guest of Captain Gervais, he was escorted to the captain's table. As he approached the table, he immediately noticed Captain Gervais. Seated with his back to the wall dressed in his crisp white uniform, the captain acknowledged Horatio by standing to his feet and extending his arms to greet him with a welcoming embrace. Eight others at the table, also, rose to their feet to greet him. In a hazy moment of introductions, it became clear that the men seated at the table were members of various faiths or beliefs.

The group was comprised of a rabbi, a mullah, an astrologer, a shaman, a hieromonk, a witch doctor, a Sangha, a pandit, and a guru.

This must be some kind of a setup. There has to be a hidden camera around here somewhere, Horatio thought to himself as he moved toward the unoccupied seat. After the introductions had concluded, each table guest returned to his seated position.

The captain explained, "Pastor Smiley, the staff of this cruise ship is responsible for meeting the needs of, as many as four thousand, passengers that we entertain each trip. Our ability to satisfy the recreational, nutritional, and emotional needs of our guests is what determines the success of our business." All seated at the table nodded in agreement.

The captain continued, "Late last night, Father Williams, who serves as one of my ship's spiritual counselors, was called away to tend to an urgent family matter. Pastor Smiley, as I explained to you earlier, our guests have expectations that must be met." He continued, "I need a clergyman to be available for anyone professing to be Christian who might experience a spiritual episode. Granted, I can't recall when such a situation as that last occurred but, there's always a first time. I don't want to be caught ill-prepared. I need your help."

"Captain Gervais, I'm flattered," Horatio began, "but, I don't know anything about serving as a counselor on a ship."

"Pastor, you probably won't receive a single distress call during your seven-day stay," the captain reassured. "Just ask anyone here at our table. I think it's fair to say that this is the most well-rested collection of clergymen you'll find anywhere." His dinner guests jovially confirmed the accuracy of his statement. "If anything," the captain continued, "you may receive a request to perform a wedding ceremony. In that case, simply direct the couple to me. I love performing weddings." He chuckled. "To make the company's proposition sweeter," the captain continued, "you will be our guest. Whatever expenses you've incurred for this vacation will be fully reimbursed. What do you say, Pastor Smiley? Are you onboard? Please, pardon the pun." Everyone laughed at the captain's quick wit.

"Captain, your offer is generous, indeed." Horatio continued, "May I have a while to pray about it?"

"Pray if you must, but do it quickly," the captain continued. "I'm sure there are other clergymen on board who would jump at this opportunity."

Horatio excused himself and returned to his cabin to pray.

In the midst of his prayer, there was a knock at his door. Aggravated at the interruption, he took his time in responding. Then, came a second knock, followed by a man's voice.

"Pastor, are you in there?" He recognized the voice as that of Albie, the cabin steward.

"Coming," he responded. Opening the door, he could see that the man's eyes were reddened from crying. "Albie, is everything all right?"

"Pastor, my mom is very ill," Albie explained. "I just received word from the hospital in Honduras. She is alone and I cannot leave to be near her. My time here will not end for twenty-four more days." He continued, "I don't know what to do."

"Albie, what's wrong with her?"

"It's her heart. She's been dealing with it for a lot of years."

"Are you a praying man, Albie?"

"Yes. I pray to God all the time, sir."

"Good. Let's pray," Horatio instructed.

During the next ten minutes, they prayed that God would move, miraculously, to heal Albie's mother. At the conclusion of prayer, Albie spoke of the presence of God being in that room as he had never experienced before. He thanked Horatio for being available to him in his time of need.

"Pastor, your prayers have power. I wish you were here all the time. So many people around here could use some real prayer." He took Horatio's hand and said in a hushed voice, "Very few people on this ship believe in prayer. So-called 'spiritual' people included." He winked and walked away.

Returning to his praying position, Horatio remembered his commitment of availability to God. *Even though I'm on vacation, I am still available and on-call to be used for whatever You have need of me, Lord, even while at sea.* He laughed, "Okay, Lord. I get the message. I'll let the captain know that I'll be accepting his offer." He chuckled as he stood to his feet and departed to give Captain Gervais his answer.

Standing in the entryway of the dining room, he could see the captain's guests sharing a belly laugh while sipping adult beverages and smoking cigars. As he drew nearer to the table, the atmosphere shifted from one of carnival to one of professional congeniality. He extended his right hand to the captain and, with a firm grip, said, "Captain, I accept your offer."

"That's wonderful news, Pastor. I'm certain you'll be pleased with your decision. Would you like a cocktail or perhaps a fine Cuban cigar?" he asked.

Searching for a way to graciously decline the captain's invitation, he responded, "No, thank you, Captain. I'm going to change my clothes and run a few laps before I retire for the evening." Bidding everyone good night, he departed.

"Oh, man," he processed aloud, "I can't believe I said that. I haven't jogged in years. Thank you, Lord, that no one asked to join me."

Wanting not to be guilty of lying, he returned to his cabin and half-heartedly suited up and went for an evening jog. Laboring to complete his first lap around the ship's Skydeck, he slowed to a walk as his leg muscles began to ache. A voice from above called down to him with a bit of a chuckle, "Hey, Pastor, you need to pray for some stronger lungs."

Looking up to see who was speaking, he saw Albie, the cabin steward, who continued to speak, "Pastor, you were puffing so hard that you caused me to be homesick. You reminded me of an old train that travels everyday through the mountains back in my country." Albie laughed.

Horatio joined in by intermittently laughing, coughing, and clutching his side. "Albie, you found me out. I'm terribly out of shape."

"That's all right, Pastor. Your secret is safe. Have a good night." Albie waved and disappeared from sight.

Horatio made his way to a deck chair where he spent a bit of solitary time adoring an amazingly cloudless, star-filled sky. With his eyes still heavenward, there came a voice to him, inquiring, "Are you the Pastor who Albie spoke of?"

His attention moved to a young woman standing alongside him.

"Yes. Hello. I'm Pastor Smiley," he replied. "How can I help you?"

For the next half hour, the woman, having the name of Anna, explained to him that her husband, Hank, experienced prolonged bouts of depression. She had used her family's savings to take Hank on this cruise to lift his spirit but, her plan was failing miserably. Now, Hank blames himself for his inability to break free from his affliction, despite his wife's efforts and his desire to do so.

"I love my husband, so much, Pastor. I don't know what else to do," Anna said with tears in her eyes.

Horatio instructed Anna to go to Hank and ask him to return with her so that they could chat. Anna expressed her doubt about Hank coming, so he promised to pray while she went to make her appeal to him.

Twenty minutes later, he heard voices approaching. Looking in the direction of the footsteps, he saw Anna and who he assumed to be Hank, walking arm in arm toward him.

"Hi, Pastor." Anna was excited. "This is my husband, Hank."

"Hank. I'm pleased to meet you," Horatio said as he extended his right hand. With a firm grip seemingly out of desperation, Hank grabbed at his hand and held on.

"Anna," Horatio began, "would it be okay with you if Hank and I talk for while?"

"Oh, I thought…. I mean, sure," she replied. Anna kissed Hank on his cheek and walked away.

"Do you mind if we sit down over here?" Horatio asked, leading Hank in the direction of some deck chairs. In the two hours that followed, he counseled with Hank about the reality of spiritual warfare. Next, he instructed Hank on how to pray, effectively. At the conclusion, Hank was a changed man.

"Oh, my God, Pastor," Hank rejoiced, "I haven't felt this good in years! How can I ever thank you?"

"Hank, don't thank me. Thank God for this little black book," he said, holding up a small bible. "It has the right answer for every situation." Hank gave him a man hug and headed off to find Anna.

Looking at his watch, Horatio decided that it was time to head back to his cabin for the night.

Day 52
January 23rd - Wednesday

Horatio emerged from a well-deserved night's rest at seven thirty. Hearing the footsteps of passengers on their way to the dining room, he decided to get ready and go, as well. He remembered the captain telling him about the eight o'clock breakfast seating at his table.

Entering the dining room, he spotted several of the regulars at the captain's table being treated as royalty and relishing every minute of it. Selecting a seat and greeting all present, Horatio began perusing the menu. Within a matter of seconds, a woman's voice over his left shoulder quietly said, "Good morning, Pastor." Not yet decided on his breakfast choice, he turned to request more time.

"Please," he began to speak, lifting his eyes away from the menu. It was Anna. "Hi, Anna. Is everything all right?" he asked, concerned about Hank.

"Oh, yes, Pastor. Everything is wonderful," she said with a broad smile. "Pastor, I don't mean to intrude, but would you like to join Hank and me at our table this morning? There are some people who would really like to meet you."

"Captain, would you mind?" Horatio asked, noticing that his host was paying close attention to the exchange.

"Not at all, Pastor. Please, we'll see each other tonight for dinner."

Horatio excused himself and followed Anna to her table. Once there, Hank stood to his feet and gave him a hug.

"Who's this wild man?" Horatio asked, jokingly.

"Thank you. Thank you, so much, Pastor." Again, Hank hugged Horatio, "Thank you." The spirit of depression that had Hank bound and wearied had, seemingly, departed.

Everyone at the table laughed. In fact, the laughter was so contagious that it drew the attention of passengers at tables nearby. Word of Hank's transformation traveled quickly. People continued to gather around the table to introduce themselves to Horatio, while telling him about their issues. It became difficult for the wait staff to perform their responsibilities. Horatio invited those who wanted to continue the gathering to meet in an activity room that Captain Gervais made available. The excitement of the moment set the pace for the remaining six days of unforgettable, life-transforming travel for the passengers and crew of this state-of-the-art cruise ship.

Each day Horatio was sought out by an increasing number of people for counseling and instruction in the things of God. Twenty-seven renewals of wedding vows were conducted, with the assistance of Captain Gervais. During this time, the healthy revenue streams that the ship routinely enjoyed from sales of alcohol, cigarettes, and gambling diminished. In contrast, revenues soared from onboard gift shop purchases as husbands lavished jewelry and services on their wives. It was as though the passengers opted to spend their money on romantic, unselfish items. There was an excitement that the captain labeled as refreshing.

Understandably, spirits of jealousy and contempt flourished in the hearts of the others who graced the captain's dining table. Looks of disdain, ill-spoken words, and even the mention of a curse was directed at Horatio. Captain Gervais could no longer ignore the wickedness that continued to fester in these religious men.

"Gentlemen," he began, "why do you take such exception to the good work that the pastor is accomplishing in his time with the passengers?" he asked of them.

"Good work?" one was heard to respond.

"This man is a fraud. A man who misleads people for the purpose of being popular," another offered.

"Why would you say such a thing?" the captain questioned.

"Look at him. He is as the pied piper. Everyone's healed! Everyone's saved! All because of his Jesus," said a third.

"Charlatan! Fraud!" a fourth began. "In every walk of faith, there are rituals that must be observed before the spirits will respond." All seated at the table nodded in agreement.

"A blood sacrifice, chants, the burning of incense—something must precede the spirit's response," the witch doctor continued, "There is no power in this man's words."

"Gentlemen," Captain Gervais challenged, "if you believe what you are telling me, prove him wrong. Prove his God wrong. Give me a reason to have him thrown off this ship, broken of spirit and reputation. Otherwise, pack your bags and consider your services to this cruise line no longer required. You have four days." With that, the captain stood up and walked away.

For the next hour, the "holy men" sat at the dinner table with drinks in hand, devising a plan that was certain to succeed in exposing Horatio as a man without power. After all, how difficult could it be? It was Horatio himself who clearly stated, "Apart from God, I can do nothing."

The plan was designed to keep him separated from his God for the remainder of the cruise. The "men of faith" would summon the gods they served to send spirits of distraction and affliction to come against Horatio, so that he would be unable and unavailable to be concerned for anyone but himself.

With the accomplishment of their plan, the "holy men" would be restored to the good graces of Captain Gervais. The "holy men," together and alone, spent the rest of their day burning incense, chanting, tossing chicken bones, reading crystals, and meditating for the power of the spirits they called on to manifest.

Horatio was completely unaware of the evil that was being perpetrated against him. Sensing a strong presence of God about him, he gave thanks.

****

Throughout the day and into the evening, passengers continued to seek him out. With more dinner invitations than he could expect to honor, he arranged to conduct a bible study in one of the ship's conference rooms. The number of cruise passengers attending the study sessions increased daily, to the dismay of his critics, the self-proclaimed holy men. By request, bible study sessions were scheduled during lunch and after dinner for the remainder of the cruise.

Day 53
January 25th - Friday

Judy is sitting in her office when her cell phone rings. It's Aviana.

"Good morning, Aviana," she greeted.

"I'd have a better morning if you would provide me with an update once in a while," Aviana jabbed. "What's going on with the application?"

"Well, as of yesterday my supervisor submitted your package for a background check," Judy explained. "Once the review is complete and as long as there aren't any complications, a series of home visits will be arranged with your case worker. Simultaneously, for the sake of expediency, you and your husband will attend our parenting course and become certified as adoptive parents. The process usually takes ninety days but...."

"Ninety days is too long, completely unacceptable," Aviana interrupted.

"As I was saying," Judy fired back, "the process usually takes ninety days but, I'll move things along, cut a few corners, and in thirty days the process should be concluded."

"That's better," Aviana continued. "It's been six days already, so I can expect Daniel to be here in twenty-four days. Right?" she pressed.

"I'll do my best."

"See that you do," Aviana insisted. "And, I want to hear from you every other day about where everything stands. Are we clear?"

"Yeah, yeah," Judy muttered as she hung up the phone.

Day 54
January 26th - Saturday

Arthur was the first to arrive for the meeting. Sitting at a corner table with his back to the wall and his nose buried in the newspaper. He learned, well, everything that Bill Nelson taught him. As the other trustees arrived, they took their positions around the table.

"Okay, let's get started," Arthur began. "I've prepared a packet for each of you to study before the church meeting. We have some pictures of our esteemed pastor in some rather compromising situations, thanks to Joe, our shutterbug. Danny, do you have the information I asked for?"

"Information?" Danny was confused.

"You know, the record of questionable petty cash payments that Smiley approved," Arthur clarified.

"Well, to tell you the truth, Pastor Smiley is as honest a person as I have ever known." Danny explained, "He pays for church supplies, travel expenses, and charitable donations out of his pocket and doesn't request the level of reimbursement that he is entitled to."

"Come on, Danny. Nobody is that honest," Arthur chastised. "You're not looking deep enough."

"Arthur, I'm telling you. If you continue down this trail, it's going to do more harm than good."

"Fine," Arthur huffed. "We'll just go with the pictures."

The other trustees agreed. They studied the pictures over a round of adult beverages and adjourned the meeting soon after.

Day 55
January 27th - Sunday

Horatio awoke to the sound of someone knocking at his cabin door.

"Just a minute!" he called out.

Sensing that someone was in need, he quickly put on his robe and opened the door. There standing in his crisp, white uniform was Captain Gervais.

"Captain, is everything all right? Is there a problem?"

The captain was by nature a sober man. For some reason unbeknownst to Horatio, there stood Captain Gervais at his door with his arms folded across his chest, his face red and his eyes fixed.

Again, he asked, "Captain, is everything all right?"

The captain tried, unsuccessfully, to maintain his composure. "Ha, ha, ha. Ha, ha, ha."

Horatio began to laugh in reaction to the way that the captain was laughing. Captain Gervais couldn't stop laughing. He placed his right hand on the wall to steady himself as he attempted to catch his breath.

"Pastor Smiley, I came to give you a difficult time about your continued absence from my dinner table."

"Oh, I apologize, Captain."

"Please. No need to apologize," Captain Gervais continued. "When I saw your pajamas with the little yellow duckies all over them, I lost it. Sorry." Regaining his composure, he asked, "Do you have a moment to speak with me?"

"Absolutely. What can I do for you?"

"Pastor, I have witnessed many things during my tenure as captain of this ship, and others." Captain Gervais continued, "I have never before experienced all that you have caused to take place with our guests. This morning, I requested of my manager the authorization to make you an offer to extend your services on board, indefinitely. They have given me their overwhelming approval, so I am here to ask you to come aboard. You will receive a generous benefits package, a luxurious cabin, and a fifteen hundred dollar weekly stipend. So what do you say?"

"Wow," was all that Horatio could manage.

"Cat got your tongue, Pastor?" the captain asked, sensing that this was an offer that Horatio could not refuse.

Again, Horatio could only respond, "Wow."

"I can have the paperwork to you by day's end," Captain Gervais promised.

"Captain, may I have the remainder of today to consider your offer?"

"Certainly, but don't make me wait too long," he cautioned. "My office is known for granting and rescinding authority at the drop of a hat."

"I promise to not keep you waiting."

"Well then, I'll expect to hear from you very soon," the Captain said as he extended his hand in friendship.

Closing the cabin door, Horatio prayed. "Lord, what should I do?" Understanding that this could well be the opportunity of his lifetime, he was both flattered and apprehensive. He was flattered by the confirmation that God was using him to affect change in others. At the same time, he was cautiously reluctant because he understood that this could be Satan's plan to reroute or sideline him from what God had begun to do at Good Shepherd.

After spending time on his knees before the Lord, but not yet hearing from Him, he got dressed and made his way to eat breakfast. As had proven to be the routine each morning, he would take only a few steps outside of his cabin when a voice would call out to him, "Good morning Pastor, will you join us for breakfast?"

This morning, it was a family of passengers that he had no recollection of having met before.

"Pastor, my name is Rusty Brady and this is my wife, Eva, and our children, Ezekiel, Stephen, and Ruth. We've heard so much about you."

The man explained, "Earlier this month, we decided to shoot the works and live the rest of our lives on the open sea, after hearing the prophet assuring us that the world is coming to an end soon. In fact," he continued, "we brought along my sisters and brothers and their families, too."

"My goodness," Horatio responded. "You are, indeed, a very generous man, Mr. Brady."

"Please, Pastor. Call me Rusty."

"Rusty, I'm not familiar with this prophecy that you're speaking about. Can you tell me more about it?"

For the next forty-five minutes, sixteen Brady family members hosted Horatio. In their time together, Rusty told him about their subscribing to the teachings of a particular prophet.

According to Rusty, this prophet heard directly from God, daily. Sometimes, several times a day. The prophet would enter into a trancelike state whereby the voice of God would speak. He would act as a scribe and record everything that God spoke, without exception. Three months ago, the prophet called for a worldwide teleconference and announced that the world will end the coming year, on Friday, September 13th. Based on this prophecy, Rusty and Eva agreed to sell their home, cars, and personal belongings and invest every dollar that they had into booking passage on cruise ships right on through September 13th. They were convinced that they had decided wisely. Horatio was in disbelief about everything the Bradys had done.

"Just so I'm clear," Horatio began, "this prophet has always proven accurate in his messages?"

"The prophet is amazing. He's always been right." Rusty was enthusiastic in his response.

"So, Rusty, you're telling me that this prophet has never missed on a single prediction?" he asked, again in disbelief.

Rusty hesitated for a moment, before responding. "Well, there was this time that he said the world was going to end. He had set the date and everything, but…."

"Wait just a minute," Horatio interrupted, "You mean this prophet has predicted the world's end before?"

Rusty was becoming a bit uncomfortable. "Only twice before," he acknowledged.

"Twice before?" Horatio was incredulous.

Rusty countered, "But, the errors were due to mathematical miscalculations or something like that, beyond his control. He explained it all and I believe him. Mistakes happen," he concluded.

"So, let me make sure I understand this," Horatio continued, "You believe in a man who you acknowledge has missed on a prophecy or two, enough to convert everything you own to cash and endeavor to spend every bit of it by September 13th?"

"Yes," Rusty confirmed.

Horatio then asked, "What are you going to do if your prophet misses on his prediction for September 13th?"

Rusty hesitated, then replied, "I don't believe that will happen, but if it does, well, I'll just have to take it one day at a time."

"Rusty, are you familiar with II Thessalonians chapter 2?"

"Thessa-what?" Rusty pondered.

"Thessalonians." Horatio continued, "It's the book of scripture after Colossians."

"Colossians? Is that in the New or Old Testament?" Rusty asked.

"New Testament," Horatio responded with a hint of frustration. Choosing to re-engage, he continued, "Rusty, I truly believe that you don't want to do anything to put your family at risk. There's a bible in the desk drawer of your stateroom. Please read verses one through twelve in the second chapter of Second Thessalonians. After dinner, you and I can meet to discuss your thoughts about the scripture. Is that okay with you?"

"Sure. That's fine. I'd like that a lot." Rusty was animated.

"Let's say seven o'clock on the Starlight deck," Horatio confirmed as he stood up to bid farewell to the Brady family members. He was grieved in his spirit at the level of influence that the false prophet had on the Bradys and, undoubtedly, countless others. The scripture "My people are destroyed for lack of knowledge" (Hosea 4:6) continued to resonate in his heart. He returned to his cabin and remained in prayer for the rest of the afternoon.

Uncertain as to whether it was a dream or a vision, the faces of Sam and Teresa Wooden, Timmy and Sara, the Heywoods and the faces of other Good Shepherd members appeared to him. Immediately, he understood that God was using these images to show him where he was needed most. With a great sense of relief, he went in search of Captain Gervais to give him the answer to his generous proposal.

****

At the captain's table, the full contingent of "holy men" was enjoying another banquet-style meal when Horatio arrived. Captain Gervais stood to his feet to greet him while the others sat defiantly. Some made eye contact with him, as he said hello. Others refused to acknowledge him. The captain addressed the snubbing with an announcement.

"Gentlemen, self-exultation and entitlement are two disciplines that I will not tolerate," he continued. "Your continued disrespect for this man of God has revealed the wickedness in your heart. Tomorrow morning when this ship docks, you will disembark and return to your home. Your service is no longer required on this ship or any other ship that is associated with this cruise line. Your severance checks will be mailed to you. Now, please excuse me as you enjoy your last supper." At that, he got up and walked away. Horatio followed close behind.

"Captain, that wasn't necessary," he explained. "I've decided to decline your offer and return home to Scituate. That's where I belong. That's where God sent me." Horatio had never before referred to Scituate as "home."

"It had to be done," the captain explained. "Those men are devils. Cancerous, pompous freeloaders."

"But Captain, I feel as though this is all my fault," he continued. "If I hadn't come to dinner tonight, none of this would have happened."

"Pastor, don't be silly. I am thankful that God directed you to my table, tonight. The undeniable presence of God in you convicted me to get rid of those men. They were of no benefit to anyone but themselves." Captain Gervais continued, "And, I am not one to easily give up. I will not rest until you agree to accept my offer."

"Thank you, Captain. Your hospitality and encouragement have blessed me immensely."

"We will speak again, soon," the captain promised. They parted company. Horatio went in search of Rusty.

As he approached the Starlight deck, he noticed Rusty standing by the railing with his head hung down, overlooking the pool below. In jest, Horatio called out, "Rusty, don't jump!"

Rusty looked up and turned around slowly. His contagious laughter and jovial demeanor were gone. Looking like he had just lost his life savings in a game of chance, Rusty was humiliated.

"Pastor, I feel like a fool," he began. "I should have read that scripture before I acted. Now, my family will suffer because I accepted the word of a false prophet. What am I supposed to tell them?"

"Rusty, I didn't come to chastise or criticize you," Horatio assured. "I knew that God would show you what you needed to do once you read the scripture."

"Did he ever," Rusty muttered. "I can't believe I was so naive."

"Rusty, whatever you do from this time forward, trust God to lead you, not a man." He continued, "Please, for the sake of your family, get to know God by studying his Word. Study it with your family so they'll get to know Him, too. He will bless you for your faithfulness and guide you through the days ahead."

"Pastor, you're a good man. I wish I had run into you before I got involved in all this prophetic foolishness," Rusty acknowledged.

"Rusty, I'll keep you and your family in my prayers."

Rusty left to rejoin his family. Horatio returned to his cabin to begin packing for his morning departure from the ship.

Day 56
January 28th - Monday

At six o'clock, the ship was back in port and the off-loading process was well underway. Passengers, who only days ago were being warmly welcomed aboard, were being hurried off the ship as though they were trespassers. The cruise line availed a continental breakfast to the exiting passengers, but gone was the leisurely, omnipresent ambiance that the guests had become accustomed to during the past week.

With his bags packed, Horatio was ready to leave by eight o'clock. He decided to skip breakfast aboard and seek out a Denny's restaurant. He had a taste for a "Grand Slam" breakfast, similar to the one that Ellen Willis had prepared that morning in his kitchen. He had never fully appreciated the beauty of family until that day. Now, he is ready for a wife and children of his own.

His attention shifted to Rene. He experienced a connection with her that was unlike any relationship he had known before. Every day since his sabbatical began, he and Rene communicated by phone and text. When he was with her, it was as though he had rediscovered a joy and enthusiasm for life that he hadn't known for a very long time. Having failed at his last romantic relationship, he was guarded about letting any emotion within him be made public. It was difficult for him to conceal his enthusiasm whenever they talked.

Lord, is this of You? he pondered, as he remembered his dream about Rene that had caused him to wake up shaken and crying. *What was that about? Was I created to be alone?* he questioned time and again. It had been thirty-three days since he had the dream and, as yet, the Lord hadn't responded to his prayers for understanding. Uncertain of the probability of a future with Rene, he couldn't deny that life with her would be a blessing. His focus next moved to her son, Daniel. He prayed often that God would reunite them and that he would share in their joy as a member of their family.

After a satisfying breakfast, he registered at a waterfront hotel and toured the area in a rented car. Horatio appreciated the break from being on-call aboard the ship. He returned to his hotel at seven o'clock and placed calls to Rene and his parents. In the course of the conversations, he mentioned that he was considering taking a road trip to Baton Rouge,

Dallas, and Denver. He chose to get a good night's rest before considering his plan further. At ten thirty, he retired for the evening.

Day 57
January 29th - Tuesday

At nine thirty, he was sleeping soundly when his cell phone rang.

"Good morning, Pastor. This is Sam Wooden."

"Good morning, Sam, is everything all right?"

"Nothing God can't handle but, I was wondering when are you coming back, this way?"

"To be honest, Sam, I hadn't really decided. I was going to play it by ear for the next two weeks," he began, "but, if you need me to, I can be back there by tonight."

"Might not be a bad idea," Sam suggested. "Those rascals on the trustee board are up to something. I can feel it in my bones."

"Sam, that's not your bones, it's the Holy Spirit speaking to you. Pay close attention. God's Spirit will never steer you wrong. I'll be home tonight. I'll call you when I get in."

"Thanks, Pastor. I'll talk to you, then."

Horatio's attention shifted to his conversation with Billy Nelson and all that he revealed about his father's wicked ways. With his father dead, it was likely that there was some confusion being conjured up by his successors. Despite the fact that Horatio was cutting his vacation short, there was a huge upside. He would get to see Rene, sooner. The times that he had spoken with her, while on his sabbatical, seemed never enough. He spent the next few minutes arranging for transportation back to Boston. After that, he had breakfast as planned. He made his way to the airport and was on a three o'clock flight home.

The final leg of his flight touched down at seven fifteen that evening. He retrieved his bags and made his way to the airport garage shortly thereafter. He stopped by the Village Mart to pick up a few items before going home. While standing in the checkout line, a voice from another aisle called out.

"Hi, Pastor Smiley. I thought you were still on vacation?" It was Timmy Andrews.

"Timmy, my friend. So good to see you. How is everything going?"

"Pastor, it's like my life is totally different. Ever since I got my head straight and started caring about Sara and the baby like I should, I've come to understand how much God loves me." He continued, "Just think, He gave me another chance at getting my life right. After I met with you that day in your office, I went home and talked with my mom. Pastor, I think that was the best conversation I've ever had with her. So many things that she spoke to me before about God I realized were true. Things that I rejected completely are now my reality. Thanks for the time you invested in me. It really made a difference."

"Timmy, you may find this difficult to understand, but the time that you shared with me blessed me more than you can understand."

Timmy was touched. "Really, Pastor?"

"Really," Horatio affirmed.

"Not trying to be a bother, but can Sara and I get together with you, again?"

"I'd love to. How is your schedule looking?" Horatio asked.

"I'm off tomorrow. Mind if I call Sara and check with her about her schedule?"

"By all means," Horatio said as he handed Timmy his phone.

Timmy called Sara at her job. She confirmed that she was off the next day. The three agreed to meet in Horatio's office at one o'clock for lunch and counseling the following afternoon. By this time, they were standing outside by Horatio's car. Timmy continued to thank Horatio for everything he helped him to understand. Returning home, he found everything as he had left it. He was in bed by ten o'clock.

Day 58
January 30th - Wednesday

At eight fifteen, Horatio awoke to the sound of a familiar knocking at his front door. It was unmistakably that of Sam Wooden. He called out, "Sam. Is that you?"

"Morning, Pastor. Okay if I wait out here while you get dressed?"

"Sam, it's too cold to stand outside. I'll meet you at the church."

"Can't do that. The trustees took my key from me a week ago," Sam explained. "Only the trustees and Reverend Bell have keys, now."

Horatio was in disbelief. "Sam, stop playing."

"Pastor, I'm not playin'." He continued, "I told you something was going on with those scoundrels. Pastor, as soon as you left for vacation, Arthur and the other trustees started acting crazy. They took my key and started talking about I can't be trusted because I'm too close to the pastor. Then they mentioned something about some compromising pictures that they are going to present at a special church meeting to have you fired."

Horatio was heated but, he tried to play it down. "Sam, come on in while I get dressed. We'll head over to the church afterward. We really need to pray."

"Pastor, I'm fine with that."

Twenty minutes later, Horatio and Sam were at the church. Before going into the sanctuary, Horatio went to his office. Everything appeared to be undisturbed and in order. Returning to the sanctuary, Sam was already deep into his prayer. Positioning himself alongside Sam, the two prayed that God would expose the wickedness that was being perpetrated against Horatio. They prayed that God's divine justice would be administered and those responsible would repent of their misdeeds. Sam discussed some of the church-related events that took place during Horatio's absence. From all that Sam explained, it was clear that this was a well-timed, concerted effort by the church's trustees to bring confusion and division into the Good Shepherd community of believers. As their conversation continued, they could hear the church's front door open.

"Hello. Pastor, are you here? Hello." The voice was immediately recognizable. It was Rene.

He became animated as he called to her, "Rene, we're in here. C'mon in."

Sam noticed the shift in his demeanor, but he chose to act oblivious to the change. Horatio walked hurriedly towards Rene and met her mid-sanctuary. It was the first time they had seen each other in sixteen days. If not for Sam's presence, an embrace was certain to have followed. They settled for a hand hold that had *I missed you* written all over it. Forgetting that they weren't alone, they began giggling, as if they were people in love.

Sam couldn't ignore it any longer.

"Pastor, is this your sister?" he chided.

Horatio introduced Rene to Sam as his "friend."

Rene said that she drove by the church daily to make sure everything was okay. When she noticed his car in the driveway, she decided to stop and say hello. That he was back was no surprise to her. They had spoken with each other regularly while he was away on vacation.

Sam and Horatio brought her up to speed on all that had gone on while he was away. She asked if any of the trustees were aware of his return. Believing that they weren't, a plan was devised to have Horatio remain out of sight until the special church meeting was to take place. He booked a room at a Marriott hotel a few miles outside of Scituate. Quickly making his exit before anyone else would notice that he was back in town, he and Sam agreed to speak again that afternoon. He walked Rene to her car and then went next door to pack up some clothes and toiletries. On his way to the hotel, he remembered the one o'clock meeting he had scheduled with Timmy and Sara. He called Timmy and instructed them to come to the hotel. He cautioned Timmy not to tell anyone about seeing him. He promised to explain everything at their meeting.

As he made his way to the Marriott, his emotions shifted back and forth between the situation with the trustees and seeing Rene. The first resulted in frustration. The second filled his heart with joy. He remembered Sam speaking of "compromising pictures" that would be presented at the church meeting. Although curious, he was confident that there was nothing to be concerned about. He lived his life as an open book. *No secrets, no worries*, he thought to himself. His focus shifted back to Rene. Seeing her, today, put to rest any doubt in his mind that she was the woman for him. A silly grin formed on his face as he continued to think about her. While the nightmare he had of Rene, Daniel, his parents, and others hadn't repeated, he was mindful to always guard against placing himself in a position of being hurt or rejected, relationally. He needed her in his life to be happy but, how could he be sure she felt the same way?

He arrived at the hotel and checked in uneventfully. He dared not leave too early for his meeting with Timmy and Sara, concerned that he would risk a greater probability of being recognized. He remained in his room until one o'clock. While waiting, he recalled his conversation with Billy Nelson. Horatio assumed, incorrectly, that the wickedness perpetrated by Billy's father had come to an end as the result of his death.

"Lord, be glorified in all of this mess," he prayed.

****

As the warming sunlight entered the room through two large windows, he recalled the touch of Rene's hand on his, her smile, and the way she made him feel when with her. It was then that he decided to ask her to marry him. At that moment, nothing mattered more to him. He prayed that God would touch her heart to accept him as her husband. Was there any chance that she would entertain the thought of a life with him as her husband? How could he propose to her without appearing to be insensitive to her grieving about Daniel? He didn't intend for his proposal to be received as a substitute for the joy that would come in her reunification with Daniel. She repeatedly voiced her belief that, with respect to Daniel, she had let God down and, as a consequence, didn't deserve to be happy.

Lord, I need your help, he prayed. At one o'clock, he put on his jacket and headed for the hotel lobby for his meeting with Timmy and Sara.

Sitting in the foyer of the hotel were Timmy and Sara looking like two adolescents instructed by their parents to sit and behave until they returned. They didn't appear to be old enough to date. Yet, there they sat awaiting marital counseling. They noticed Horatio entering the lobby and waved to him. They moved to the coffee shop to continue their conversation. Horatio asked if either had made mention to anyone about their meeting. They assured him that they hadn't. He went on to explain all that he had learned about the special meeting scheduled for Sunday at the church. Timmy and Sara promised to be present. He asked for an update of all that had taken place with them since they last met. Sara was still working for an employment agency as a receptionist. She told Horatio that she was presently assigned to working part-time at the Mercy Ministries' Home for Children. His mouth dropped wide open.

"Sara, did I understand you to say Mercy Ministries?"

"Yes, Pastor. Are you familiar with them?" The look on his face caused her to ask, "Is everything okay, Pastor? Is something wrong?"

He asked Sara if she knew of a little boy in the care of the orphanage named Daniel. "He's five years old," he added.

"No, Pastor. I can't say that I do." She continued, "I'm not very familiar with much of anything that takes place outside of the office area. Lately, everybody's been pushing to get through the agency's latest round of adoption applications. That's why they brought in a few of us temps," Sara explained.

"When did the adoption event take place?" Horatio asked.

"Actually, it took place last week," she said.

"Last week? Sara, I need you to find out if anyone took out adoption papers on Daniel," he instructed. "Get back to me with anything that you can find out. Okay?"

"I'll look into it but, please understand, I'm only a temp. Most of the files are confidential, so I don't have access to them. I'll try but I can't promise a whole lot."

"Sara, whatever you can find out would be greatly appreciated," he said. "I met a young lady there about a month ago. She was the receptionist. Her name was something Vega."

"Do you mean Sheila?"

"Yes. That's her. Sheila Vega," he recalled. "A really sweet, young lady."

"We eat lunch together," Sara continued. "You know, Pastor, maybe Sheila can help us find out if there is anything going on with Daniel."

"That would be great." Horatio appeared to be encouraged.

His obvious interest in Daniel came without explanation, so he decided to share a bit of Daniel's history. After sharing his reason for being so concerned about Daniel, he concluded with a statement that surprised even him.

"I'm in love with Daniel's mother," he confessed.

Timmy and Sara were so happy for him that they began fist-pumping and hugging each him. Timmy asked, "Does she know about your feelings, Pastor?"

Horatio acknowledged his apprehension and gave a few reasons why. Understanding that certain boundaries were not to be crossed between a pastor and his flock, he was guarded in how much information he shared about his personal life.

Sara promised to find out everything she could about Daniel. Horatio gave them his cell phone number and instructed her to keep him in the loop about anything having to do with Daniel. They spent a while discussing God's precepts for holy matrimony according to scripture. After their time together, Timmy and Sara said good bye, committing to be at the Sunday worship service.

Horatio returned to his room and placed a call to Sam as promised. Sam's wife, Teresa, answered and told him that Sam was at work. She asked if Sam could reach him at his at home, when he returned from work. He told Teresa that Sam would be able to contact him on his cell phone. After the call ended, he continued to think about Daniel's possible adoption and the emergency church meeting. That was enough to make his head start to ache.

He called Rene at eight o'clock to say hello. Not wanting to cause her any unnecessary stress, he decided not to mention anything about his conversation with Sara. After his call with Rene ended, he ordered dinner and watched television for the rest of the evening.

Day 59
January 31st - Thursday

Throughout the night and into the morning, Horatio pondered all of what Sara had spoken about taking place at Mercy Ministries. Looking over at the clock radio, he could see that it was eight forty-three.

"I feel like I didn't sleep a wink last night," he mumbled. He couldn't remember being this tired since his sabbatical began. "Can't go anywhere I might be seen. Can't let anyone know I'm back in town. Man, this is like being in prison," he muttered. *I need to see Rene. It's about time I tell her how I feel. I wonder if she can meet me for lunch?*

He called her on her cell phone. "Good morning, Ms. Brock."

"Good morning, Pastor Smiley," she responded.

At the sound of her voice, he began to feel better. They chuckled mischievously. "How is your morning going today?" he asked.

"It's crazy around here. We're getting ready for our annual operations audit. Every year the main office puts us through the wringer. They're always looking for a reason to justify terminating the senior employees, so they can bring in younger, lower-paid college kids in the name of efficiency."

"That's a shame."

"Yeah. Its criminal the way they treat experienced people."

"So, it sounds like accepting my invitation for lunch would be out of the question?"

"I'd love to but I wouldn't feel right taking time away with all that's going on here," she responded, disappointedly.

"Probably just as well. Someone from the church might have recognized me. Okay if I give you a call tonight?"

"I'd like that." She sighed.

"Well, then, guess we'll talk later," he conceded. "Bye-bye for now." Horatio remained in his hotel room reading, praying, and channel surfing for the remainder of the day.

Day 60
February 1st - Friday

George and Mattie were sitting at their breakfast table examining the calendar that Mattie received at the New Year's Eve Watch meeting. Today was her blotch date and she was excited. Recalling first-hand accounts of the way God moved in Henry Williams' and Jenny Murray's circumstances, Mattie eagerly awaited her blessing.

"George, how do you think God is going to bless us today?"

"My goodness, Mattie," George replied. "Weren't you paying attention?" He laughed. "Did you honestly miss it?"

"Miss what?" Mattie was puzzled. "What did I miss?"

"Babe, we woke up this morning holding onto each other. We have a warm comfortable home." He continued, "Our health and finances aren't the greatest, but the Lord makes sure we have what we need."

Feeling convicted, Mattie agreed, "You're right, party pooper."

Just then, they heard a vehicle pulling into the driveway. Looking out, they immediately recognized it as the Willises' truck. George got up to open the door.

"Good Morning, Ellen. Good morning, Ted. What brings you here so early this morning?"

"This should speak for itself," Ted said, smiling as he placed an envelope in George's hand.

"Well, now, what's this?" he asked as he removed the document from the envelope. "Praise God. It's the occupancy certificate, Mattie."

"That's wonderful," Mattie responded. "Good job, you two."

"It wasn't anything we did. It was the favor of God," Ellen explained. "The building inspector who processed the application remembered approving your property, years ago. Ted had to sign an affidavit that he would install the required smoke and carbon monoxide detectors before anyone could occupy the building. Ted informed him he had already installed them, so the inspector signed the occupancy certificate, right then."

"Yeah," Ted added. "God is truly amazing. Then, the guy laughed and said something about 'Bill Nelson must be turning over in his grave.' Not sure what he meant by that. Anyway, the guy told us to call him if he could help us with anything else."

"Ted, I do believe that you're beginning to understand how wonderful God is." George chuckled.

"Must've had something to do with the woodshed time you spent with our pastor," Mattie said. Everyone laughed.

"Well, what say we head over to Mercy Ministries and give them a copy of the certificate. That's the last item on the application they need to get us approved."

"With pleasure," Ted responded.

Mattie and Ellen chose to remain at home while George and Ted left to drop off the paperwork. Once there, George and Ted went into the reception area of the administration building. They introduced themselves and asked the receptionist to page Cora, their case worker. A few minutes later, Cora appeared.

"Hello, Mr. Heywood and Mr. Willis. How are you gentlemen doing today?"

"Good morning, Cora," George began. "We just received the Occupancy Certificate for our building, hot off the press. We wanted to get it to you right away."

"Wonderful," Cora said. "This completes your foster care certification package. I'll enter the information in your file and contact you as soon as we have a client for you."

"Thanks, Cora. We appreciate that," Ted said.

"Say hello to Mrs. Heywood and Mrs. Willis for me."

"We sure will. You have a great day," George said as he and Ted exited.

****

George and Ted returned home, directly. As they pulled into the driveway, they could see Mattie and Ellen standing at the door, urgently waving them inside. Presuming there was a problem, Ted ran to Ellen and Mattie to see what was going on. George was close behind.

"What's wrong?" he asked.

"Ted, everything's fine," Ellen assured him.

"We received a phone call…," Mattie began as George walked through the door.

"Phone call? From who?" George asked.

"George, relax and just listen," Mattie said. "Cora called from Mercy Ministries. She said that her supervisor is looking for a host home for five siblings ranging in age from four to eleven years old. She asked if we would be interested. Ellen and I told her that we would call her back after you returned home and had a chance to discuss it."

"Wow. You hear that, Ted?" George asked.

"Yeah, talk about moving fast," Ted began. "We expected that it would be at least two or three months before we got a single placement. But five ... NOW?"

"And, to turn the pressure up a notch, Cora needs an answer before noon today," Ellen added.

"Ephesians 4:6 tells us, 'Be anxious about nothing but in everything by prayer and supplication with thanksgiving, let your request be made known to God,' so let's pray," George suggested.

"Good idea," Mattie said.

The four went into the renovated living space for prayer. In that time, they prayed that God would confirm that it was he who brought the opportunity to them. At the conclusion of the prayer, they agreed to not respond to Cora until God responded to them. It was ten forty-five. After a few minutes more in the renovated section of the building, they returned to the kitchen.

****

At eleven o'clock, the Heywoods' telephone rang. George answered the call. It was Cora.

"Heywood residence," he announced.

"Hi, George. It's Cora."

"Cora. I know that we owe you a twelve o'clock telephone call, but...," George began. "We're here together. Is it okay if I put you on the speaker?"

"Certainly, of course. I'd like that," Cora began. "Good morning. I apologize for hounding you all about this placement," she began. "I could get fired for this, but I feel the need to discuss the client's situation and, more specifically, why I am reaching out to you as I am. This discussion needs to take place quickly and in person. May I come by so we can talk?"

"Yes, please come over," George replied.

"See you in twenty minutes," Cora promised.

****

Cora's car was heard pulling into the driveway right on schedule. Soon following, came a knock at the door.

"Cora, come on in," Mattie greeted her. George, Ellen, and Ted were sitting at the table.

"Please, Cora," George said as he and Ted stood to their feet, "sit down."

"Thank you," Cora replied as she sat between Mattie and Ellen. "A few days ago, five children were found living in an abandoned house in Springfield. Their mother's body was found lying on a piece of mattress in a room adjacent to where the children were sleeping. From what I understand, she died of natural causes. The family had been staying in this filthy, boarded-up building for less than a month, according to people in the neighborhood. The two older children tried to care for their younger siblings as best they could."

"Oh, my Lord. Those poor children." Mattie shook her head. Cora continued, "The mother had a history of health problems but she didn't seek medical care because, according to the children, they would be taken from her if she was hospitalized. The family lived as nomads in squalid, inhumane conditions, as a result. No heat, no running water. Just the clothes on their back and the love of a dying mother."

"Those poor children," Ellen grieved.

"Yeah, and it gets worse." Cora elaborated, "The children have no known relatives. They're all alone. Their grandparents are deceased. Their father's whereabouts are unknown. That's why I brought this opportunity to you."

"Why us?" George asked.

"All I can tell you is that I believe this is where these children belong. I am thoroughly convinced that they will be loved and nurtured here the way God intended." Cora continued, "I am relatively new to the Mercy Ministries organization, but I have worked in the state's foster care system for fourteen years. For some time now, I've heard about the good things that you have done for the children in your care."

George and Mattie were flattered. They were unaware of any recognition they had earned as a result of the care and encouragement they had shown their clients, so many years ago.

"Really? You know about that?" George asked.

"George, to this day the standard of care that you and Mattie established remains unequalled," Cora confided. "The union of the Heywood and Willis families as foster care providers represents the best hope for these children. They need to live together in an environment with foster parents who are truly committed to their well-being."

"Wow. I don't know what to say," George responded.

"Please, say yes. I promise that you won't regret it," Cora said.

"Is there any chance of meeting the children beforehand?" Ted asked.

"No. Our agency's policy is very strict on that." Cora emphasized, "Way too many problems with preplacement client-provider interviews."

"But suppose it's not a good fit?" Ellen asked.

"Tell you what," Cora began, "I'll let the Heywoods answer that question."

"We pray," George continued. "We pray that if it is God's will, He will work it out. And if it isn't, well, He will work that out, too."

"Got it," Ted said.

"And, how," Ellen confirmed.

"Cora, we'd appreciate a few minutes to discuss all that you've shared with us. This is not a commitment to be casually considered," Mattie explained.

"I agree. Whatever your decision, I need to know your answer, one way or another, by three o'clock this afternoon. The children are being discharged from University Hospital, today. If I haven't arranged for their housing by three o'clock, this case will be placed with another agency."

"Duly noted," George replied. "We'll call you with our decision before three o'clock. Promise."

Cora left to return to her office.

It took only a few minutes for the group discussion to conclude in unanimous agreement to accept Cora's proposal. Each and all were enthusiastic about the opportunity to introduce stability, joy, and encouragement to the five forgotten children. George called Cora and informed her of their decision. She was delighted and asked them to meet her at Mercy Ministries right away to process the paperwork.

****

That meeting concluded, quickly. In the course of preparing for the children's move, Cora arranged to have five beds delivered to the Heywoods' residence in time for their arrival.

After returning to the Heywoods' home, Ted and Ellen scrambled to return to their motel room and pack up their clothes and personal effects for the relocation to their new home. George and Mattie agreed to pick up Noah and Becky after school.

****

With the assistance of Noah and Becky, George, Mattie, Ted, and Ellen had the children's bedroom picture-book perfect, in time for their arrival. Cora promised to call when she was on her way.

At six thirty, the call came to let them know that the children had just been discharged from the hospital. Cora's plan was to stop along the way to buy burgers and fries for the children. George assured her that everyone there was ready and waiting to meet them.

****

Cora and the children arrived at the Heywoods' home at eight o'clock. She ushered in three of the five children.

"Welcome," George invited with a smile as he held the door open.

Cora and three of the children waited in the kitchen. She sat at the table with Mattie and Ellen, while the siblings remained standing. Appearing to be emotionally spent, it was difficult for them to respond to George's invitation with equal enthusiasm. Noah and Becky appeared from an adjoining room. Noah welcomed Jeremiah, Elijah, and Hope as Becky looked on shyly.

"Dad, is it okay if they watch the movie with us?"

"If Mr. and Mrs. Heywood have no objection, that'll be fine," Ted responded.

"That's a good idea. You children go enjoy your movie." Mattie continued, "I'll bring some popcorn and water to you in just a minute. And remember, feet on the floor, not on the chairs," she cautioned. The children understood exactly what was expected of them.

"That's my bride. You've still got it, Babe," George chuckled. It was clear that Mattie was the disciplinarian and George was a soft touch.

"Now, isn't someone missing?" Mattie asked.

"Yes. Faith and Charity are still out in the car. Charity is having a tough time with everything that's happened. Faith asked to be left alone with her for a while longer," Cora explained.

"Can I be of help in any way?" Mattie asked.

"Not just yet. I'm going to trust in Faith's power of persuasion," Cora replied. "From what I understand, she handled things very nicely before and during their time at the hospital."

"Don't let them stay in the car too much longer. It's thirty-nine degrees outside," Ted cautioned.

"I'll give them five minutes more," Cora said.

Five minutes elapsed without any indication of Faith and Charity heading toward the house. Cora's concern for their safety caused her to be distracted from the conversation taking place with the Heywoods and the Willises.

"Cora, may I make a suggestion?" Ellen asked.

"Of course."

"I'd like to go out to the car with Becky and invite the girls inside."

"Ellen, as soon as I saw Becky, that very thought came to mind." Cora chuckled.

Becky was summoned to the kitchen where Ellen explained the situation to her. "Becky, there is a shy, little girl outside who we would like to invite to come inside and share some popcorn with us. We need to go introduce ourselves to her."

Always, 'Mother's little helper,' Becky responded, "Okay, Mommy. Can I bring her my coat? It's cold outside."

"That's a great idea," Ellen said as she hugged her daughter and went in search of the girls. Soon after, Ellen and Becky returned with Faith and Charity close behind.

"Faith, Charity, please say hello to Mr. and Mrs. Heywood and Mr. and Mrs. Willis," Cora instructed.

Faith walked over and hugged Mattie. "Thank you for inviting us into your home," she said.

"Faith, the pleasure is ours," Mattie responded as Faith continued to cling to her.

"And, what's your name, young lady?" George asked.

"This is my friend, Charity," Becky announced.

"Charity," George repeated. "That's a very pretty name," he continued. "Charity, would you and Becky like your very own bowl of popcorn to enjoy while you watch the movie?"

Charity's eyes grew wide, "Yes, thank you," she responded.

With a bowl of popcorn in hand, Becky led Charity into the adjoining room to watch the movie. The children enjoyed the movie, the popcorn, and their newfound friends.

Faith was tired, but thankful, for the generosity that she and her siblings received. She was escorted next door to the Willises' residence where she, along with her brothers and sisters, would stay. As she went from room to room, tears formed in her eyes. Each room was spacious enough to easily accommodate three beds. There was a bathroom for the girls and one for the boys. Everything was perfect.

She hugged Ellen and Cora and continued to say, "Thank you. Ms. Cora, you were right. This is a nice home."

They left to retrieve the children from the other building. The children's reaction to their new home overshadowed any evidence of sadness or anxiety that was previously present. Laughter could be heard throughout the building. All of the children were asleep in their beds by ten thirty. It had been a long, eventful day for them. It had also been a long day for Cora, the Heywoods, and the Willises. Before leaving, Cora promised to return the following morning to assist in getting the children settled in.

Day 61
February 2nd – Saturday

"Breakfast in ten minutes. Rise and shine, guys!" Ted called out with a voice that was sure to awaken the deepest of sleepers. Little faces appeared in the hall doorways, to see what the commotion was about.

"Breakfast in ten minutes," Ted repeated. "Wash up, get dressed, and last one to the kitchen has to wash dishes."

At that, the level of responsiveness increased significantly. The sound of laughter and teasing caused Ted to chuckle.

"Thank you, Lord, for our new home," he said.

****

In the kitchen, two folding tables were positioned end-to-end to accommodate everyone. Ellen worked the pancake griddle. Faith served the food and Becky poured the juice. The interaction taking place between the children caused Ted and Ellen to join in. God had unexpectedly increased the Willis family member count to nine.

In the middle of a dream-sharing discussion, George, Mattie, and Cora came to visit. "Good morning. Look at all the happy faces." Mattie laughed.

"Reminds me of mornings here long ago," George said, as he hugged Ted and Ellen.

"This is wonderful, just wonderful," Cora added.

Faith rose from her chair, walked over to Mattie, and gave her a big hug. "Good morning, Nana."

"Nana?" Mattie asked. "Faith, I like the sound of that." She chuckled. "I thought I heard you call me 'Nana' last night when you hugged me," Mattie continued, "but, I wasn't sure."

"Nana?" George repeated. "Mattie, is there something you want to share with me?" George chuckled.

"Well, George, remember the summer I went to care for my sick mother?" Mattie said with a straight face.

"Woman, your mother was never sick a day in her life," he recalled aloud. George's eyes grew wide.

Mattie attempted to maintain her best poker face to no avail. The kitchen erupted with laughter. "I had you thinking, Babe." Mattie laughed.

"George, you should have seen your face," Ted mused.

"That's all right, Poppa. Don't let them tease you," Faith encouraged.

At that, Mattie and George's eyes met. "What did you call us, child?" George asked.

"Nana and Poppa," Faith responded. "Isn't that your names?"

"Child, we haven't been called Nana and Poppa for more than twenty years. Wouldn't you say, Mattie?" George asked.

"Oh, my. Fifteen years, at least," Mattie confirmed.

"How did you know about that?" George asked Faith.

"Our mother told us," she explained. "She always talked about the time she lived with Nana and Poppa."

"Your mother? What's your mother's name, child?" Mattie asked.

"Courtney Gillespie."

George and Mattie's mouths were agape. "You're my little Courtney's children?" Mattie asked, taken aback. "Oh, George, they're Courtney's babies. Children, come give your Nana a big hug," she invited. The children quickly ran to Mattie and George and received a loving hug.

"This is wonderful." George was giddy.

"I wanted to tell you earlier, but our agency's policy prevented me from mentioning it," Cora explained. "These are Courtney's children and, from what I understand, she never stopped speaking about her time with you, both."

"My mother let me wear the ring that you gave her as a Christmas gift," Faith offered, while proudly displaying the ring.

"George, look at this. Remember we gave our girls those rings for Christmas? And, look here, it says, 'Faith, Hope, Charity.' This is amazing! Who would have guessed that Courtney would give birth to three beautiful daughters named Faith, Hope, and Charity. I can't believe this, George. This is amazing."

"Amazing doesn't begin to describe what's taking place, here," George agreed.

The Willises were as excited as were George and Mattie. Ted set up three more folding chairs so George, Mattie, and Cora could join them for breakfast. Ellen continued cranking out pancakes while George and Mattie recalled humorous events that involved Courtney.

The stories that were exchanged about Courtney by George, Mattie, and her children held everyone's interest. At times, there was laughter and other times, tears.

The conversation continued until noontime, when Cora informed the Heywoods and Willises that she brought along some clothing vouchers. The children were instructed to clean their rooms, shower, and return quickly, so that they could go shop for clothes. Excitedly, the children complied. George and Mattie remained at home while two vehicles shuttled the group to various department stores where dreams delayed would no longer be, dreams denied.

Returning home four hours later, the children emerged from the cars with arms full of bags and boxes. Mattie invited everyone in for supper. Cora excused herself, promising to return the following week. A meal of meatloaf, corn, mashed potatoes, and gravy was enjoyed by all. The evening concluded with preparations being made to attend Good Shepherd's Sunday morning service.

Day 62
February 3rd - Sunday

Horatio checked out of the hotel and was on his way to the church by ten fifteen. He intended to be tardy in his arrival to guard against being seen by the trustees or their supporters. Good Shepherd's Sunday morning church service always began promptly at ten thirty. By the number of cars in the parking lot and along the roadside, it was clear that the church was packed. He entered the foyer and immediately was greeted by Darryl Burch, head usher.

"Pastor, so good to see you," Darryl said, extending his right hand. Horatio, placing his finger to his lips, motioned that the man be quiet. Darryl responded accordingly and, in a hushed tone, Horatio promised to explain it all to him, later.

Darryl whispered, "Pastor, I know all about what those trustees are trying to do. Sam told us what was going on but he didn't tell us that you were going to be here, today."

Again, Horatio placed his finger to his lips and asked, "Are there any seats at the back of the sanctuary?"

"Let me take a look." Darryl disappeared through a set of double doors and quickly returned having located a seat to one side, obscured by a structural support column.

Horatio took his seat and began scanning the congregation to identify those in attendance. First, his eyes moved to the front left corner of the sanctuary where the trustees occupied the first two pews. He observed that their corporate demeanor was one of smugness, as usual. Reverend Bell was so deep into his sermon that he didn't notice Horatio's entrance.

Next, he located the Woodens, the Heywoods, the Brocks, the Willises, and many more of the faithful church families. The message and its delivery by Reverend Bell was unemotional. Several of those in attendance struggled to remain focused.

After the benedictory prayer was given, Arthur Mutton stood to his feet and requested that all who were not going to stay for the church meeting leave quickly. With the exception of Reverend Bell, not one person moved from their seat.

At that point, Arthur called the meeting to order. He took his position behind the lectern and began his presentation. As he read from a statement, unanimously, approved by the trustee board stating the purpose of the meeting, Horatio moved from his position at the rear of the church to sit in the pew with the other trustees. A majority of church members, witnessing his return, stood to their feet, applauding. The trustees became noticeably uneasy, as an *Oh, CRAP!* expression registered on each of their faces.

Arthur attempted to complete the reading of the prepared statement, but began to stutter and sputter, like an engine that was running out of gas. At that point, he summoned the other trustees to join him on the platform. Reluctantly, they came forward and stood with him. Continuing on, he referred to Article 28 of the church's bylaws that stated: "Having the majority consent of the trustee board, a vote of no confidence in pastoral leadership may be called in a meeting of the general membership of Good Shepherd when evidence of inappropriate or contradictory conduct is supported by any church member or investigatory agency."

Immediately, a barrage of boos and objections were directed at the trustees. "Who's bringing these outrageous accusations against our pastor? Show your face!" a man's voice blurted out.

"Show us your evidence!" a woman demanded.

Horatio reflected on his nightmare about the meeting that had taken place in the school gymnasium. While he fully appreciated that the voices were energized in a show of support for him, he stood to his feet and asked for calm.

"Please, let the trustees speak. Give them the opportunity to present their case." He continued, "I'd like to know what I am being accused of."

The voices were quieted. "Arthur, you have the floor. Continue. Please."

Horatio could sense a shift in the atmosphere as he prayed for God's divine justice to enter in. Arthur attempted to stay on point with his evidence by producing four photographs from a manila envelope. "These pictures will explain everything," he said as he passed them first to the other trustees who, in turn, passed two of them to Horatio.

The other pictures were, intentionally, given to church members for effect. Two photos were of Horatio and Kelli Brock hugging at the coffee shop. Another was of him speaking to Thad, the hair stylist, at Bill Nelson's funeral service. Studying the photos, Horatio asked, "This is your evidence? Are you suggesting that these pictures indicate inappropriate behavior in some way?"

The trustees stared accusingly, but did not respond. Another picture made its way back to him. He identified it to be a picture of him sitting on a bench along Front Street, at night, holding Sara's hands as they prayed.

Horatio, again, demanded, "How in God's name are these pictures incriminating?"

Uncertain as to whether it was his unexpected presence or the realization that their evidence was too weak to withstand any measure of scrutiny, the trustees stood looking at each other, searching for a worthwhile response.

Finally, Arthur managed to blurt out, "Bill Nelson said you couldn't be trusted. These pictures confirm his suspicions."

"Don't you dare mention my husband's name," Mrs. Nelson called out, as she walked hastily to the front of the church and stood alongside Horatio. "Arthur, you and the rest of you men ought to be ashamed of yourselves," she continued. "I know my husband had his issues, but don't try to pin this foolishness on him. Either take ownership of this nonsense or walk away."

The church erupted in applause and laughter. A chorus of "Amen!" resonated throughout the sanctuary.

Mrs. Nelson wasn't finished, yet. She was not a woman to be easily calmed. "It's because of you, trustees, my husband included, Lord bless the dead, that I stopped coming to Good Shepherd. I couldn't stand to listen another minute to you pompous knuckleheads conspiring to build monuments to yourself at the expense of the church's financial integrity and the good people who never did you any harm. Arthur, what's going on with that building fund money that the trustees are managing for the church? Do you want to tell everyone what you all plan to do with that money or should I?" Mrs. Nelson was mad.

Arthur was flustered. While he stood there having a *Lord, make me invisible, please* moment, his cohorts slithered away like serpents off the platform.

Mrs. Nelson continued, "The whole lot of you trustees need to repent, apologize, and tender your resignations."

Horatio reached over and took Mrs. Nelson's hand. He walked onto the platform with her. He motioned to Arthur to hand over the microphone and Arthur, sheepishly, complied. Cheers and applause continued.

"Members of the Church of the Good Shepherd," Horatio began, "In the presence of all here today concerning this matter of the trustees, each and all, Mrs. Nelson has presented a motion to relieve them of their responsibilities. What is your pleasure?"

Sam Wooden, standing in front of the platform pointing his finger at the trustees one by one, spoke two words that will forever haunt the five men: "YOU"RE FIRED!"

A wave of "I second the motion" surged throughout the sanctuary. Children who had no understanding of what they were endorsing repeatedly shouted, "YOU'RE FIRED!"

"It's great to be home." Horatio chuckled. "I missed you, all. Trustees included." The congregation laughed and continued to applaud. "Would any trustee wish to rebut the unanimous position of the church membership?" he asked.

There before the church stood five speechless men who could only respond with their bobble-like heads moving from left to right.

"Members of Church of the Good Shepherd," Horatio began. "Are you ready for the question?"

"Yes," was the unanimous response.

"All in favor of accepting the resignations of the trustee board members, respond with a vote of 'Yea!'" he instructed.

Seemingly every voice, young and old, responded in the affirmative.

"And, now, will the votes of 'Nay' be made known?" he requested. Not a nay vote was uttered.

"The vote is carried unanimously," he stated. "Danny," Horatio continued, "as the church's treasurer, I'd like to meet with you tomorrow to sort out the finances. I know that you are very close to Arthur and the others."

"Pastor," Danny began, "you don't have to worry about me. Just tell me when and where you need me to be. I haven't had a good night's sleep in three years, taking orders from these guys."

"Well, hopefully we'll all get some quality sleep from now on." Unsure as to whether or not Danny could be trusted, Horatio set the meet time at five thirty the following evening. After, further, conversation with Danny, he chatted briefly with several church members.

Searching the audience for Rene, he couldn't locate her. Assuming that she had somewhere to go or something to do, he planned to call her later. Deacon and Mrs. Brock greeted Horatio with a hug and an invite for dinner. He explained that he wanted to take the remainder of the day to go home, unpack, and decompress after being gone for the past two weeks. He promised to meet them for lunch the next day and get caught up on his experiences while away.

Excited at the opportunity to speak with Rene and hear her thoughts on the result of the church meeting, he called her that afternoon and again later that evening. Her voice mail answered both times. He left a message asking her to return his call as soon possible.

Day 63
February 4th - Monday

At nine thirty, Horatio called Deacon. "Good morning, Deacon. Am I catching you at a busy time?"

"No, not at all, Pastor. Just getting caught up on the news. I don't know why I bother," he continued, "It never gets any better."

"I know what you mean, Deacon. These days, a little bit of good news has to carry us a long way. Who knows how long it will be before we'll hear more?"

Not quite sure what Horatio was alluding to, Deacon responded, "You can say that, again."

"So, are we still on for lunch today?" Horatio asked.

"You better believe it. How's noon?"

"Noon's fine," Horatio agreed.

"Great. See you then." The call ended.

****

Horatio remained in his office for the remainder of the morning, preparing to deliver the 'news' about his feelings for Rene that he would, soon, share with Deacon and Mrs. Brock. He believed that his intentions would be well received, but was there something that Deacon and Mrs. Brock knew about Rene's feelings for him that they weren't sharing? He was reminded of the phone messages that he left with her the day before. She hadn't, yet, responded. Had something shifted in their friendship that he was unaware of? Painfully, he revisited his previous romantic relationship in Virginia Beach that had crashed and burned. Was he self-deceived in expecting a better outcome in his desire to share his life with Rene?

"Lord, please be with me, on this one. I'm asking for your help. I need Your blessing," he prayed.

The time to leave was fast approaching. He freshened up and locked down his office. Making a quick stop at the Village Mart, he picked up a bouquet of flowers for Mrs. Brock. Driving to the Brock's home, he listened to a Christian radio program. The program host

303

was teaching according to the scripture: Proverbs 18:22. Immediately, he recited the scripture aloud, "Whoso finds a wife finds a good thing and has favor with the Lord." He was convinced that this was God's response to his prayer. "Thank you, Lord! I double thank you, Lord!" he shouted enthusiastically while letting loose with a flurry of fist pumps.

Within 15 minutes, Horatio was standing at the front door of the Brock residence with a bouquet of flowers in hand. Ideally, he would have been presenting the flowers to Rene on bended knee. *All things in time*, he reminded himself as the door swung open.

"Pastor, come on in," Deacon welcomed him with a hug. "Are those for me?" he chided.

"No way, Deacon, my friend. These are for your bride." Horatio laughed. "Aside from the flowers, how are you doing this fine day?"

"Great."

Entering the house, Horatio called out, "Hello, Mother Brock."

"I'm in here," she responded from the kitchen.

"Good afternoon. Beautiful flowers for a beautiful lady," Horatio said, presenting the flowers to her.

"Oh, my goodness. They're beautiful. Thank you." She blushed as she sniffed and named each flower in the bouquet. "Pastor, come sit down. I hope you like beef stew. I cooked up a big pot."

"I love beef stew almost as much as I love your daughter." He laughed.

"What did you just say?" Deacon asked, as though he wanted to be sure that he heard correctly.

"I said: I love Rene," he repeated. "I'm in love with your daughter and I want her to be my wife."

"Oh, my God, Pastor. Are you serious?" Deacon was excited. "When did all this happen? Rene didn't mention a word about this to me."

"Oh, Pastor," Mrs. Brock echoed. "Deacon. Please, take a breath," she cautioned. "Have you told her, Pastor?" By this time, Deacon and his wife were locked in an embrace in the moment of a long, overdue celebration.

"No, I haven't told her yet." He went on to explain, "I didn't want to mention any of this to her without speaking to the both of you first and, hopefully get your blessing."

"Okay. Okay. Pastor, you've got our blessing. Deacon and I couldn't be happier," Mrs. Brock emphasized. Deacon remained speechless.

"Thank you, so much. Your support means the world to me," he confided.

"You said Rene doesn't know, yet?" Deacon remembered. "When are you going to tell her?"

"Well, my plan was to speak with her after I had spoken with you," Horatio explained. "But now, I'm not sure when the time might be right."

"What do you mean, son?" Deacon asked.

"I'm not sure," Horatio began. "It seems as though something is going on with her that she hasn't shared with me. I was hoping that you might be able to let me in on whatever it is that she's dealing with."

"Now that you mention it," Mrs. Brock pondered, "she was a bit quieter than usual, yesterday, after church."

"Well, I didn't notice anything different," Deacon chimed in.

"Deacon, as involved as you were in watching your precious football game, this house could have burned down around you and you wouldn't have noticed," Mrs. Brock reminded him.

"It was a good game," Deacon acknowledged.

"I called Rene twice and left a message but, so far, she hasn't called me back. That's not like her."

"Maybe Kelli can shed a little light on this. Rene might have said something to her." Mrs. Brock continued, "Kelli should be here at three-thirty. She's never late for beef stew. In the mean while, let's eat before the food gets cold." Horatio and the Brocks enjoyed the stew, the conversation, and thoughts of sharing their future together as family.

Promptly at three-thirty, Kelli's car was heard pulling into the driveway. Horatio's car was parked in plain view, so it was no surprise that he was there, when she walked in.

"Hi, Mommy. Hi, Daddy. Hi Pastor," Kelli said, walking into the kitchen. "Everybody's all smiles. What's going on?"

"Have a seat, Kelli. We've got great news to share with you," Deacon informed.

"After the kind of day it's been, I can use some good news. What's going on?"

"If I may," Horatio began, "I've just shared with your mom and dad my feelings for Rene. I'm going to ask her to marry me."

Kelli jumped up and gave him a great big hug. "Pastor, thank you so much for loving Rene." Kelli continued, "She'll be so happy. God knows she's due a boatload of happiness, after all she's been through. Can I see the ring?"

"The ring? The ring!" Horatio was caught off-guard. "In all the excitement, I forgot about the ring. I need to buy an engagement ring right away."

"By the way, what's going on with Rene?" Kelli asked. "She was acting really weird yesterday after church. Is everything okay with her?"

"I was going to ask if you had any idea about what's going on," Mrs. Brock said.

"I have no idea."

At that moment, the house telephone rang. Mrs. Brock answered the call. It was Rene, calling to let her parents know that she would be at their house in a few minutes.

"Oh, no. I've got to go." Horatio jumped up from the table. "Please don't mention anything about what we spoke of today. I need to buy a ring before I say anything to her."

The Brocks promised to say nothing about his visit or anything that had been discussed that afternoon. Deacon agreed to give him a call after Rene left. Horatio was out the driveway within the next three minutes, careful to return home via a route that would not cross with Rene's.

Not long after the taillights of his car cleared the Brocks' driveway, Rene's car was heard pulling into the very spot that his car occupied. Deacon was certain that she recognized Horatio's car leaving out.

"Hi, Daddy. Hi, Mom," Rene said, hugging and kissing her parents, as they met her at the door. "Where's Kelli? I see her car out front."

"In here eating Mom's stew," Kelli called out from the kitchen.

Everyone adjourned to the kitchen, taking a seat at the table. Deacon struggled to maintain his usual demeanor. He was still on cloud nine, as he continued to process all that Horatio had shared, earlier. Mrs. Brock kept a close watch to make sure he didn't spill the beans.

"So, Rene, where did you run to so quickly after church?" Mrs. Brock asked.

"I had something to do, so I didn't hang around."

"It must have been real important the way that you rushed out without saying a word to any of us," Kelli said. "You were mad about something. That much was obvious to anyone who knows you, Rene."

"Look, Kelli. I told you that I had something to deal with. So deal with it." She was agitated.

"Rene, what's gotten into you?" Deacon demanded.

"Daddy, did you get a good look at that picture that was being passed around in church yesterday?"

"What picture? What are you talking about, Rene?" He was puzzled.

"The picture of Kelli and our dear pastor locked in a loving embrace," Rene continued. "It made me sick to my stomach. Some sister you are…."

"Rene, you have no idea what you're talking about!" Kelli interrupted.

"Don't I?" Rene countered, "You and Pastor have been found out. I can't believe I was so gullible. He would never agree to meet with me unless 'Kelli was there to chaperone.' How could I be so stupid? I was so blind. Falling for that chaperone rule of his."

"You are stupid, if you believe any of that, Rene. Don't you have any understanding of what's going on here?" Kelli asked.

"That's enough," Mrs. Brock interrupted. "Rene, have you asked Pastor about the picture? At least give him the opportunity to explain what it was all about before you remove him from your Christmas card list."

"Mom, I don't think that any explanation our beloved Pastor can give me will redeem himself or Kelli."

"Rene, I love you and I understand that you have experienced more than your fair share of disappointment," Deacon began, "but, knowing Pastor as I do, I think you're wrong on this one. He's a good man, an honest man. A man of God. Don't be so quick to burn this bridge. Enough said?"

"Okay, Daddy. I'll speak to him," she promised. "And, he better not confirm what I'm already believing or this family will be looking for a new pastor and quite possibly be minus a younger daughter."

"Oh, I'm so shaken. NOT!" Kelli responded.

"Now, everybody be quiet, please. Eat some stew and show each other some respect," Mrs. Brock insisted.

The atmosphere around the dinner table had shifted from jovial to guarded for the remainder of the evening.

****

Before going home, Horatio stopped by the jewelry store on Front Street. In all the excitement, he forgot the store was closed on Mondays. He decided to wait until the following morning to begin his search for Rene's ring.

Day 64
February 5th - Tuesday

Horatio called the jewelry store at nine thirty. Timmy answered the phone. "Good morning, Front Street Jewelers. Tim, speaking."

"Timmy, it's me, Pastor Smiley."

"Hi, Pastor. Is everything okay?"

"Timmy, everything is wonderful, just wonderful." He was animated. "I'm going to propose to Rene."

"Sounds like a man in love to me." Timmy chuckled.

"It's that obvious, huh?"

"Like my shop teacher used to say, 'No bout a doubt it.'" Timmy laughed.

"So, it shouldn't surprise you that I need to come by and take a look at some rings."

"What time are you coming by?"

"I'll see you in twenty minutes, the good Lord willing."

"See you then, Pastor," Timmy said, as the call ended.

Within five minutes of concluding his phone call with Timmy, Horatio's cell phone rang. The call screen indicated that it was Rene.

"Well, good morning, Ms. Brock. I was beginning to think that you were upset with me." He was relieved.

"Now, Pastor. What could you possibly do to cause me to be upset with you? I wanted to call and apologize for not returning your calls, sooner. Someone I knew as a friend had deceived me and the hurt caused me to disconnect for a while."

"Rene, I'm so sorry to hear that. Are you okay? Anything I can do?"

"Please, just pray for me," she requested. "It hurts to think of someone as a friend, only to find out that the relationship was necessary for them to achieve an ulterior motive."

"Yeah, I've been down that road before," he replied. "Tell you what, how about having dinner with me tonight?"

Here it comes again, Rene processed inwardly. *Now, he's going to ask if Kelli will be available to chaperone. Lord knows he wouldn't want to violate his precious little rule number one. I'm so tired of jumping through this clown's hoops. Time for a curve ball.* "Can't do it tonight," she countered. "How about tomorrow?"

"Tomorrow is fine. Are you up for another trip to Baha Bob's restaurant?" he asked.

"Do you want me to ask Kelli to come along as chaperone?" she positioned.

"Doesn't she work the night shift on Wednesdays?" Horatio asked.

"Oh, that's right. Wednesdays. No Kelli," She paused, "Seems like you're more familiar with her work schedule than I am," she said, struggling to remain calm. "So, what other things have you noticed about my sister?"

Refusing to respond to her question, he redirected the course of conversation. "Are you sure you're feeling all right, Rene?" Horatio sensed that something wasn't right.

"I'm fine. Just dealing with a nagging headache."

"Well, I'm praying that you feel better, in Jesus' name. I'll call you tomorrow."

"Thanks, Pastor. Looking forward to it. Bye, bye." The call ended.

Horatio accepted that Rene's headache was the cause of her being out of sorts. Without further thought about their conversation, he quickly made his way to the jewelry store in search of the perfect engagement ring.

Timmy was on the phone when Horatio arrived. "Sara, can you call me at lunchtime? Great. Talk to you, then. Okay, I'll be sure to give him the message. Promise. Bye."

"How's Sara doing today?"

"She's doing fine," Timmy paused. "Oh yeah, she was saying something about a lot of activity taking place at Mercy Ministries. She promised to let you know what's going on when she gets more information. They've got everybody working overtime."

"I wonder what's up? I hope everything is all right with Daniel," Horatio processed aloud.

"Pastor, you know how Sara is." Timmy explained, "She sees you as a father figure and wants to know what you think about things."

"A father figure, huh?" he chuckled.

"Maybe that was a bad way to say it," Timmy caught himself. "I meant to say a big brother."

"I appreciate that; either way I'm flattered. Now, let's talk about the engagement ring that I want to walk out of here with, today. I'm talking about a ring so perfect in its cut, clarity, and brilliance that it will take Rene's breath away when I place it on her finger."

"Pastor, I've got just the ring for you," Timmy said.

Retreating to the back office for a moment, he returned with a tray of diamonds that were amazing. At the center of the tray was one stone that rendered all the others pale by comparison.

"That diamond is magnificent," Horatio acknowledged while pointing, but daring not to touch it. "How much does something like that cost?"

"About a year's pay, after taxes." Timmy chuckled. "It's priced at fifteen thousand, but I'll see if my boss can do better."

"To be perfectly honest, I had a budget of ten thousand dollars," Horatio confided.

"Pastor, there are some very nice stones here that fall within your price range." Timmy continued, "How about this one?"

"No, not that one," Horatio responded.

"Well then, how about this one, here?" Timmy asked as he pointed to another.

After considering and quickly rejecting several other stones, he instructed Timmy to call his boss to discuss a cash sale price for the diamond at the center of the tray. Timmy complied and within a few minutes, Horatio negotiated a price with the store owner. For thirteen thousand five hundred dollars, the jeweler promised to have the stone mounted and ready for pick up the following day. He hugged Timmy in celebration of his purchase of the perfect engagement ring.

****

Back in his office, he phoned Sam Wooden to request that he lead the Wednesday night prayer meeting.

"Good morning, Sam. Hope I'm not catching you at a bad time."

"Nonsense, Pastor. Never a bad time to speak with a man of God."

"I appreciate that, Sam. And Sam, I appreciate your friendship."

"Now, you know that goes both ways, Pastor. Is everything all right? You're not dying or anything, are you?"

"No, Sam. I'm fine. In fact, I couldn't be better."

"Whew! That's good to know. So, then, what's going on?"

"Sam, my friend, I am about to propose marriage to the most beautiful woman in the world," Horatio announced.

"Pastor, I don't know how to break this to you, but Teresa is already married."

"Teresa? Oh, your wife." Horatio chuckled. "She must be right there beside you."

"Boy, Pastor, you catch on quick." Sam laughed. "You're gonna make Rene a real good husband." Sam and Horatio laughed at each other's comic genius, while Teresa was laughing in the background.

"Sam, I need you to stand in for me at prayer meeting tomorrow night, if you can. Can't be in two places at the same time, you know."

"I know what you mean. I'll let my boss know that I need tomorrow night off. I'm sure he won't mind, being slow time of season and all."

"Thanks, Sam. This means a lot to me," Horatio continued. "Oh, by the way, say nothing to anyone about my plan until the deed is done, if you know what I mean."

"Gotcha. Not a word," Sam promised. "But I do expect a full report, not a single detail left out." He chuckled.

"Done. You'll be duly apprised," he promised. "Talk to you later, Sam." The call ended.

Horatio spent the next few hours preparing for his dinner date with Rene. Making stops at the barber shop and dry cleaners, he was back at his office before four o'clock.

The remainder of the afternoon and evening was spent practicing the art of delivering the perfect proposal.

****

At five thirty, Rene's cell phone rang. It was Kelli.

"Hey, Sis. Can you talk?"

"Yeah, I'm just closing down for the day," Rene explained. "What's going on?"

"I wanted to call and apologize for yesterday," Kelli began. "I should have been more understanding…"

"Understanding of what?" Rene responded, defensively.

"Well," Kelli continued, "you said that you were dealing with something and I should have let it go at that."

"Yeah," Rene acknowledged. "I'm hoping everything will be resolved soon."

"Whatever it is that's going on, please don't stress. God will work it out for you," Kelli encouraged.

"I sure hope so." Rene sighed. "I'm so tired of people playing me." She didn't want to say anything more about what she was dealing with, so she attempted to change the topic of conversation. "I've got a dinner date with Pastor tomorrow night," she said, listening closely to Kelli's response.

"That's great! Where are you going?"

"Baha Bob's."

"Boy, you and Pastor are meant for each other," Kelli continued. "You both like Baha Bob's and Mom's stew."

"When did he ever get to eat Mom's stew?" Rene inquired.

Kelli immediately recognized a shift in Rene's demeanor. Certain that she had divulged something that she should not have, she attempted to diffuse Rene's agitation.

"Oh, Pastor stopped by yesterday to speak to Daddy. While he was here, Mom gave him some stew."

"That's funny," Rene pondered aloud. "He didn't say anything to me about that when we spoke."

"He must have forgotten to mention it," Kelli offered.

"Were you there while he was eating his stew?" Rene asked.

"Not at first," she explained. "He was there when I stopped by after work."

"Kelli, I have to go. I'll talk to you later." Rene ended the call abruptly.

"Bye," was all that Kelli had the opportunity to say, uncertain of whether or not Rene heard her.

"That does it!" Rene was steamed. "Who does he think he's playing with? Using me to get to my sister. Oooh! All that stuff he fed me about his precious nightmares and past heartbreaks. Well, Pastor Smiley, get ready for a nightmare that you will never forget." Rene was feeling every bit the part of a woman scorned. On her way home, she stopped by Mercy Ministries Home for Children. There, in her car, she sobbed.

"Daniel. I miss you. Oh, God help me," she cried out again and again.

At seven thirty, Rene's cell phone rang. She let it ring until the call was routed to her voice mail. Ten minutes later, it rang, again. The call went to voice mail. By eight fifteen, five calls had come to her phone. The first four were from Horatio. The fifth was from her parents. She chose to return her parents' call first.

"Rene. Are you all right?" Mrs. Brock asked without saying hello. It was obvious from the tone of her voice that she was very concerned.

"Hi, Mom. I'm fine."

"Where are you? Tell me why you're crying," Mrs. Brock insisted, sensing the hurt in Rene's voice.

"I'm just sitting in the parking lot of the orphanage, Mom."

Believing that her guilt and separation from Daniel was the reason for the emotional struggle that Rene was experiencing, Mrs. Brock moved away from her line of questioning. Endeavoring to bring comfort to her daughter, Mrs. Brock encouraged Rene to share with her all that was in her heart.

"Rene, mind if I come and sit with you?"

"Mom, that's not necessary. I'm fine." Rene was fragile and uncertain of whom, if anyone, she could trust. Her parents, Kelli, and Horatio had demonstrated by their actions a knowledge of something that they dared not share with her. She chose to go it alone until she could be sure of who could be trusted and who could not.

"Well, if you change your mind, let me know," Mrs. Brock offered.

"Thanks, Mom. Will do. Promise. Love you. Good night." The call ended.

Within a matter of seconds, her phone rang, again. It was Horatio.

"Hello, Pastor."

"Pastor? My, that sounds distant. What happened to Ace?" he asked light-heartedly.

"One of those days, I guess."

"Are you okay?"

"Yeah, I'm fine. Thanks for asking." She continued, "I heard you were at my mom and dad's yesterday."

"Er. Ah." He was at a loss for words. "Didn't I mention that?"

"No. You didn't," she said with noticeable firmness. "Why didn't you tell me?" she pressed.

314

"I'll explain it all to you when we have dinner tomorrow," he promised.

"All right. Until tomorrow, then. I've got to run. See ya."

Rene ended the call. She was thoroughly convinced that he was romantically interested in Kelli. She felt used in the way he befriended her to score points with Kelli and her family. The scorned spirit that was present in her before his call was now multiplied a thousand times. "Pastor, you're playing with the wrong person," she promised. "I'll make tomorrow night a night that you won't soon forget." She was so angered by all she understood, that her hurt became secondary to revenge. She spent the balance of the evening devising her payback strategy.

****

After his call with Rene had ended, Horatio became increasingly convicted for his attempt to downplay his deception.

"Lord, forgive me," he prayed. "She deserves much better than that from me."

He understood that Rene had been badly, perhaps permanently, scarred by the selfish and deceptive actions of others whom she loved and trusted earlier in her life. Certain that he would be vindicated and forgiven after his full explanation of the events of the day before, he retired for the evening. He slept very well.

Day 65
February 6th - Wednesday

Rene couldn't sleep a wink all night. Wide awake, she reached over and slammed the off button on her clock before the alarm had a chance to sound off at the usual time. She was deeply hurt and wanted revenge. As her body lay limp and her head throbbed with excruciating pain, Rene found strength from within to lift herself from her bed, make her way into the bathroom to prepare for a day of payback. Fueled by renewed memories of every romantic heartache and relational betrayal that she experienced as a consequence of wanting to be loved and appreciated, she pieced together an elaborate plan that would undoubtedly expose Horatio as the callous, unethical, self-centered fraud that he was.

At work, the hands on the clock moved slowly but Rene's mind was operating at breakneck speed. She concocted a strategy for her dinner meeting with him that would test any man's mettle. By ten o'clock, the final detail of her ingenious plan was in place. The plan required a perfectly timed introduction of two ingredients during her dinner date.

First, Ghost pepper flakes, also known as Bhut Jolokia, a medicinal fruit of India that is twenty times hotter than Cayenne pepper and two hundred times hotter than jalapenos.

Second: phospha soda, a liquid citrus-flavored laxative that is guaranteed to move the immovable. Finally, she needed to manufacture a convincing reason for them to travel to Baha Bob's in her car.

Coworkers bearing witness to her spontaneous, diabolical-sounding laughter as she fine-tuned her plan asked her to share what was going on but, she declined.

At eleven o'clock her cell phone rang. It was Horatio.

"Well, good Wednesday morning to you," he began. "Hope you're feeling better."

"Oh, I'm feeling much better, thank you."

"I'm happy to hear that. You seemed a bit on edge last night."

"Sorry about that. I had a pain in my neck that took a while to work out."

"Are you sure you're feeling well enough to keep our evening plans, tonight?"

"Oh, I wouldn't miss it for the world," she assured him, following up her response with a chuckle.

"Great." Horatio was animated. "Mind if we take your car? Mine is in the shop and won't be ready until tomorrow," he explained.

"Sure. No problem. Pick you up at six?"

"Six is perfect. See you then. Bye-bye."

Rene was delighted about not having to concoct a lie to get Horatio to travel with her in her car. While it was easy to acquire a bottle of phospha soda, she surfed the internet to locate Ghost pepper flakes. Twenty minutes later, she had connected with a local herbalist and arranged to have the most obscure ingredient of her recipe for revenge delivered to her office before three o'clock. Sensing the joy of victory before her confrontation with Horatio even began, she drove to Mercy Ministries Home for Children during her lunch break.

There sitting behind the wheel of her car, she made her son a promise: "Daniel, I believe with all my heart that God will bring us back together. Never, again, will I place my trust in cleverly crafted words spoken by any man who claims that our reunion is his priority. I love you, Daniel, and I will not rest until I hold you in my arms, again."

For the first time she could recall, in all her visits to the orphanage, not a tear was shed. In an epiphanic moment, she realized that her burden of overwhelming sadness had evolved to an attitude of profound determination. Nothing outside of an act of God could deter her from carrying out her plan to set Horatio straight. He was the walking, talking representation of every man in her life who had used her friendship in pursuit of their self-serving interests. She returned to her office and remained there until five thirty.

****

She called Horatio five minutes before she and her accomplices arrived at his home. With one vial of phospha soda and another containing the Ghost pepper flakes tucked safely inside her purse, Horatio's evening to remember was about to begin. Turning off Kent Street onto First Parrish Road, she could see him standing curbside in front of his house. Displaying his usual boyish smile, he waved as though he was genuinely happy to see her.

For a moment, Rene took pause to reconsider her plan. *Could he possibly be so wicked or was he just clueless?* she thought to herself. As she brought her car to a stop, the passenger door opened and he climbed inside.

"My, you look radiant tonight. You look like you really are feeling much better," he said.

"Thanks, I'm feeling better by the minute."

"Well, great then," he continued, "I hope you're ready to relax and enjoy some of Baha Bob's finest."

Rene, concealing any indication of being distracted or out of sorts, chose to engage him in light conversation.

"Yeah. I'm really looking forward to that fully-loaded nacho appetizer we ordered last time. And, oh my gosh, what was the name of that lemonade drink you let me taste?"

"That was the Lemon Explosion," he recalled.

"Oh, yeah. The Lemon Explosion. We definitely have to start the evening with those two treats." Rene chuckled.

"I'm sorry that Kelli couldn't join us," Horatio continued, "I know she likes Baha Bob's, too."

That was all the confirmation Rene needed to proceed with her plan. I knew it, she processed, inwardly. The only thing this butthead cares about is hooking up with my little sister. Well, after tonight they're welcome to each other. She struggled to maintain her bubbly persona on their way to the restaurant.

****

Inside Baha Bob's, several dining booths were available but, in keeping with Horatio's rule number one, he requested to sit at the counter to avoid the appearance of any impropriety. A waitress wearing the name tag Koko appeared and took their appetizer order. Putting her plan in motion, Rene excused herself to freshen up, while Horatio remained seated. Outside his field of vision, she sought out the waitress in the service area.

"Hi, Koko. My name is Rene. Can I speak with you a minute, please?"

"Hi, Rene. What can I get for you?"

"Koko, my boyfriend brought me here tonight for the last supper."

"The last supper? What does that mean?" Koko asked.

"He's giving me the kiss off, the 'see ya around,' the 'nice knowing you," Rene explained.

"That's cold-blooded." Koko appeared disgusted. "What makes men so mean?"

"I, certainly, don't understand their thought process but, I will tell you this," she assured Koko, "I'm going to teach him a lesson he'll never forget."

"What do you have in mind?" Koko asked with heightened interest.

Rene, in her explanation of how much Horatio liked spicy food and lemonade, shared with Koko her plan to "introduce" him to pepper flakes and a "flavor enhancer" for his lemonade. Koko roared with laughter at her plan.

"Rene, thinking back, I wish I had your kind of creativity, more times than I can remember."

"It's not creativity as much as it is taking a stand." Rene explained, "Any woman who trusts her innermost thoughts and emotions to some self-centered man who uses her friendship to get close to her sister has earned the right to the last laugh. Wouldn't you say, Koko?"

"Last laugh? Last laugh?" Koko was incredulous. "No, Rene. I'd need to see some part of his male anatomy in a jar or a box or something, if my man ever tried playing me like that. I feel your pain and I'm willing to help, but I can't do anything that will get me fired. I need this job."

"Don't worry, Koko." Rene explained, "All you have to do is give me a signal when our order is ready. I'll figure out some way to excuse myself and make it over to the food service area. I only need about ten seconds to sprinkle the pepper flakes on the nachos and pour the flavor enhancer into his lemonade. Is that okay with you?"

"Yeah, that's real easy." Koko was at peace. "In fact, you don't even need me for that. You see the message board over the service area?"

"Oh, yeah. I see it," Rene confirmed.

"Well, the last three numbers of your order slip, five-eight-nine, will appear on the message board when your dinner is ready for pickup," Koko explained. "All you need to do is watch the board, then make your way over to the counter before I pick it up. I'll tell the other waitresses to mind their business."

"Thanks, Koko. You're the best." Rene was excited. Koko put her finger to her lips, as if to remind Rene to tone down her enthusiasm. She left to service another table. Rene headed back to her table, reminding herself to focus her attention on the message board.

"Is everything okay? I was becoming concerned," Horatio said, as she sat down.

"Oh, Pastor. Everything is just fine. Don't worry yourself about me," she said coyly.

Horatio appeared a bit uneasy but she pretended not to notice. "Rene," he paused to clear his throat. "Excuse me," he continued, "The reason that I invited you to dinner tonight is that I have a confession to make…."

Just then, Rene noticed the number five-eight-nine light up on the message board.

"Please hold that thought just a minute, Pastor," she said as she grabbed her purse, got up, and made her way back to the service area.

Horatio was appreciative for the distraction. He considered it an opportunity for a final rehearsal of his marriage proposal. He was so focused on executing his plan to perfection that he paid little attention to Rene's retreat to the other side of the restaurant.

At the service counter, she quickly produced the container of pepper flakes and sprinkled a generous portion atop the platter of nachos. Next, with precision, she took a small vial containing three tablespoons of phospha soda and emptied the contents into Horatio's glass of lemonade. Koko, while taking an order from another diner, watched and waited for Rene's all-clear signal. Rene returned to her table and apologized to Horatio for her sudden departure. He appeared to be more anxious now, than before. She couldn't discern whether her leaving the table or his impending confession was the cause of his uneasiness.

"Back again," she announced. "Now, what is it you were saying: something about a confession or something?"

"Oh, yes. The confession," he, seemingly caught off-guard, recovered.

"One order of nachos, fully-loaded, and one large Lemon Explosion," Koko said, as she approached their table. Setting the items down, Koko asked, "Anything else I can get for you two?"

"Thank you, no," Rene responded. Koko departed.

"My, the nachos look amazing," Horatio said as he lifted a heap of them onto his plate. Rene nodded in agreement.

Looking directly into her eyes, he said, "These nachos, as amazing as they appear, pale in comparison to you, Rene."

"Thank you, I think," she wasn't sure what he was leading up to. She began processing, *Would this 'confession,' that he was about to launch into conclude with 'I don't deserve a person as amazing as you so, I'm going to start dating Kelli.'* Or, *You're so amazing. You're like a sister to me. So can we just be friends.* Bracing for the worst, she sat quietly while he continued.

"Rene, what I'm trying to say, or rather ask, is will you marry me?"

She was in shock. Unable to do anything more than sit there, she observed him rising up out of his chair, kneel before her on bended knee, and present her with the biggest, brightest diamond ring that she had ever seen. In a surreal moment, she couldn't remember whether she responded to his proposal or not. She didn't remember moving her lips or nodding her head, but she could hear Horatio's voice saying: "Thank you, Rene. I love you so much. I'll try to be the best husband ever. We've got to call our parents and let them know."

As Rene's mind and emotions returned to real time, she was crying tears of joy while, passionately, hugging her fiancé. The ring, now firmly on her finger, was beautiful.

Koko laughed and called out, "Get a room, you guys." The restaurant's staff and patrons, observing what was taking place, stood to their feet applauding the soon-to-be newlyweds.

"Waitress, can my fiancee and I be moved to a booth, please?"

"Certainly, sir," Koko continued. "Please, right this way."

Horatio and Rene were seated in an intimate booth where they sat side by side, no longer concerned about violating Horatio's rule number one. As soon as the food was placed at the center of the table, he reached for some of the nachos on his plate.

"No! Don't eat that," Rene cautioned, emphatically.

"Why? Is there something wrong?"

She had no intention of informing him of what she had done to his food. Thinking quickly, she responded, "The nachos are cold. Let me ask for a replacement."

"Nonsense. These look too good to throw out," he said.

As he reached to gather some up and eat them, Rene snatched the nachos from his fork and shoved the full measure of the forkful into her mouth. A burning pain that she had never before experienced or imagined exploded in her mouth and found its way into every extremity of her body, simultaneously. Her eyes watered, her breathing became short, and her face flushed. Desperate for relief from the excruciating, full-body burn sensation, she chugged down the tainted Lemon Explosion.

"Horatio, I'm gonna be sick," she struggled to excuse herself as she ran to the lady's room.

Koko, bearing witness to the situation, swooped in and removed the platter of nachos and lemonade to prevent him from consuming any of the order. After depositing the uneaten portion of the appetizer in a trash receptacle, she ran to the ladies room to check on Rene.

There, Koko observed Rene kneeling on a wad of paper towels to protect her knees from coming in direct contact with the badly soiled floor around the commode. Clutching her stomach as she emptied the contents of everything within, Rene cried out, "God, please forgive me." Her head was so deep inside the bowl that her face was not visible.

"Drink this, Rene," Koko instructed, handing her a glass of milk. Lifting her head and turning her body to see what Koko was suggesting, she reached for the glass. She slowly nursed down the milk, trying to keep it from coming back up. Koko called out to the other waitresses to alert them that she was taking her break. They agreed to cover her tables until she returned. Then came a knock on the bathroom door. It was Horatio.

"Rene, honey. Are you all right? Do you want me to come in?"

"No, stay out. I'm fine. I'll be out in just a minute," she responded, trying to calm his concern. At that moment, Rene's digestive system began to bubble up. *Oh, my God. The laxative is getting ready to kick in*, she thought to herself. *I've got to get home, right now.*

"Horatio, are you still there?" she called out.

"Still here. What do you need me to do?"

"Please gather up my coat and get the car ready. I need to make a dash home."

Koko exited the restroom and took Horatio by his arm. "She took a bullet for you."

"What are you talking about? What are you saying?" he asked.

"Something about those nachos wasn't kosher and she sensed it. She tried to stop you from eating them so you wouldn't have to go through what she's going through," Koko explained.

"Wow. I had no idea."

"That's a special lady you have there," Koko said with a wink.

"Yes, she certainly is." Horatio was in full agreement.

With the grace of God, they returned safely home, making only two pit stops along the way. At Rene's request, he dropped her off at home and continued on to his house in her car. She promised to call him if she needed anything.

****

During the course of the evening, Horatio received phone calls and texts from each of the Brock family members, his mom and dad, Sam Wooden, Timmy and Sara, and others. He was not aware of them. At the time Rene picked him up, he had shut off his phone to avoid any hint of what was to come. Clearly, his planned proposal was not a well-kept secret. He was eager to report that all went well, but was apprehensive to do so without Rene's participation. He decided to wait until the next day to share the news with everyone, expecting that she would be feeling better. He went to bed at ten thirty.

Day 66
February 7th - Thursday

Concerned for Rene's recovery, Horatio called her. She answered after the sixth ring.

"Hello?" She was disoriented, uncertain whether she was dreaming or awake.

"Hi, how are you feeling?"

"What time is it?" she asked.

"Four fifteen," he replied. "Did I wake you?"

"That's okay. I don't mind receiving phone calls at four fifteen in the morning from the wonderful man who just asked me to share the rest of his life with him." She chuckled. "And, yes, I'm feeling better. Thank you."

"Are you feeling well enough to make a few phone calls?"

"Phone calls at four in the morning?" She didn't think he was serious.

"Well, some very special people have called to ask how everything went last night at the restaurant, and I think that they would appreciate hearing all about it even at this hour." He chuckled.

"You're so mischievous, Pastor Smiley." She joined him in the moment. "Let's do it."

Three-way phone calls were placed to the homes of Rene's parents and then to Horatio's parents. It was six thirty when the second call was concluded. Deacon wept throughout the call while Mrs. Brock and Horatio's mom wanted to know every detail about the evening. Horatio's dad ministered to them through scripture and personal experience on the keys to a Godly marriage.

After the calls ended, Horatio and Rene agreed to meet for a light lunch. Rene was continuing to heal but she decided to take a sick day from her job. She told him that she was headed back to bed and asked that he call her at eleven thirty. The call ended.

****

The familiar knock of Sam Wooden was heard at Horatio's door before eight o'clock.

"Pastor. You in there?" Sam called out before Horatio could open the door.

Horatio decided to have a bit of fun with Sam. As he slowly opened the door, he stuck his head out. Looking Sam squarely in the eye, he greeted him.

"Morning, Sam. How was Prayer Meeting last night?"

"Prayer Meeting?" Sam repeated, seemingly caught off guard. He expected to hear all about the engagement.

"Yes. You know, Wednesday Evening Prayer Meeting. How was it?" Horatio asked, again.

"Well, it was all right, I guess."

"How many were there?" Horatio continued with the questioning.

"Ah, maybe fifteen, I guess."

"That's great, Sam. Thanks for the update. Talk to you later. I've got to run." He eased the door closed. Horatio remained positioned behind the door, but did his best to imitate the sound of footsteps walking away.

Recalling the confused look on Sam's face, he did all within his ability to contain his laughter. It was obvious that Sam didn't understand that he was joking with him. Still positioned inside the door, he listened for any indication of Sam's leaving. Unable to tell, he slowly pulled the door open. There was Sam, standing there looking directly in Horatio's eyes.

"So, how'd everything go last night?" Sam asked, emotionless.

Horatio roared with side-splitting laughter. Sam laughed so hard his eyes watered. "That gull turd had absolutely no chance of taking flight. You know that, right?" Sam asked, still doubled over from laughing.

Horatio, regaining his composure, gave Sam a hug. "Sam, Sam, Sam, my friend. It was an evening to remember." He was animated. "Rene said "yes" and then she saved my life by eating some contaminated food. Long story short, we're getting married."

"Now, that's what I wanted to hear. Praise God!" Sam shouted. "Can I tell my wife?"

"Sam, you have my permission to shout the news from the highest rooftop." Horatio laughed.

"Well, my work has begun. Talk to you later, Pastor." Sam headed up the street.

****

Horatio was seated behind his office desk at ten thirty when the phone rang.

"Good Shepherd, Good morning. Pastor Smiley, speaking."

"Bonjour, Pasteur Horatio. This is your friend, Captain Gervais. How are you doing today?"

"Captain, so good to hear from you." Horatio continued, "How are things on the high seas these days?"

"The high seas miss you, Pasteur. In fact," Captain Gervais continued, "the general manager of the cruise line has given me instruction to do what is necessary to recruit you as a full-time member of our corporate clergy staff. Our Reservations Division has received an impressive number of inquiries asking about your cruise itinerary. Apparently, people have heard of, shall we say, your outstanding 'ability' to provide counsel and comfort. They want to see you, again. What do say, my friend?"

"Well, Captain, I am flattered. Last night I became engaged to marry to the most beautiful, wonderful woman on earth. Now, what do you think she'd say if I accepted your offer to leave her for months at a time?"

"Yes, I appreciate your point. Your fiancée would most certainly find it difficult to believe that your proposal to share your lives together forever was sincere. But, congratulations on your good fortune. Perhaps, your bride would enjoy living aboard one of the world's most prestigious cruise ships. She'll be pampered like a queen, every day. No cooking. No housework. Just enjoy life together. You should ask her what she thinks of my proposal."

"Captain, you have a way with words." Horatio chuckled. "I'll ask her, but we have responsibilities here that we simply cannot walk away from."

"I understand, but I remain hopeful. Would it be acceptable if I contact you next Wednesday when I return to port?"

"Next Wednesday will be fine, Captain," Horatio agreed.

The call ended.

****

At eleven thirty, Horatio called Rene. "Hi there. Are you still feeling well enough to go to lunch?"

"Wouldn't miss it for the world, even if I, just, watch you eat." She chuckled.

327

"Music to my ears. Can't wait to see you," he confessed. "In fact, I'm leaving now. Hope you don't mind me showing up a few minutes early."

"Well, I can do better than that. I just walked out the door and I'm on my way downstairs." She laughed. "Come get your bride, Ace."

He couldn't leave fast enough. "Being in love is amazing," he thought aloud.

Twenty minutes later, he was in front of Rene's apartment building. She waved as she hurried to get into the car. He attempted to stop the car, disembark, run around to the passenger side and open the door for her, but that wasn't going to happen. Rene was belted into the passenger seat before he could remember bringing the car to a complete stop. Giggling like little children at the opportunity to be together again, they drove away without any idea of where they would have lunch.

"What do you have a taste for?" he asked.

"I don't know. Something light, I guess. Maybe a salad."

"I have an idea." He suggested, "What do you say we make a surprise stop by your parents' house after we pick up some salad fixings?"

"That would be fun. They'll be so surprised." She was giddy. That decision proved to be priceless.

Deacon was in the yard and Mrs. Brock was inside when they turned into the driveway.

"Lord, Jesus!" Deacon shouted loudly enough that Mrs. Brock ran to the front door to see what the commotion was all about. In the Brock family's driveway, two generations were locked in a joyous healing embrace that was as medicine to the soul. The remainder of the afternoon was spent laughing, crying, planning for an August wedding, praying, and giving thanks. It was a very good day, long overdue. Horatio and Rene left in time to pick up his car from the repair shop. Phone conversations continued throughout the evening. Their last call for the day ended at ten thirty.

Day 67
February 8th - Friday

Convicted about missing so much time from work, Horatio was positioned behind his desk at seven forty-five. The message indicator signal was blinking on his answering device. Hitting the play button, the recorder announced, "You have one new message marked 'urgent.'"

"Hi, Pastor. This is Sara. Please contact me via text to let me know when we can meet. I'm not able to receive personal calls at work. This is very important. Thank you."

Concerned that something bad had happened with Timmy, he immediately responded to her text, informing her that he was available to speak.

An hour passed without hearing back from her. His increasing concern caused him to walk to the jewelry store and see if he could find out anything more from Timmy's boss. Standing at the door of the Front Street shop, he noticed that the lights were off and the door was locked. A sign on the door reminded him that the store didn't open for another forty minutes. Timmy didn't have a cell phone, so there was little else to do but return to his office and wait for Sara to contact him. In the minutes that followed, he received a text response from Sara alerting him to expect her call during her lunch break.

****

Sam Wooden and four other members of Good Shepherd were scheduled to be installed as trustees during the Sunday morning church service. In recognition of the newly appointed trustees, Horatio recruited the assistance of several church members to organize a fellowship brunch. Volunteers, enthusiastically, welcomed the opportunity to prepare homemade dishes, desserts, and decorations. The event signaled the beginning of a new chapter for Good Shepherd's family. Under the watchful eye of Bill Nelson's trusteeship, a church-sponsored celebration, for any reason other than to benefit his personal interests, would not have been approved.

****

Precisely at twelve noon, the church phone rang. It was Sara. She was distraught.

"Pastor, something's going on with Daniel." She continued, "I'm not sure what it is, but I've got a really bad feeling that he is about to be moved out of here."

"Oh, Lord. No. This can't happen." He couldn't accept what he was hearing. "Sara, are you sure? What have you seen? What have you heard?"

"Pastor, there was some kind of Adoption Open House here, about two weeks ago. I wasn't involved with organizing the event but, afterwards, I was given a stack of applications to file." She continued, "The applications included notes about possible matches with children at the Home…."

"What kind of notes?" he interrupted.

"Notes about the gender, age, and ethnicity that the applicants express a preference for," Sara explained. "Several calls came into the office late last week from this one lady who was determined to get in touch with Mrs. Monahan. I know that I took at least three phone messages from the woman. Yesterday, as we were closing the office down, the woman called again. Mrs. Monahan wasn't there so the woman left the message for her saying that she and her husband can't wait for Danny to arrive. I snuck the file into the ladies' room so I could get a closer look at the case history. The entries didn't make any sense. From what I observed, it seems as though six months of activity was backdated. A total of nine procedural requirements that began last summer were entered into the file on the twenty-fourth of last month, within a thirty-minute time frame. All of these entries were posted one day after the Adoption Open House occurred. Something's fishy about this. Pastor, there is only one child named Danny at the Home, that I know of. When I realized what was taking place, I called you right away."

"Sara. I'm in shock." Horatio sighed. "Rene will never be reunited with her son," he muttered. The silence was uncomfortable.

"Pastor, nothing is too big for God to handle," Sara continued. "You taught me that when we spoke that night on Front Street. You told me that God is able and you were right."

"Wow. I can't believe I spoke that. Forgive me, Lord." He was convicted. Sara's words reminded him that God's power is unequalled. "Sara, I need you to find out everything you can about this for me. We need to be absolutely sure of the situation before I mention anything to Rene."

"I understand, Pastor," she replied. "I leave work at five o'clock. I'll call you as soon as I'm in my car."

"Call me on my cell phone," he instructed. "You have that number?"

"I've got it. Talk to you later." The call ended. It was seven minutes after twelve.

****

During the next five hours, Horatio's thought process was operating in high gear. Rene's happiness meant everything to him. Inundated by a barrage of "what-ifs" and "how-abouts," his heart became increasingly heavy because he had no solution that could bring Rene even the slightest bit of hope.

"Perhaps Sara was mistaken in her assessment of Daniel's pending adoption. After all, she's only been working at Mercy Ministries for a few months."

Unable to wait for Sara's five o'clock call, he decided to do a bit of snooping around on his own. He remembered Sheila Vega, the Mercy Ministries' receptionist. "I'll give Sheila a call and see if she can give me more insight about the adoption process." Calling on his cell phone to avoid being recognized by the caller identification system, his call was answered on the second ring.

"Good afternoon, Mercy Ministries. Can I help you?"

The voice was, immediately, recognizable as Sara's. Horatio quickly hung up the phone. Certain that Sara would in some way recognize his phone number, he began to stress.

"What the heck was I thinking? What's wrong with me?" He chastised himself for his bone-headed move. He prayed that, should Sara put two plus two together, she wouldn't consider his taking matters into his own hands as a vote of no-confidence in her. He remained in his office until Sara called a few minutes after five o'clock.

"Pastor, I wasn't able to come up with much more than what I shared with you earlier. I had to cover the phones all afternoon," she said. "I asked a friend to meet me for lunch, tomorrow. She's worked for Mercy Ministries for a while and I know she can help me understand the process better."

"Would that friend be Sheila Vega?"

"Yes, she's an awesome resource." Sara continued, "We're having lunch at Joe's, at one o'clock. I was thinking that Timmy and I could meet with you afterward."

"That will be great. Just let me know where and when. I'll wait for your call."

****

Assuming the role of protector, Horatio chose to withhold the events of the day from Rene. While still seated at his desk, his cell phone rang. It was her.

"Hey, Rene. How is your Friday going?"

"Okay, I guess," she replied. "I've been burdened with a sense of heaviness pretty much all day. I keep trying to focus on you, your handsome face, and your beautiful smile to move away from it but, it won't leave me. Something is wrong. I know that something is seriously wrong." Horatio didn't respond. "Are you there?"

"Yeah, I'm here."

"What's the matter, honey? You seem to be distracted."

"I'm sorry. Just one of those days you'd like to be over and done with," he explained.

"Want to talk about it while I give you a shoulder rub?" she asked.

"Mmm. Sounds good. I don't think I've ever had a shoulder rub."

"Well, Mister Smiley, prepare to be pampered," she chuckled. "Do you want to come to my place? I can whip up something to eat."

"Sounds great. I'd like that. Say six o'clock?" he asked.

"Six will be fine. See you then." Rene hung up.

Horatio began to have second thoughts about his decision to accept the invitation. Loving her as he did, how could he withhold the truth about Daniel's situation? Thinking aloud, he muttered, "That wouldn't be love; that would be wrong. Lord, what should I do?" he pondered. "I need your direction in all of this."

He closed the office and went home to freshen up. After a quick stop at the Village Mart to buy some flowers and dessert, he was on his way to Rene's apartment. Determined to stay the course of nondisclosure, he labored to convince himself that he had chosen wisely. *Lord, help me. Please*, he continued to pray. He exited the car and climbed the stairs to her apartment.

She greeted him at the door with a beautiful smile and a kiss.

"Welcome. Come on in," she invited with outstretched arms. Any other time Horatio would have been on cloud nine. A Friday evening to be shared in the company of a beautiful woman who loves and appreciates everything about you, after three years of being alone, would be every man's desire. Tonight, however, he finds himself between a rock and a hard place. As the evening progressed, he began to reconsider his strategy. Eventually, he abandoned it, altogether.

"Rene, there's something that I need to discuss with you…," he began. He brought her up to speed on everything that he understood to be taking place with Daniel. Rene was devastated.

The evening was spent praying and comforting her with the assurance that God wasn't going to let anyone or anything cause her reunification with Daniel to be frustrated. Sitting on the sofa he held her, lovingly, until she drifted off to sleep in his arms. Occasionally, she would sob quietly and reach out to be sure that Horatio hadn't left from her side. He vowed, inwardly, that he would never leave her alone. He understood, more than ever before, the extent of the heartache that she suffered in her times of loneliness.

Day 68
February 9th - Saturday

Watching the sun rise over the Atlantic Ocean from her living room window, they continued cuddling on the sofa until eight thirty. The decision was made to take a ride to the Bagel Barn to pick up some fresh bagels and coffee. It had been a long restless night and their ability to proficiently process the simplest of ideas was a challenge. Standing at the service counter of the Bagel Barn, "Home of 28 Varieties of Bagels," each ordered a plain bagel and a cup of coffee. Unable to decide whether to return to Rene's apartment or ride around until Sara called, they remained in the Bagel Barn parking lot.

Rene had an idea.

"We need to share this with my parents. After all, Daniel is their grandson. They'd be hurt if we didn't tell them."

"Tell them what?" Horatio asked. "We're not sure of anything, just yet. Why not meet with Sara, first, to get a better understanding of the situation. After that, I promise we can go directly to your parents' house and fill them in."

"Fair enough," Rene agreed.

They drove to Nantasket Beach and sat in the car, watching seagulls and joggers brave a brisk northeasterly wind. At ten thirty, he dropped Rene off at her apartment and continued on to his house to shave, shower, and wait for Sara's call.

His cell phone rang at two thirty-eight. It was Sara.

"Pastor, Sheila just left. We need to meet right away."

"Rene and I can come to you, now. Where are you?"

"I'm at Joe's Restaurant on Route Fifty-Three. But, can we get together at the Stuffed Pig? Timmy is working until five o'clock and, I'd like for him to be a part of the discussion," she explained.

"Well, can you tell me anything at all about how your meeting with Sheila went?"

"Pastor, it hasn't quite settled in, yet. Rather than tell you what I got out of it, I prefer to share all that Sheila confided in me. Then, you can give me your take on it. I can tell you this, though: we need everyone we know to pray, nonstop, for God to intervene."

Horatio had a sick, sinking feeling in the pit of his gut. Sensing that Rene's reunification with Daniel was not going to happen, he endeavored to appear encouraged, as he called to alert her that he was on his way.

"Hi. Ready?" he asked.

"I'm ready. How long before you'll be here?"

"Fifteen minutes. See you then. Bye-bye."

Horatio, intentionally, kept the exchange short. He didn't want to give Rene a chance to ask for an update. Along the way to her apartment, he pondered the best way to prepare her for the devastating news that Sara would soon reveal to them. Rene needed a measure of strength beyond what he couldn't provide.

He prayed, "Father, in the name of Jesus, help us. Please bring unification to this family. You are the true and living God. There is nothing too great for you. Today, more than ever before, families are under attack. Let not the plan of Satan be successful in his continued declaration of war against the family structure, as you have created it to be. Please keep this family from becoming another casualty in the battle to stand as believers in you, Lord. Amen."

As soon as he spoke the word "Amen," he heard in his spirit, "I am with you." The strength and clarity of the voice was so obvious that at first he thought that the words were spoken by someone on his car radio. Reaching to turn up the volume, he realized that the radio was powered off.

"Thank you, Lord."

Minutes later he was positioned in front of Rene's apartment building. She hurried to the car, attempting to conceal any evidence of physical or emotional weariness.

"Hi again," she said. "Where are we meeting Sara?"

"She asked us to meet her at the Stuffed Pig Diner."

"I've heard of that place," Rene said. "Their food is supposed to be pretty good."

"Yeah, I've eaten there before. The food is excellent." He labored to appear upbeat.

"What's wrong, Horatio?"

"Just processing."

"Please, don't worry. Everything is going to work out according to God's plan. In fact, I believe that He's already worked it out."

Horatio couldn't believe what he was hearing. "Oh, my God. Thank you, Lord." He explained, "Rene, I've been praying since I received Sara's call. I asked the Lord to strengthen and protect you from any source of affliction that might come against you to cause sadness, depression, fear, and anything else that would attempt to discourage you or diminish your faith in Him."

"Well, I've been praying, too. In fact, since you told me about the meeting with Sara, I've been praying like I've never prayed before. It's obvious that darkness has come against us." She explained, "I was, profoundly, comforted when in the middle of my prayer this morning, I heard someone say, "I am with you.""

Horatio was so taken aback that he pulled the car onto the roadway shoulder. "What did you say?"

"Say about what?" Rene responded, seeking clarification.

"About someone saying something," he inquired. "Tell me about that. What happened, exactly?"

"It was something that I haven't experienced in a long, long time," Rene recalled. "In fact, I've probably heard it only once or twice, before. Anyway, the same voice I heard years ago said, clear as day, 'I am with you.' That was all I needed to hear to let me know that God was fully at work in whatever it is that we're meeting Sara about."

"Rene, I love you so much," he said, reaching over to embrace her. "I believe it, too. God has already worked it out." As the embrace concluded, he pulled the car back onto the roadway and continued along to their meeting with Sara and Timmy.

****

Sara was sitting in a booth sipping from a cup of hot chocolate when Horatio and Rene walked in. Standing to her feet, she motioned them over.

"Hi, Sara. This is my fiancée, Rene Brock, Daniel's mother. Rene, this is my friend, Sara Reynolds."

Sara stood up and reached out to embrace her. "You are just as I pictured you to be," Sara said, continuing to hug Rene while being mindful of her baby bump.

"I am?"

"Yes. You are," Sara continued. "I am so happy to meet you. The way that Pastor's face lit up when he told Timmy and me that he was in love with you clinched it for us. We knew that you had to be really special." Horatio's face became as red as a perfectly boiled lobster.

"He said that?" Rene was flattered. "Honey, that's so sweet." She kissed him on the cheek.

"Too much information, Sara," he said, causing everyone to laugh.

"What's going on?" Timmy asked as he approached the table. "Sounds like I missed out on one of Pastor's jokes." Noticing Horatio's reddened face, Timmy asked, "Sunburn, Pastor?" The circle of laughter expanded to include nearby customers and staff members.

Timmy directed them to a room nearer to the back of the restaurant to continue their discussion. After Timmy was introduced to Rene, Sara brought Horatio and Rene up to speed about the situation involving Daniel.

"Earlier this week, Sheila and I were given a stack of adoption applications to forward to outside fact checkers that Mercy Ministries uses to verify the individual's CORI, employment, character references and credit information. On each application, the prospective 'match' child's name is mentioned. On Thursday, one applicant's vetted file was received and I delivered it to Judy, Mrs. Monahan's assistant. I know that I shouldn't have but, I read the file. That was wrong. I'll probably be fired if anyone besides Sheila finds out about it. I wasn't familiar with the applicant's name but, I immediately recognized Daniel's picture." For the next twenty minutes, Sara delineated the glaring red flags that she noticed while reviewing Daniel's file. She concluded her summarization of events with the statement: "I believe that someone is calling in a favor and Daniel is the payment."

Rene tried to remain calm, but with each additional detail that Sara revealed she became increasingly anxious. Tears that had, gradually, welled up, began to roll down her cheeks.

"Are you okay?" Horatio asked. "Can I get you anything?"

"I'm sorry," Rene said as she wiped a tear from her eye. "Please, Sara. What else did the file say about Daniel?"

"I didn't notice anything more about your son, but the woman who's requesting Daniel must have learned that the background check process was completed. She kept calling and asking questions about the adoption vote. I told her that she would have to speak with Mrs. Monahan but, she wasn't available at the moment. I offered to take a message. She just kept calling and calling. She must have called eight or nine times during Thursday and Friday alone."

"I wonder how she found out, so quickly, about the background checks being completed?" Timmy asked. "Something doesn't seem kosher."

"My question, exactly," Sara pondered. "Obviously, this woman has clout with someone inside Mercy Ministries. The adoption vote is the final hurdle for her. Once the vote takes place, it will be a done deal for Daniel."

"I believe that if Daniel is meant to be with us, God will cause it to happen," Rene said, trying to remain encouraged.

"Rene, I wonder if it's too late for us to put in a reunification application for Daniel?" Horatio said as he stroked his chin.

"I don't see how that would be possible, given my history." She sighed.

"Well, maybe we can request a delay in the process until we can be married." He explained, "Then, it wouldn't be your history but, our future that should be considered. We need to get married right away, Rene"

"Oh, Horatio. I was thinking the very same thing," she gushed. "I love you, so much."

"Awwh. You guys are so cute." Sara laughed.

"Sara, can you believe it? Our Pastor is getting married before us. I thought we had him beat." Timmy chuckled.

"Timmy, Proverbs 18:22 tells us: 'A man who finds a wife finds a good thing,'" Horatio recited. "I've waited all my life for the Lord to send her to me. Forgive me, Lord," he said, looking Heavenward and taking Rene's hand, "I don't see any reason to procrastinate. Do you?" he asked. Rene blushed while everyone laughed at her reaction.

"Timmy, Sara, we appreciate your help and encouragement in all of this craziness," Rene continued. "Please, Sara, keep us current on anything that you find out. Daniel means everything to me."

"I will," Sara promised, as she gave Rene a hug.

Horatio and Rene returned to her apartment. Along the way, they agreed to wait until the following day to speak to her parents about Daniel's situation. He stayed with Rene long enough to be sure that she was okay. After that, he returned home to prepare for Sunday's church service and the installation ceremony for the newly appointed deacons.

Day 69
February 10th - Sunday

The morning light came, too, quickly. Only a moment ago, Horatio had glanced over at the alarm clock. It was three thirty. How did nine o'clock come so soon? He let loose a yawn big enough to cause his eyes to water.

"Lord, give me strength," he petitioned. He knew that this was the start of what would prove to be a very busy day. With the grace of God, he managed to gather himself and be at the church on time. He took a moment to peek inside the kitchen and community room to check in with the volunteers working on the after-sermon fellowship. The table settings, inclusive of red and white floral arrangements, were beautifully designed and the aroma of home-cooked foods filled the building.

His sermon was based on the scripture John 16:33 ("In this world you will have trouble, but take heart"). He taught about the strategy of deception that Satan has so successfully used to separate generations of God's people from their faith and from each other. "Social engineering and government legislation have diminished the presence of God in our homes, in our schools, and in the Body of Christ. A house divided will not stand," he cautioned. Reciting Ephesians 6:13, he said: "Put on the full armor of God, so that when the evil day comes, you may be able to stand your ground and, after you have done everything, continue to stand."

At that, the congregation stood and applauded. He asked the incoming trustees to come to the front of the church. As the men took their positions, Horatio came and stood with them.

"Friends of Good Shepherd," he began, "each of these five Godly men, who stand before you, has been chosen to serve our church in the capacity of trustee. I know them. You know them. They are men of integrity, charity, and humility. They love the Lord and are priests of their home." He continued, "Will each candidate's wife come forward with a bible and stand beside your husband, please?"

Teresa stepped to the front and stood with Sam, as did the other wives with their husbands. He read aloud the character traits and responsibilities of clergy and elders, as required in I Timothy Chapter 3. With their right hand placed firmly on the bible held by their wife, each candidate recited the trustee's oath of service. There was not a dry eye in the sanctuary. A new season of leadership for Church of the Good Shepherd had officially begun. Horatio requested that the congregation move into the community room to continue the fellowship.

"Everybody, please. Before we adjourn to the community room, can I have your attention?" Sam summoned. "For those of you who haven't heard yet, our pastor is about to become a married man." A chorus of cheers went up. "Pastor. Are you going to introduce the future first lady of Good Shepherd or shall I?"

Horatio walked to Rene and escorted her from the third row of pews. Arm in arm they walked to the front of the church.

"Everyone, this beautiful lady is Rene Brock. She has, mercifully, accepted my proposal of marriage," he began. "Please pray with me that God will give her the strength and patience to not grow weary in loving your pastor."

Everyone rejoiced at the good news. The fellowship continued until three thirty that afternoon. Afterward, Horatio and Rene went to her parents' home to discuss Daniel's situation with them.

****

"Look at this gorgeous couple," Deacon announced with outstretched arms, as Horatio and Rene walked in.

"Hi, Daddy. Hi, Mom. Wasn't church service wonderful today?"

"Couldn't have been better if we had two services," Horatio replied, chuckling. "The presence of the Holy Spirit was amazing."

"It was as though a breath of fresh air entered in, as those fine men stood at the front of the church with their wives beside them." Mrs. Brock shared, "It blesses me when I see the next generation step up to the plate and take their responsibilities, seriously."

"Speaking of the next generation," Horatio continued, "Rene and I are here to discuss a situation that involves Daniel."

"Daniel? Is everything all right?" Mrs. Brock tensed up. "What's wrong, Rene?" Her demeanor became like that of a lioness prepared and able to protect her cub.

"Mom, we don't know much at this point," Rene prefaced. "Horatio learned through someone at the church that an application for Daniel's adoption has been filed with Mercy Ministries."

"Application? Nobody's taking Daniel away from this family," Deacon jumped up and pounded his hand on a tabletop. "Horatio, Son, what's the plan?"

"Well," Horatio responded, "Rene and I plan to get married tomorrow and file our own application for reunification with Daniel, ASAP."

"Oh, thank you, Lord," Mrs. Brock sighed. "Rene, what are you thinking about all of this?"

"Mom. Daddy. I'm ready to go get my son. It's time," she responded resolutely.

"Hallelujah!" Deacon jumped to his feet. "Son. I mean Pastor, what do we do now?"

"We pray," Horatio answered. "And Deacon, from now on, you're Dad, I'm Son."

Deacon relished the correction. "Thanks, Son," he replied laughing as he embraced his son-in-law.

They adjourned to the kitchen table and prayed. Their prayer petitioned the Lord, in His infinite wisdom, to take the lead and be glorified in the process. Having agreed to, immediately, pursue the marriage license process, Horatio and Rene made plans to meet the following day, during her lunch hour, at Scituate's Town Hall. By the time their visit ended, the spirit of anxiety that weighed heavily, earlier on, had evolved to a spirit of good old "Brock determination," as Deacon liked to call it. Horatio and Rene departed for their respective homes. The exchange of frequent phone calls and texts between them concluded at eleven o'clock.

Day 70
February 11th - Monday

Horatio called Rene at eight o'clock to say good morning. They spoke long enough for her to assure him that she was fine and would meet him at the town clerk's office at twelve thirty. He was preparing to go to his office when there came a knock at the door.

"Coming," he called out. Opening the door, he was surprised to see that it was Arthur Mutton.

"Arthur?" he said, reflexively. "What brings you here? Is everything okay?" In the three years that Horatio served as pastor to Good Shepherd, Arthur never once darkened the parsonage doorway. By his appearance, he had aged ten years since Horatio last saw him.

"Pastor, I haven't had a moment's rest since that nightmarish church meeting," Arthur sulked. "I haven't slept. I don't eat. My life has been turned upside down. My wife keeps telling me that I need to apologize to you." He explained, "She says if you forgive me, I'll be able to rest again. Kind of like a curse being lifted. You know what I mean? So, will you forgive me, Pastor?"

"Arthur, I don't harbor any ill will against you. What benefit would it be to God, if I did?"

"I don't understand you. Bill and I spearheaded the attempt to run you out of the church. In fact, we had every intention of running you out of town. And now, you tell me that you have no hard feelings toward me? This doesn't make sense."

"Arthur, I know all about what you and the others were trying to do to me. God showed me everything. Nevertheless, Jesus instructs us to walk in love, in season and out of season. Do you understand what that means?"

"Of course, I do," Arthur responded. "I'm a good person. I used to go to church every Sunday."

"Arthur, the more you speak the clearer it is that you don't understand. Where in the Bible does it say that being a good person or going to church every Sunday assures anyone of salvation?" He explained, "The Bible says nothing of the sort. It says: 'If you confess with your mouth that Jesus Christ is Lord and you believe in our heart that he was crucified of flesh, resurrected from the dead, and ascended to heaven, as our Savior, you shall be saved.'"

"Yeah, yeah, I know," Arthur responded. "And, don't forget about Mary.

"Mary? Who's Mary?" Horatio inquired.

"You know, Mary. Holy mother of God," Arthur offered. "According to what the Roman Catholics believe, she can get you saved, too. She has pull with God because, you know, she's Jesus' mother."

"Are you serious, Arthur?" Horatio was taken aback. "You're really beginning to scare me."

"Listen, Pastor. I understand everything that I need to know just fine," Arthur responded, defiantly.

"Arthur, if you understand everything so well, why would it seem nonsensical if I tell you that I harbor no hard feelings toward you?"

"Because it's impossible for anyone to live according to that discipline," Arthur admitted. "It's not even practical, so why try? And what do you mean God showed you what we were up to? What the hell do you mean by that?" Arthur was frustrated.

"First of all, Arthur, God doesn't expect anything more than we, as his creation, are able to do. If you see any instruction that God gives as being impossible, I would suggest that you get to know Him better." Horatio continued, "And, Arthur, I will tell you this: when your heart is ready to receive, the Lord will give you wisdom, discernment, and protection. He doesn't withhold anything from us that we need to live triumphantly. Nothing is impossible when you learn to trust in Him more than you trust in yourself." He had Arthur's complete attention. "As far as the way in which God showed me what you, Bill, and the others were up to, well, I would encourage you to ask Him to reveal it to you." Horatio chuckled. "Like they say, Arthur, 'No Jesus, No Peace. Know Jesus, Know Peace.' Have a nice day. I've got to get ready for an appointment." He eased the door closed and then moved to a window to observe Arthur get into his car and drive away.

Unaware, Arthur had confirmed exactly what God had revealed to Horatio in his dreams. The former trustees of Good Shepherd were the demonically-influenced hypocrites who were determined to run him out of town.

"Lord, you never cease to amaze me," he thought aloud.

****

At nine thirty, Horatio's cell phone rang. Recognizing the caller's number, he answered.

"Sara, what's the latest with Daniel?" he asked, expecting more bad news.

"Pastor. They're really fast-tracking his adoption vote. It's scheduled to take place at three o'clock this Friday," she whispered. "Sheila says everything they're doing goes against standard procedure."

"Sara, I agree. This is crazy," he acknowledged. "One thing that God has taught me during my faith walk is this: if something doesn't make any sense naturally, it makes perfect sense, spiritually. And this situation that's taking place with Daniel screams: spiritual warfare."

"Yeah, Sheila's like, what's up with this…?" Sara confirmed. "And, she ought to know."

"Listen. Rene and I are meeting at the clerk's office at noon to get our marriage license. After that, we'll look for a justice of the peace to perform the ceremony," he explained. "Then, I need to pick up an adoption application and get it back to Mercy Ministries right away, so it will be on record before the vote takes place."

"An application for reunification is what you need." Sara explained, "It's a different process but, if you can get the application back to me right away, I'll ask Sheila to bring it directly to Mrs. Monahan."

"Oh, Sara, that would be awesome." Horatio was encouraged. "I'll see you at your office before the close of business today."

****

Horatio was sitting in his car at twelve twenty when Rene arrived. She parked alongside his car. He was so deep in prayer that it took the sound of her car door closing shut to quicken his attention as to what was taking place around him. Looking up at Rene, he saw, in her face, every emotion that she attempted to conceal. A modest application of makeup did little to camouflage the concerns that oppressed her. Eyes dimmed with worry, a smile less broad, and a voice weakened by bouts of crying. Still, there was something about her countenance that caused him to see her as the most beautiful woman in the world.

Exiting his car, he, lovingly, embraced her and said, "Don't worry, Rene. Everything is going to be okay. Promise." She held on to him and his promise as would a drowning person clinging to a life preserver. He had absolutely no way of guaranteeing his promise and he knew it. *Lord, we need your help*, he prayed inwardly.

They quickly made their way to the clerk's office and, after presenting sufficient identification, completing the application process and paying the twenty dollar fee, the clerk instructed them to return in three days and pick up the license.

"Three days…." Horatio sighed. "We don't have three days."

"Sir, I'm sorry but that's the law," the clerk explained.

"Miss…," Horatio began.

"It's Mrs., actually. Mrs. Dooley."

"Ma'am. Mrs. Dooley. We're in a tight spot here," he explained. "We have to get married right away. Our son's future hangs in the balance. We don't have three days. Three days will be too late."

"Mrs. Dooley, is there any way around the three-day wait period?" Rene asked. "My fiancée is not exaggerating. If we don't get married right away, any chance that we have to be reunited with my son could be lost, forever."

"Oh, my. Let me think. Wait just a minute," she instructed. The clerk retreated to a desk at the rear of the counter area and made a phone call. Horatio and Rene joined hands and whispered a prayer that a solution would be found. Mrs. Dooley returned with, what appeared to be, good news.

"According to state law, there is only one way you can bypass the three-day wait period," Mrs. Dooley said. "You have to go to the courthouse and get a judge to grant you a waiver."

"How long does that take?" Horatio asked.

"I don't know. I've never seen it done before," the clerk acknowledged. "Perhaps someone at Hingham District Court can answer your question."

"Hingham District Court…?" Rene repeated, nervously.

"Yeah, it's about ten minutes from here. You'd better get going. Courthouse might be busy," Mrs. Dooley advised.

"Thanks for your help, ma'am," Horatio said, as he and Rene turned and walked hurriedly, arm in arm, out the door.

Rene was, unusually, quiet along the way to the courthouse. Horatio attributed her disconnect to the pressure she was experiencing. If the court refused to grant the waiver, the wedding ceremony couldn't take place until Friday. In all likelihood, that wouldn't allow sufficient time to file an application before the scheduled adoption vote. He gazed at Rene from the corner of his eye as she, stoically, looked straight ahead.

"Rene. A penny for your thoughts," he said, attempting to engage her in conversation.

With her eyes fixed on the roadway, she responded, "I think that maybe we're getting in God's way."

At that, Horatio pulled the car onto the roadway shoulder. "What? I don't understand. What are you saying?"

"Maybe, we should just wait the three days and then get married," she muttered.

"If we do that, we won't have enough time to get our application in before Friday's vote," he reminded her. "Rene, are you having second thoughts about marrying me?"

Rene, positioning herself to look directly into Horatio's eyes, replied, "Honey, I love you so much. No one has ever made me feel as happy as you do. Being your wife would be like a dream come true for me."

"So then, what's going on, Rene? You need to be honest with me."

"I don't want to step foot inside any courthouse ever again, Horatio. Hingham, especially," she tensed up. "People, there, remember me. Every time I've been in a courthouse, something bad has happened. I always come away feeling like I had just been raped while everybody stared, pointed, and laughed. And, now you're asking me to return to that very same place with the same people in their authority flexing positions, to plead for their help, in order to be rejoined with my son? Well, I'm sorry but, I am not interested in giving them another opportunity to humiliate me."

"But Rene, you spoke about trusting God. What happened?" You're not giving him a chance. We prayed and prayed again that God would make a way in all of what's going on," he reminded. "Now, you're telling him, 'Lord, this situation is bigger than you.' Isn't that what you're saying?"

"No. I didn't mean it that way, Horatio. You don't understand," she replied, defensively.

"Then, help me understand, Rene. This walk of faith to be reunited with Daniel is every bit as important to me as it is you. We have nothing to gain by sitting on our hands for the next three days. Absolutely nothing to gain but, so much to lose. Rene, I have lost enough. You've lost enough. Remember the similar dream we shared when we were so close to being happily joined in marriage. The dark forces rose up against us to make us believe that neither of us was worthy of being happy or loved?"

"I remember," she nodded in agreement.

"I believe that God is about to bless us. I also believe that before this whole thing is over, Satan is going to come against us with every weapon he has. He'll attempt to discourage us, divide us and render us defeated. Let's do what God has given us the understanding to do and fight for our son. Please." Horatio's eyes welled up.

"You're right. I'm so sorry for allowing fear to diminish my faith." Rene leaned over the arm rest and embraced him, before planting a big kiss on his lips. It was the first time that the husband-and-wife-to-be had publicly kissed. Realizing what had just taken place, they blushed. They proceeded to the courthouse after he reached over to plant a loving kiss of his own on her lips.

****

At the courthouse, they located the civil clerk's office and stood at the counter, waiting to be helped. Within a few minutes, a woman came forward to assist them.

"Hi, are you folks being helped?"

"Not yet," Rene responded.

"Well, then. How can I help you?"

"We were told by the clerk at town hall that we could come here to get a marriage license waiver," Horatio explained.

"A waiver?" The woman was puzzled. "What do you need the waiver to do?"

"It will let us get married right away and not have to wait the three days," Rene explained.

"I've worked here for four years and I've never heard of anything like that," the woman continued, "Let me ask my supervisor about it." She called out to a woman at the other end of the counter, "Betty, do you have a minute? I need your help."

The clerk, after explaining the situation to her supervisor, returned and suggested that they come back to the courthouse the following morning. She assured them that, if they would leave the marriage application with her, she would forward it to the clerk magistrate for review before the morning session commenced. She promised to list their hearing first on the case docket. "Easy in, easy out," she said.

Encouraged by the turn of events, Horatio and Rene left the courthouse all smiles, hand in hand. They drove back to Scituate town hall so Rene could pick up her car and return to work. Before parting, they agreed to talk on the phone, later.

Horatio drove directly to the office of Mercy Ministries to pick up the application. Sheila was seated behind the receptionist desk.

"Hi, Sheila. How are you doing today?"

Looking up, she smiled and said, "Hi. I remember you. You were here around Christmas time. What brings you here, today?"

"I'm here to pick up a reunification application," he replied with a big grin.

"You have a child in foster care?"

"Not yet, and with the grace of God, I plan to keep it that way,"

Sheila was baffled. "I don't understand."

"My fiancée has a beautiful son here. We're getting married tomorrow," he explained. "As soon as the marriage license is signed and recorded, we're filing the application for reunification."

"Oh, that's wonderful." Sheila was excited. "What's her son's name?"

"His name is Daniel."

"Daniel!" she exclaimed. Her eyes grew wide. "Do you know Sara?"

"Yes, I do. I'm her pastor," he replied. "In fact," he whispered, "Sara has been keeping us apprised of everything that's been taking place with him."

"I know all about Daniel's situation," she whispered, in response. "Something about it stinks to high heaven. I told Sara that."

"Sheila, Sara thinks a lot of you. She knows that you have a heart for the children in Mercy Ministries' care. Daniel's mother and I want him home with us. Will you help us?"

"Pastor, I'll do whatever I can," she promised.

With that, she turned and reached into a file cabinet drawer. Retrieving a folder containing reunification applications, she removed one and placed it in an envelope. Handing it to him,

she instructed, "Fill this out and bring it back to me with a copy of your marriage license as quickly as you can." She continued, "When you do, I'll give you a date-stamped receipt to prove your application is in the system before the vote takes place on Friday. It may buy you a little more time to advocate for Daniel's reunification, but I can't say for sure how much. I'll put your application in the director's hand myself."

"Sheila, thank you so much. I'll see you tomorrow." Horatio thanked God for touching Sheila's heart. On his way back to the office, he noticed an ominous cloud bank on the horizon. The wind velocity had increased to the extent that he sensed it pushing against the car. Caught unaware, he processed aloud, "Whoa. Where did that gust come from?"

Earlier in the week, local weather reports had predicted a storm that had a fifty-fifty chance of producing plowable amounts of snow. Horatio was so focused on Daniel's situation and the marriage license that he had disconnected from the news and weather reports, altogether. Now, realizing that might have been a mistake, he turned the radio on just in time to hear a local weather report advising of significant snowfall, commencing at dusk.

Lord, please don't let the weather cause a problem in getting us through this process, he prayed. An occasional snow flurry settled on the windshield of his car, as he drew nearer to his office.

At four thirty, he sent Rene a text. After a series of back and forth ideas, she promised to call him as soon as she was safely home.

****

"Hello. Hello," Sam Wooden called from the church foyer at five fifteen.

"In here, Sam."

"Pastor, I was passing by and saw the lights on. The trustees were supposed to meet tonight but, I left messages for everyone that we'd have to reschedule because of the storm. When I saw the lights, I figured maybe someone didn't get the message," Sam explained.

"Do you think the storm is really going to be that bad, Sam?"

"Pastor, it looks like the weather people got this one right. Have you looked out the window? It's getting serious outside."

"I came in about an hour and a half ago. It was only flurrying," Horatio explained. Getting up from his desk chair, he made his way to a window. Looking out, he exclaimed, "Oh, no! Lord, no. Not now. Please."

The roads, lawns, and rooftops were completely cloaked in white. It was as though it had been storming for hours.

"What's the matter, Pastor?"

Horatio detailed the events of the past seventy-two hours as much as he could recall. Sam was deeply grieved. He had never, before, seen his pastor this deflated.

"Pastor, how can I help?"

"Sam, pray with us that the courthouse will be open tomorrow, so Rene and I can get the license. Get in touch with as many prayer warriors as you can think of and ask them to pray for us," he pleaded.

"Done. I'm on it," Sam promised. "Now, I suggest that you think about making your way next door. Try to get some rest. You and Rene have a busy day ahead of you tomorrow. In fact, mind if Teresa and I tag along as witnesses to the momentous occasion?"

"We'd like that, a lot."

"All righty, then. I'll give you a call about eight thirty, weather permitting. Good night."

Horatio closed down his office and went, directly, home.

****

Rene called him at six thirty. "Hi, honey. Sorry, I'm so late. The roads were covered."

"Just knowing that you're safe and sound is all that matters. How was the rest of your afternoon?"

"It was difficult. Kind of like a rollercoaster. Know what I mean?"

"I know exactly what you mean. One minute victory is within reach, the next minute you feel like you're going down for the last time."

"Horatio, honey. Thank you for loving me. I wouldn't have the strength to attempt any of what we're doing for Daniel without you."

"And, Rene, I wouldn't want to go through this with anyone but you. It's going to be real interesting tomorrow morning if this storm doesn't blow out of here within the next couple of hours."

"Do you think we're going to have a problem getting to see a judge?" Rene asked.

"Lord, I hope not. You know how quickly municipal buildings close during snowstorms. We took the option of finding another courthouse that might be open, off the table, when we agreed to leave the paperwork with that clerk."

"Just a little more for God to work out, I guess." Rene chuckled.

They spoke for hours, paying no attention to time. Laughing, planning, enjoying their relationship as only best friends could. They said good night at eleven o'clock.

Day 71
February 12th - Tuesday

At six thirty, Horatio awoke to the sound of wind-driven ice pellets hitting against his bedroom window. Jumping up out of bed to assess the after effects of the storm, he stood motionless at what his eyes beheld. Nothing moved on land or in the air. The snowstorm was still in effect and displayed little interest in leaving town, anytime soon. Silhouettes of snow-covered cars, abandoned by their drivers for lack of traction, littered the road. The intensity of the northeast wind caused four-foot snowdrifts to form in every direction. This was the biggest snowstorm that Scituate had experienced since the monster blizzard of '78. He attempted to call Rene repeatedly to alert her to what was taking place outside but, the cell signal failed. Fully convinced that there was nothing he could do to until weather conditions improved, he returned to bed.

Horatio was, finally, able to connect with Rene at ten thirty. "Thank God. I've been trying to reach you all morning."

"Same here," Rene replied. "I tried calling and texting you. When I didn't hear back, I began to worry."

"It's been one of those mornings," he explained. "I was so resigned to wait for the cell phone signal to be restored that I completely forgot to try calling you on the landline. Sorry, didn't mean to stress you."

"The news is reporting that municipal buildings won't reopen until Thursday," Rene informe d.

"Thursday? Are you sure? That doesn't sound right."

"Check for yourself. It's on every channel."

"Oh, my God, Rene. What more can go wrong?" he sighed.

"Honey, I know that you're doing the best you can," she continued. "If getting Daniel back is what God intends, no snowstorm, no judge, no adoption vote will keep it from happening. You told me yesterday: 'Give God a chance.' You said that we have to trust Him. I was feeling so vulnerable, so weak in my faith when you reminded me that nothing is too difficult for God. So, honey, let me ask you: how are you feeling now?"

"Vulnerable and pretty darn weak," he chuckled. "Rene, I love you."

****

The first snowplow passed by Good Shepherd at twelve thirty that afternoon. Every media outlet continued to loop news footage of snow-clogged roadways and weather-related cancellations. The governor of Massachusetts declared a state of emergency, until further notice. Weather forecasters predicted that the snowstorm would dump as much as an additional foot of accumulation before winding down and moving away, tonight.

****

Phone calls, text messages, and emails kept Horatio and Rene in contact with each other until the storm departed. By nine thirty, that evening, more than three feet of snow had fallen. It was a foregone conclusion that life as normal would not return to Scituate or the surrounding area for two days, at least. If there was at all a silver lining to be found in the events of the past twenty-four hours, it would be the very real likelihood that Friday's scheduled adoption vote would be delayed, giving Horatio and Rene sufficient time to get married and submit their application for Daniel. They bade good night to each other at eleven o'clock.

Day 72
February 13th - Wednesday

Snow removal equipment moved aggressively in every direction throughout the night. The distinct vibration and clanging of each passing snowplow caused Horatio to believe that the declared state of emergency would soon be lifted. The regional travel ban was scheduled to expire at three o'clock this afternoon. The official announcement returned autonomy to cities and towns in the Metropolitan Boston area to determine when schools and municipal offices would re-open. The announcement, further, stated that nonessential, state-run buildings and agencies would remain closed until further notice.

"There's no way they can consider courthouses as nonessential buildings," he reasoned aloud. "Courthouses are as vital as police stations and hospitals. Lord, please let the Hingham court house be open."

At four o'clock, he trudged to the church to escape the boredom of cabin fever. Good Shepherd's weekly prayer meeting was scheduled to begin in two hours. It was a foregone conclusion that the meeting couldn't, safely, take place. As he watched the church's plowing contractor clear the parking lot and walkways, his phone rang. It was Captain Gervais.

"Pasteur Horatio, how are you doing, my friend?"

"Hello, Captain. I'm fine, thank you," Horatio responded, unenthusiastically.

"But, you don't sound happy to hear from your friend," the captain observed.

"I apologize, Captain. This has been a very difficult week for me." Horatio explained.

"You are the man of God who works wonders for so many people," the captain reminded him. "Why should you be so discouraged?" After hearing the account of what Horatio was dealing with, Captain Gervais could only respond, "This situation is impossible. What are you going to do?"

"Captain, I'm going to continue trust God. Pray and trust God," Horatio repeated.

"I don't want to appear insensitive, but have you given further thought to my proposition?"

"Captain…." Horatio sighed.

"Say no more," the captain offered, apologetically. "Please call me when you are able. In the meanwhile, I will pray for you and your loved ones."

"Thank you, my friend. I appreciate that," Horatio said.

The call ended.

****

His response to Captain Gervais continued to resonate in his spirit.

"So much coming against us, Lord," he cried out. *Rene and I need to come together in prayer*, he processed. At that moment he called her. "Rene, there's no prayer meeting tonight. Mind if I come over so we can pray together?"

"Do you think it's wise to travel? We should probably just pray over the phone," she suggested.

"I've noticed a few cars traveling through town, so I should be okay. With so much at stake, we can't let a little snow or ice defeat us." He continued, "And don't forget that 2 Kings 7:3 reminds us: we should not sit here 'til we die. So I would really like to come over and pray with you."

"I'd like that a lot," she acknowledged.

"Great. I'm on my way."

Cautiously making his way to her apartment, he arrived at five thirty. After a moment's embrace, they breathed a sigh of relief.

"Oh, Horatio, what more could possibly happen?" she asked, teary-eyed. "I've believed for so long that I was fighting a battle that couldn't be won. Now, you've been undeservedly brought into all of this because of me. I'm so sorry, Horatio."

"Rene, it's not our battle. The battle belongs to God," he said as he wiped a tear from her cheek. "Only God knows what's ahead of us and only He can work it out. In fact," he paused, "I believe that he already has. And, whatever the end result, we'll be fine."

"It seems as though every time I'm able to take a step forward away from my past, something wicked comes along and knocks me backward, again. It's like someone has put a curse on me," she explained.

"That's why I'm so glad to have you in my life, Rene. I'm reminded of the poor choices and situations in my past that I could have handled differently. You represent everything that's good and possible. Through all you've experienced in life, you continue to be strong for Daniel and yes, for me. It's never about you, Rene. You are the most loving, caring, and determined woman I've ever known."

"Really?" She blushed.

"From the first day I arrived in Scituate, I've been praying unsuccessfully against darkness and failure. It's become a way of life for me," he said. "Since I met you, while the presence of darkness and evil has intensified, I no longer feel like I'm all alone in this."

"Well, I'm certainly glad to have you in my life, Pastor Smiley," Rene confirmed with an embrace. They sat down to pray when his cell phone rang. Recognizing the incoming call was from Sam Wooden, he answered.

"Sam, is everything all right?"

"Actually, I'm not sure, Pastor," Sam began. "Seems we have a good number of prayer warriors here for weekly prayer but our pastor has gone missing."

"What did you just say, Sam?" Horatio asked. Wanting Rene to hear the reason for Sam's call, he activated the speaker feature before Sam could respond.

"I said you've got about thirty prayer warriors waiting here at the church for our pastor to come and lead us," Sam repeated. "Will you be joining us? We've got to get busy praying that God will open up those courthouse doors bright and early tomorrow morning, so he can get this wedding done." Sam chuckled.

"Sam, that's wonderful news. We're on our way. See you, all, in twenty minutes," he promised. They leaped up and down with joy. God had sent others to stand with them in this very difficult time. They recognized Sam's call as confirmation that God had heard their prayers and was responding to them.

"Horatio, this is wonderful. We're not alone," she said. "You said that God is with us. You were right."

"Thank you, Lord," he laughed as he gave Rene another hug.

****

Arriving at the church, they counted thirty-six cars in the parking lot. During storms past, the church provided off-street parking for neighbors to facilitate the safe clearing of snow from public streets and walkways. Tonight, however, every one of the cars in the lot had carried someone to prayer meeting to stand in support of Horatio and Rene.

They heard Sam's voice leading the prayer, as they entered the church. By this time, more than fifty people were gathered in front of the altar with hands raised, engaged in fervent prayer, petitioning God to move in their pastor's situation. As Horatio and Rene advanced toward the altar, words of encouragement and vows of support were received. The prayer was interrupted, momentarily. In that time, Horatio spoke of his appreciation.

Taking hold of Rene's hand, he addressed those present.

"Tonight you have chosen to risk your safety to come and stand with us in this difficult time. Your very presence means more to us than words can express. The Lord speaks to each of us in times of testing. He reminds us that He is with us. He hasn't forsaken us. But too often, voices of doubt or the appearance of overwhelming circumstance cause us to believe that we can't win. Rene and I were at the precipice of falling into the abyss of doubt when Sam called to inform us that you had come to pray. My brothers and sisters in Christ, the unselfish, loving act that you have demonstrated by standing with us here tonight has caused the voices of doubt and failure to be silenced. We thank the Lord for you and the victory to come."

Everyone applauded and Sam led the group in a chorus of "How Great Thou Art."

The prayer meeting ended at eight thirty. A number of those present asked if they could come to the courthouse hearing in the morning as a show of support. Horatio assured them that their presence wouldn't be necessary, since getting the paperwork shouldn't be problematic. He promised to keep them up to date with all that occurred. Rene and Horatio returned to her home just long enough to discuss their planned trip to the courthouse. Horatio was home and in bed by ten fifteen.

Day 73
February 14th - Thursday

"Good morning. Happy Valentine's Day," Horatio greeted as Rene entered his car.

"Happy Valentine's Day to you, too. Did you manage to sleep at all?"

"Not a wink," he replied, chuckling. "How about you?"

"Ditto," she said.

"So, what do you think the Lord has in store for us today?" Horatio asked.

"Ask me that after I've had a cup of coffee." Rene chuckled.

"Excellent comeback. You're in rare form this morning. Isn't it wonderful to be able to laugh in the midst of a storm?"

"Ask me that after I've had my coffee," she responded, straight-faced. After stopping at a coffee drive-thru, they continued on to Hingham District courthouse.

****

As they neared the courthouse parking lot, their hearts sank.

"Oh, my Goodness, the courthouse is closed." Rene sighed. "There's no one here except a couple of snowplows."

Horatio was silent. Searching for an encouraging word, he found none. Their car couldn't advance more than twenty-five feet inside the lot entryway because the snow hadn't, yet, been cleared.

"Hold on. I'll be right back," he said, as he exited the car.

Uncertain of his course of action, he found himself standing outside feeling frustrated and without a plan B. From his vantage point, he observed two pieces of heavy equipment pushing the snow away. A pickup truck was parked alongside the courthouse. Flagging down the driver of the larger plow truck, he called out:

"Any idea on when the courthouse will reopen?"

The man, seemingly unable to hear his question, rolled down his window and barked, "Hey, you need to move that car out of there. Courthouse is closed. You're blocking the access for our other equipment."

"I'm not staying," Horatio explained, "I'm just trying to find out when the courthouse is going to reopen."

"I don't know, buddy. Does it look to you like I work in the courthouse? I don't get paid to talk. I drive trucks. That's all," the man responded, dismissively.

Horatio recognized that a demonic spirit was influencing the man's attitude so he prayed: "Lord, hold back the darkness. Grant me favor with this man, in Jesus' name."

At that moment, the truck driver applied his air brake. A loud "Whooosh!" from the truck's undercarriage caused the fluffy snow to blow back into Horatio's face. The truck door flew open and the cigar-chomping man climbed down from the cab of the truck. Rene observed the interaction and processed it as though the man was ready to fight Horatio.

Reflexively, she opened her door to hurry to his assistance. Before the man's second foot came in contact with the ground, Horatio was braced to defend himself. As the man turned to face Horatio, his disposition changed completely. The truck driver stood all of five feet, four inches tall. Horatio's six-foot frame towered over the man and his familiar, youthful smile had been replaced with a stern look.

"Sir, if you go over by the door where that pickup truck is parked," the truck driver began, "and give a couple of solid raps, someone will open up the door for you. Maybe they can tell you when the court will reopen."

"Thank you," Horatio responded as he turned and headed in the direction of the door.

Rene, witnessing the exchange, chuckled and returned to the car. *That's right, buddy. You better not mess with my man.*

Horatio noticed a set of footprints in the snow by the pickup truck leading to a side door. After a few minutes of knocking, an elderly man resembling a custodian appeared.

"Can I help you?" the man asked.

"Yes, thank you," Horatio began. "The other day my fiancee and I dropped off some paperwork that had to be signed by a judge," he explained. "I wanted to get the paperwork back since there's nobody here to sign it, today. Maybe we can get it signed at another courthouse. I don't mean to be a bother, but this is an emergency," he emphasized.

"The courthouse should reopen tomorrow. I'm sure that this can be resolved first thing, then," the man offered.

"Sir, tomorrow may be too late to save our son," Horatio hung his head.

"Too late to save your son?" The man's curiosity was piqued. "My, this certainly sounds dire. Please, step inside. Let's keep the heat in. Now, what's this all about?"

In the next few minutes, Horatio explained the history and urgency of the situation involving Daniel's upcoming adoption vote. In the middle of the conversation, his eyes grew wide.

"Oh, no. Rene," he remembered. "My fiancee is outside. I left her in the car."

"Do you want to go back and bring her inside while I try to locate your paperwork?" the man asked.

"Yes, thank you. That would be wonderful," Horatio said as he turned to go and retrieve her. He trudged back in the direction of the car to find that Rene had moved it to keep the lot entryway clear for other vehicles. He observed her praying as he approached. Startled at the opening of her door, she recoiled.

"Sorry. Didn't mean to sneak up on you."

"That's okay. I saw you go inside. Any news?"

"Not sure, yet. The custodian is trying to locate the paperwork for us. The courthouse isn't scheduled to open until tomorrow, so if we can get the paperwork, we may be able to find another courthouse that's open and have them approve it. Otherwise, we will have satisfied the three-day wait requirement by tomorrow morning so we can get married without the court's sign off, anyway."

"Is that going to give us enough time to get the application back to Sara?"

"I'm praying that she'll get our application to the director in time," he said. "Come on."

They secured the car and walked to the side door of the building. After a few knocks, the door opened up. As they entered the building, Rene's eyes met with the custodian's. She froze.

"Ms. Brock, it's been a while. How have you been?" the man asked. She didn't respond. Her face became flush, as if she'd seen a ghost.

"Rene. Are you all right?" Horatio asked.

"Good morning, Judge Young," she responded.

"Judge Young?" Horatio was shocked. "You're a judge? I thought you were…."

"Yes, Mr. Smiley. I am a judge. Come inside and let's find out what's going on with your paperwork."

Horatio noticed that Rene was very uncomfortable. Her discomfort became a distraction in their ability to respond to Judge Young's questions about Daniel. Unsuccessful in his attempt to locate the paperwork, the judge, mercifully, invited Rene to return to their car while asking Horatio to remain. She couldn't leave fast enough. Horatio was led back to the judge's office.

"Mr. Smiley, sit down, please. The road to hell is paved with good intentions," the judge began as he sat behind a very large desk. "I'm not sure that I would be comfortable signing your waiver. You appear to be a very nice young man, but please understand this noble act of marriage rescuing this damsel in distress, as it were, appears to be based on kindness, not love. I may be the last of a dying breed, but I believe that no marriage has a snowball's chance in hell of enduring, if it is not based on a relationship of love of the highest order," the judge explained. "Your fiancee is known to me and to the court system. A person's actions, not their words, says a lot about them. Your fiancee's demeanor a few minutes ago displayed a level of discomfort or dishonesty. I'm not certain which of the two it is but, either way, that causes me to be greatly concerned. Greatly concerned. Are you getting my drift, young man?"

"Judge Young, I mean you no disrespect but, you couldn't be any more wrong about Rene Brock if you tried. While it's true that the reason for moving up our wedding date is a desperate attempt at, quite possibly, the only chance we'll ever have of reuniting her with her son, make no mistake: I love this wonderful, beautiful woman with all of my heart. No woman has ever loved and inspired me as she has. She is my gift from God and I will do everything within my ability to show her the love that she is so deserving of. No matter what the opinion of Rene you may have, as you consider her past or ponder statistics, I would encourage you to read John 8:7. Do yourself a favor," he said as he stood up to leave.

"Let he who is without sin cast the first stone," the judge recited. "One of my favorites. How is it that you are familiar with that scripture?" the judge asked.

"As a pastor, I am expected to know all scripture and live accordingly," Horatio responded.

"You're a pastor? Where's your church?"

"I pastor at Church of the Good Shepherd in Scituate."

"Good Shepherd? I've heard about Good Shepherd," Judge Young continued. "It's the white church by Scituate Harbor, right?"

"Yes, that's right."

"Doesn't George Heywood attend your church?" the judge asked.

"Yes, sir. He and his wife are good people and dear friends of mine."

"Pastor, your fiancee continues to wait, patiently, outside in your car. Seeing that I cannot locate your waiver form in the clerk's case file, it must be with one of the other judges. If you will leave your phone number, I'll have my law clerk contact you first thing tomorrow morning. You can come and have your application presented then."

"Thank you, Judge Young. Rene and I appreciate your help." Horatio smiled, graciously, and shook his hand.

Exiting through the side door, he walked slowly to the car. Rene was slouched down in her seat, resembling a deflated doll. Uncertain of how much of his conversation with Judge Young he should share with her, he prayed that God would guard his words. Rene propped herself up at the sight of Horatio's appearing, attempting to convey a façade of strength.

"Wow, you were in there for a long time," she said, as he opened the door. "How did it go?"

"Well, he couldn't find the paperwork so, we have to come back tomorrow."

"But we don't have to deal with him, do we?" Rene began to tense up.

"I don't think so. He said that another judge already has the forms."

"Thank God for that. Horatio, I'm so sorry for the way I acted in there," she explained. "I don't know what came over me. It was like an out-of-body experience. Seeing Judge Young, again, caused me to become paralyzed with fear. I couldn't move. I couldn't speak."

"What was it about him that upset you so? He certainly remembered you."

"Judge Young presided over the case against Daniel's father," she replied. "I was called in to testify as a witness for the prosecution because of the history of physical and emotional abuse I experienced throughout my relationship with him. At that time, I was 'tore up from the floor up' as the saying goes. The defense attorney was well informed about every one of my shortcomings and he capitalized on them, big time. By the time the trial was over, I came out of the exchange looking like I was the biggest deviant on the face of the earth. At the time, Daniel was already in the state CPS system. After the verdict for Daniel's father was read, Judge Young asked me about my future intentions. I told him that I hadn't been involved with alcohol or marijuana since being free of that relationship. I let him know that I had a full-time job and an apartment. At that point, he offered to personally advocate for me if I could pass a screening test. I declined his offer because I wasn't telling the truth. I was so nervous about the trial that I had smoked and drank the night before I was scheduled to testify. Judge Young referred to me as disingenuous and said that I wasn't ready to be responsible for the care of an infant child. Receiving every word the judge spoke as true, I signed a document that gave custody of Daniel to the state. I have lived with the guilt of my weakness in that moment ever since."

"Rene, with the grace of God, by this time tomorrow this whole marriage license thing will be behind us."

"Thank Heaven for that much," she said. "Do you think it would be a good move to fill out the application for Sara today and date it for tomorrow?"

"Absolutely. Just one problem, though. I can't make it home without one of your wonderful kisses. What do you say?" He laughed as he leaned into her.

She gave him a hug and kiss so satisfying that he completely dismissed the sting of Judge Young's unflattering comments and Rene's recollection of her past.

"Hungry?" he asked.

"Famished," she replied, chuckling.

"Good. I know a place where we can get some excellent pasta and sauce." He laughed as they drove to his house.

****

"Judy, this is Aviana. I called you three times yesterday. You haven't returned any of my calls. I'm not happy. Listen to me, you witch: no more voice mails! If I don't hear back from you before twelve noon today, I will make sure that you rue the day you slept with my husband and everyone else. Hope you and whomever you're lying with, today, have a nice, disease-free morning. Call me." She slammed the phone back on its cradle for effect.

****

Horatio's phone rang at eleven thirty. It was Sam Wooden.

"Morning, Pastor. How'd everything go at the courthouse?"

"Lousy, Sam. The courthouse was closed so, we have to try again, tomorrow."

"Pastor, don't be discouraged. You know the devil is real mad. He's going deep into his bag of tricks but the battle is already won. We've got the victory, in Jesus' name."

"You're preaching to the choir, my friend." Horatio chuckled. "I'll let you know when something happens," he promised.

"Thanks. I appreciate that, Pastor." The call ended.

****

At eleven forty, Judy returned Aviana's call.

"Judy, Its about time you got back to me. What do you have for me?" Aviana demanded.

"A current list of the area's top-rated dentists," Judy fired back.

"What are you talking about?" Aviana was puzzled.

"You'll figure it out when you're picking your teeth up off the floor."

"Are you threatening me, you witch?" Aviana challenged.

"I don't need to threaten you about anything, Aviana. I'm just telling you that I've penciled you on my schedule two times: first, I've got you scheduled for a good old-fashioned butt whipping. I'm going to knock every artificially whitened tooth out of your surgically-enhanced face. Then, five minutes after that, I'm going to dutifully place a list of local dentists in the palm of your pampered little hands."

"Oh, really?" Aviana snickered. "And, when is that supposed to happen, Judy?"

"Immediately after you call and leave me another message like the one you did this morning. In fact, don't bother me ever again. If you think I'm to be played with, try me. I dare you." Judy slammed the phone down.

Aviana called Barry, upset about the manner in which Judy had spoken to her. "I'm a good person, Barry. People are so mean to me. I miss my Julep so much," she cried.

****

Horatio and Rene enjoyed the rest of Valentine's Day watching movies and eating popcorn while they filled out the application. Rene had taken a vacation day from her job and activity at the church was limited because of the snowstorm. They placed "I love you" telephone calls to Mrs. Smiley and Mrs. Brock. At ten o'clock, he drove Rene home. Horatio agreed to call her in the morning as soon as the court confirmed that their paperwork was ready for pickup.

Day 74
February 15th - Friday

At ten fifteen, the courthouse Clerk called Horatio.

"Good morning. Is this Horatio Smiley?"

"Yes, speaking."

"Mr. Smiley, the petition you filed is scheduled to be heard at four thirty this afternoon," the clerk informed. "You should be there with Ms. Brock by four fifteen to allow for sufficient time."

"Four fifteen?" he sighed. "Ma'am, I'm sorry, that's not going to work. Four fifteen will be, too, late. Can I come now and take my paperwork back?"

"No, sir. The paperwork has already been given to the judge. Your attorney will have to file a petition to suspend the hearing and request that your paperwork be withdrawn from the docket." The caller explained, "It's very likely that your attorney won't be given a hearing date before the middle of next week."

"The middle of next week? The middle of next week?" he repeated. "Lady, you're breaking my heart, here."

"I'm sorry, sir, but that's the way the court system works," the clerk explained, apologetically. "Please be here at four fifteen. Please dress appropriately." The call ended.

"Oh, Lord. How am I supposed to break this news to Rene? She'll be devastated," he agonized. "There's absolutely no way that we'll be able to get the application to the orphanage in time. Lord, I need your help," he cried out. "Please, tell me what to do."

In that moment, the name of a local attorney who advertised heavily on television came to mind. Locating the attorney's phone number, Horatio called his office.

"Good morning. May I speak with Attorney Fullercrapp?"

"Who's calling, please?" the receptionist asked.

"My name is Pastor Horatio Smiley."

"Please hold, sir," the receptionist instructed. After a while, she returned to the phone. "Excuse me. Did you say you were a priest?"

"No, ma'am. I'm the pastor of a nondenominational church."

"Thank you. Just one moment, please. Attorney Fullercrapp will be right with you."

"Good morning, Pastor Smiley. Attorney Fullercrapp here. How can I help you?"

Horatio was so stressed that he couldn't savor the comic relief in the attorney's introduction. "Attorney, I need you to file a motion for me this morning at Hingham District Court. It has to be done right away," he emphasized.

"Slow down, Pastor," the attorney instructed. "Tell me exactly what's going on? Then, I can let you know what needs to be done and how much it's going to cost you."

Horatio explained the situation up to the point of receiving the phone call from the clerk's office that morning.

"Let me make a call to the clerk's office. I'll let you know what I find out. Your case is my number one priority. Remember, Fullercrapp doesn't mess around." The attorney chuckled.

Ninety minutes had passed since he had spoken with the attorney. It was eleven thirty when Horatio's cell phone rang. *Thank goodness*, he thought as he quickly lifted the phone from its holster.

"Hello," he answered, expecting a full report from the attorney.

"Hi, honey. How'd you make out at the court?" It was Rene.

"Oh, hi." He appeared to be distracted.

"Boy, the bloom sure fell off this rose quick enough. I thought you'd be happy to hear my voice," Rene quipped.

"Sorry. You caught me a bit off guard. I'm expecting a return call from someone," he explained.

"Anyone I know?"

"No, at least, not yet." He sighed.

"Horatio, you sound so burdened. What's wrong?"

He took Rene through the events of the morning, in detail.

"Four thirty will be too late to file the application and delay the vote," he continued. "I knew you would be devastated. I'm so sorry, Rene." She was silent. "Rene, are you there?"

"Yeah," she replied, attempting to hold back her tears. "We were so close, Horatio. So close to bringing Daniel home. And, to make matters worse, I can hear Satan laughing at us. He's rubbing our noses in this."

"What are you talking about?" he questioned.

"Think about it," she explained, "We've placed our trust in some attorney named Fullercrapp. It's going to be real embarrassing when this guy proves to be aptly named. Everyone will look at us like we're idiots."

"Won't be my first time, how about you?" He chuckled.

"Horatio, we shouldn't be trusting anyone but God," Rene insisted. "Call and cancel whatever arrangement you've made with that attorney. He's probably in his office right now preparing a bill for something he had no intention of doing, anyway. We just have to accept the outcome, whatever it is. After all, God knows what's best for all of us. I'm fine with it, if you are."

"You always know just what to say. You're right, maybe God isn't finished with this, yet."

"Do you want to ride to the hearing together or meet at the courthouse?" she asked.

"Let's ride together. Strength in numbers, you know," he rationalized. "I'll pick you up at three thirty. I love you."

"I love you, too," Rene countered. "And, don't worry, I promise not to do anything rash. I'm still believing that God is able."

"I'll call Fullercrapp now." *What was I thinking?* He chuckled, as he hung up the phone.

****

Horatio was in his office reading scripture when the desk phone rang.

"Church of the Good Shepherd. Pastor Smiley, speaking."

"Pastor Smiley, Sheila from Mercy Ministries," the voice announced in a hushed tone.

"Hi, Sheila. I have the application with me but, I won't be able to submit it until later this afternoon," he explained.

"Pastor, that may not be necessary. I think it's too late."

"Too late for what? I don't understand."

"About fifteen minutes ago, Mrs. Monahan's assistant, Judy, and the attorney for Mercy Ministries rushed Daniel away," she said. "I noticed that Judy was carrying a suitcase. I don't think Daniel's coming back."

"But, they didn't even take the vote. Wasn't the vote scheduled for later today?" Horatio was frantic. "This is wrong! They can't get away with this."

"Pastor Smiley, I don't know what to tell you. I'm so sorry."

"What about Sara?" he asked. "Do you think she might know anything about this?"

"Sara didn't come to work today, so I doubt that she would know anything, at all, about what's taken place," she explained.

"My God, just when you come to believe things can't get any worse...," he agonized. "I'm beginning to feel like Job must have felt. His torment grew worse each day. Through all his suffering, he never abandoned his faith in God and it pleased God. Job was greatly blessed because of his faithfulness. And, Lord," he spoke, looking heavenward, "we refuse to abandon our faith, no matter what may come against us. I know that you must have an awesome blessing in store for Rene and me. Satan knows it, too, and he is livid. He's doing everything he can to separate us from our faith. Please keep us in your prayers, Sheila."

"Pastor, I have been praying so much that things would have worked out for you. You know how passionate I am about family reunifications."

"I know, Sheila, and we appreciate your prayers. Remember, it's not over until God says it's over. Keep on believing," he encouraged.

"I will. I promise." The phone call ended.

His conversation with Sheila caused him to focus more on God than on his circumstance. Feeling squeezed on every side but confident that nothing is too difficult for God, he prayed:

Father, your thoughts and your ways are beyond my comprehension. Let your will be done in this situation. Rene and I trust in you completely. Take away our desire for anything that is not of you. Please, comfort Rene as only you can in this time of disappointment. In the Name of Jesus Christ I pray. Amen.

He decided to withhold Sheila's update from Rene because of his concern that it would be too much for her to bear. He understood that she was struggling to remain strong. At two thirty, he closed down his office and prepared to meet her.

Along the way, he decided to stop for gas. He and Rene had discussed finding a justice of the peace, getting married, and filing the application with Mercy Ministries before five o'clock. Given that the hearing was scheduled for four thirty, they understood that it was a very ambitious plan that would only be accomplished with God's help. A single delay in their plan could prove to be catastrophic. Meanwhile, Horatio continued to figure out what might have actually taken place with Daniel. He believed that despite what Sheila confided, a legal challenge to Daniel's placement with the adoptive parents could be entertained. He prayed that he was right. It was imperative that the reunification application be received by Mercy Ministries before the close of business today. He dared not mention anything about Daniel's departure from the orphanage, until the hearing was concluded.

****

As he stood beside his car pumping gas, he saw Sam Wooden and his family driving by. He waved but Sam didn't notice him. Close behind the Woodens' car was Timmy and Sara. Soon after, the Heywoods and the Willises rode by. *Everyone sure is busy, today. Coming and going in all directions,* he pondered.

Returning to the matter of Daniel and specifically the best way to bring Rene current with all that Sheila shared, his stomach began to knot up. *Lord, the last thing I need is an ulcer. Bind up this stress, please, in the Name of Jesus.* The pain diminished. After fueling up, he continued on to meet Rene. He called her five minutes before arriving, so that she would be ready.

She was standing inside her front door when he arrived. Bounding down the steps fully energized, she got into the car. Before Horatio could say hello, she reached over and kissed him.

"Too much caffeine today?" He chuckled. Inwardly, he was relieved to see that she wasn't stressed or withdrawn. The mention of the word "courthouse" was usually enough to cause her to tremble. *Maybe she won't be as devastated when I tell her the news about Daniel*, he pondered.

"How was your afternoon?" she asked.

"Frustrating, to be sure. How was yours?"

"Great," she teased, "Ask me what I did, today."

"Okay. Hey, Rene, what did you do, today?"

"I went to Mercy Ministries and I sat in my car and made a promise to Daniel that before this day was over, you and I would file the application to bring him home with us." She was excited. Horatio didn't hear a word after "Mercy Ministries and…." He struggled to stay focused but, failed miserably. He didn't respond. "Horatio, did you hear me?"

"I'm sorry, Rene. I was distracted. Please, tell me, again."

She repeated the details of her visit to Mercy Ministries and the resulting promise she made to Daniel to no avail. Horatio continued in his distraction, thinking only about her response to Daniel's move. Rene attributed his inability to focus on the pressure of accomplishing all that they had planned. They arrived at the courthouse at four o'clock.

****

Entering the courthouse lobby, they passed through security and were directed to the clerk's office. As they stood at the counter waiting to be served, they recognized the clerk who had accepted their paperwork on Monday. She motioned that she would be with them, momentarily.

"Hi, Mr. Smiley and Ms. Brock," the clerk greeted as she approached. "I'm going to ask you to be patient just a moment longer, while I retrieve your paperwork." She disappeared through a door at the back of the room and soon reappeared holding a manila file. In the time she was gone, Horatio and Rene observed the way they were being scrutinized by the clerk's office staff. Obvious gazes and whispers began to unnerve Rene.

"Horatio, do you see how they're looking at me?"

"They're looking at us," he acknowledged.

"No, they're looking at me. They probably pulled my file," she muttered.

"I'm going to ask you to follow me to Judge Young's chamber," the clerk instructed. Horatio and Rene looked at each other curiously. Rene appeared anxious. Horatio took her hand.

"Aren't we supposed to be in the courtroom?" he asked.

"I just do what I'm told," the woman replied. Opening the door to the judge's office, she directed them to sit down. "Judge Young will be with you shortly." She left the room.

A moment later, Judge Young walked in. Horatio and Rene stood to their feet.

"Pastor Smiley, Ms. Brock, please be seated," the judge requested. "I understand that you are on a mission to get some type of application filed for your son, Ms. Brock, but I thought it necessary to speak with you and Pastor Smiley before proceeding with the hearing." He continued, "Ms. Brock, I wanted the opportunity to speak to you candidly, as I did with Pastor Smiley the other day. Is that all right with you?"

"Yes, that's fine," she responded, gripping Horatio's hand tighter.

"May I call you Rene?"

"Yes, Your Honor."

"And Pastor Smiley, may I call you Horatio?"

"Yes, Your Honor."

"Splendid," Judge Young continued. "Rene, would you, please tell me why is it you want to marry Horatio?"

"Excuse me?" Rene asked, unsure of why the judge would ask such a personal question.

"Why do you want to marry Horatio?" the judge repeated.

"Because I love him," she responded. "Why do you ask?"

"The last time we spoke, you were in my courtroom and I asked you a direct question. Do you remember what that question was?"

"Your Honor, I remember that you asked me several questions."

"That's fair." He continued, "Do you remember me asking you why you would allow yourself to remain in an abusive relationship, as you were, and your answer was…."

"Because, I love him," she sighed.

"Exactly," the judge continued, "so, before we go into the courtroom and I rule on your waiver petition, I just want to be sure that I understand your motivation for entering into marriage with Horatio. I'm going to listen very carefully to what you tell me and consider your answer. So, please, indulge me."

Horatio was positioned to stop the interrogation, as soon as Rene showed any indication of being uncomfortable. To his amazement, she stood to her feet, looked Judge Young squarely in his eyes, and offered her response:

"Your Honor, I love Horatio with every fiber of my being. I would lay down my life for him without a second thought and I know that he would do the same for me." She continued, "When you and I last met, I was a mess. The morning that I appeared in your courtroom followed a night of drinking. Before that day, I hadn't had a drink in months. I knew it was the wrong thing to do, but I convinced myself that it wouldn't be a problem."

"But it was, Rene. Look what it cost you," Judge Young recalled.

"You're right, Your Honor. But more than that, look what it cost my son," her eyes began to well up. "I knew that I couldn't pass that screening test. I understood there would be a consequence for my poor judgment. I prayed that God would forgive me. I had absolutely no understanding that I would never see or be with my son, again. Every day my heart aches and I ask God to forgive me for the damage I've caused my son and my family." Rene sat down and began to sob. Horatio hugged her and stood to address the judge.

"Your Honor, it's clear that the wait time for the marriage license has been satisfied, so whether you sign the waiver or not, Rene and I will be married today." He continued, "Your questions have struck deep into wounds that haven't, yet, healed. Why do you persist in asking these questions? Why is this so important to you after all this time?"

"Rene. Horatio. Please listen carefully to what I'm about to say. Our court system is extremely guarded in the way cases are evaluated and adjudged. When the court issues a ruling, it is expected that each decision is based on fact, not on emotion. Courts expend a considerable amount of time and expense in deciding cases and, for that reason, courts do not like to reverse any decision it makes. We as judges take our responsibility quite seriously. Rene, I apologize for any part that I might have played in causing you any hurt, today, or at any time, before. Again, I am first human and second a judge. I, too, make mistakes."

"Thank you, Judge Young."

"I am going to ask my clerk to escort you to courtroom number three while I put on my robe. It's time we proceed with the hearing of your waiver application, if you are agreeable to that."

"That's fine. Thank you, Your Honor," they responded, respectfully.

The clerk returned and escorted them to a vacant courtroom, asking them to be seated in the front row and wait for the judge to enter. Horatio and Rene had lost track of time during their meeting with Judge Young. It was four forty-five.

"Horatio, we are way behind schedule. There's no way we're going to make it to Mercy Ministries before five o'clock, even if the judge does approve the waiver," Rene said. "You have to call Sheila and ask her to wait for us."

"Good idea," he responded. Immediately, his attention went to the reality that Daniel was no longer at the orphanage. Knowing what he knew, a call to Sheila would only make him look stupid and prolong his deception. He didn't know what to do but, he knew he couldn't just sit there. Obviously, Rene would suspect that something wasn't right.

As he stood to his feet, the courtroom door opened. It was the clerk.

"Mr. Smiley. Ms. Brock. There's been a mix-up. Will you follow me, please?"

They walked, quickly, behind her to a different area of the courthouse. They understood that the clerk didn't want to be tardy for the judge.

"Hurry, please. Just up ahead through those double doors," she instructed.

The clerk held the door open as Horatio and Rene rushed inside. Before the door closed behind them, they were greeted with, "SURPRISE!"

A keyboard began to play "Here Comes The Bride."

Horatio and Rene were stunned. They stood at the entryway of a conference room that had a standing room, only, gathering of family and friends who had come to witness the courthouse event. They looked at each other, questioning if one or the other had played a role in the surprise. Standing there, their supporters circled around them. Deacon and Mrs. Brock hugged and kissed them. Stepping aside, Horatio's parents stepped in.

"Mom. Dad. This is amazing. How did you know about all of this?" he asked, as he hugged them. "Mom, Dad, this is Rene. Rene, can you believe this?" He laughed. "Everybody, these are my parents," he shouted.

A side door to the room opened and Judge Young, the courtroom clerk, and a stenographer entered the room. True to his demeanor, he was clad in his judicial garb. He offered a smile, as he stepped to the front of the room. For the record, the clerk announced that the hearing was called to order.

"All rise. This session of Hingham District Court is called to order. Justice Wilbur Young, presiding. All cell phones off and no talking. Please be seated. Now, hearing docket number CV1019-17, in the matter of Horatio Smiley and Rene Brock. Applicants, please step forward."

There was no elevated seating position in the conference room, so Judge Young decided to stand behind a lectern for the benefit of all to witness his ruling on the waiver application. Horatio and Rene came forward and stood before him. In their nervousness, they held hands.

"In the matter of the applicants' waiver to be married immediately, let the record show that this court hereby gives its full consent and well wishes," Judge Young declared.

The courtroom erupted in applause.

"Order in the court!" the courtroom clerk barked.

Instructing the Courtroom stenographer to go off-record, Judge Young addressed the audience.

"Family members and friends of these two exceptional people, it is my understanding that there is a desire to be married before today is ended. Am I correct in my understanding?" he asked Horatio and Rene.

"Yes, Your Honor. We would like nothing more," Horatio said. Rene nodded in agreement.

"It' been brought to my attention that you intend to locate a justice of the peace and complete the marriage ceremony. Is that your plan?"

"Yes, Your Honor," Rene responded.

"Well, you know, Rene and Pastor, I'm pretty good at performing wedding ceremonies, if I do say so myself." Judge Young winked.

"Oh, Your Honor, could you? Would you, please?" Rene asked.

"But, with all that's been going on, I didn't bring the rings," Horatio said. "If you'll give me an hour, I can find a jewelry store and pick up some rings for the ceremony."

"Son, I'm an old man. In an hour from now, I expect to be at home, sitting in my favorite chair talking to my wife," the judge said, chuckling. "What do you say we make do with what the Lord has provided and have ourselves a wedding, right now?"

"That's fine with me. Is that okay with you, Rene?" Horatio asked.

"That's perfectly fine with me," she replied, smiling.

"I'm going to ask Mr. Brock to walk with his daughter out to the lobby and escort her back inside when the signal is given," Judge Young instructed.

Deacon wiped his eyes of joyful tears as he took Rene's hand and walked with her to the lobby.

"Pastor, I'm going to ask you to identify your best man to stand with you during the ceremony," Judge Young continued. "I'd like everyone else who is able to stand and form an aisle for the bride and her father, as they walk to the front."

"Sam, will you stand with me?"

Sam couldn't have made it to the front of the room quicker if a rocket had been strapped to his back.

"I'm here, Pastor," he announced.

With everyone in position, the judge cued the keyboardist to begin playing the wedding march. The signal was given to Deacon and Rene to enter. The accumulation of joyful sobs and sniffles of all present paled in comparison to the tears of joy that Deacon wept. Mrs.

Brock handed him a handful of tissue, as he passed by. Rene was radiant, appearing angelic, as she drew nearer to where Horatio was standing. He was so nervous that his knees became weak.

Deacon presented Rene to Horatio and stepped away. The Brocks and Mr. and Mrs. Smiley stood together during the ceremony. Judge Young smiled at Horatio and Rene and began to speak.

"Dearly beloved, we are gathered here, today, in the presence of God and these witnesses to join Horatio and Rene in matrimony…."

Upon conclusion of the exchange of the wedding vows, Judge Young asked for the rings. "May I have the rings?"

Horatio and Rene were puzzled. It was obvious that the judge had forgotten that there were no rings to be exchanged.

Again, the judge asked louder, "May I have the rings?"

Horatio took a step forward to remind him about the rings, when the side door to the conference room opened. In walked Judy escorting Daniel, as he dutifully balanced a velvet pillow with two rings.

Rene couldn't believe her eyes. Horatio was speechless.

"DANIEL! My baby! Oh, Daniel!" she cried. She took Horatio by the hand and they ran to embrace Daniel, midway. They fell to their knees, experiencing simultaneous episodes of rejoicing and crying.

"Oh, Daniel. I've missed you so much," she repeated, as she kissed and held him, closely.

Horatio wept, unashamedly, and said, "Thank you, Lord. Thank you, Lord Jesus."

Deacon, Mrs. Brock, and Kelli ran to the front of the room and joined the reunion. Every eye in the room filled with tears, including Judge Young's. Cries of "Praise God," were repeated again and again.

After a few minutes, Judge Young asked Horatio and Rene to return to their positions so, the ceremony could be concluded. In that time, Horatio and Rene refused to release hold of Daniel. The three joined hands for the duration of the ceremony.

Given the circumstance, Judge Young considered it appropriate to include Daniel as an integral part of the ceremony.

"Daniel, this is your mommy and daddy," Judge Young began. "When you leave here today, you are going to go home with them, do you understand?"

"Yes," Daniel responded, as he nodded his head.

Overcome with joy, Rene's knees buckled but, Horatio caught her before she collapsed.

"Mommy, are you all right?" Daniel asked.

"Yes, Daniel. Mommy's fine, now." Rene smiled.

Throughout the ceremony, Daniel was adorable and very well-mannered. He would, occasionally, turn around and blow kisses to the Brocks. The vows concluded with the exchange of wedding rings. Horatio kissed his bride.

"I love you, Rene Smiley." He laughed.

"I love you, Horatio Smiley," she responded.

Daniel looked into Rene's eyes and said, "I love you, too, Mommy."

"I love you so much, Daniel. And, I'm never going to let you go. Is that okay with you?"

Daniel hugged her neck and kissed her on the cheek. Turning to Horatio, he asked, "Are you my daddy?"

"I am, if you'll have me." Horatio smiled.

"Are you my son?" Horatio asked.

"I am, if you'll have me." Daniel laughed and hugged Horatio's neck.

"Daniel, I'd be honored to have you as my son," Horatio said.

"Okay, Daddy. Can we go home now?"

Witnessing the exchange, Judge Young spoke, after asking Horatio, Rene, and Daniel to turn and face their family members and guests.

"Ladies and Gentlemen, it is my privilege to introduce to you, the Smiley family."

Everyone cheered, wept, and congratulated the newlyweds.

While the celebration was in high gear, Judge Young requested that Horatio and Rene escort him to his office for a moment. They followed close behind.

"Please, sit down," he began. "I know that your family and friends are waiting, so I won't keep you long. Rene, hold on to this," he said, as he handed her an envelope.

Rene took it, expecting that it was the court-approved waiver that she and Horatio had requested.

"Thank you, Your Honor."

"I want to apologize for believing, at any time, that you cared more about yourself than you did your son," the judge began. "The document in that envelope nullifies the state's right of protective custody over Daniel. You have demonstrated to me and to this court that you are indeed a very good mother. Some time ago, I learned that a restraining order was issued, prohibiting you from being on the property of Mercy Ministries. I instructed the clerk's office to notify me of any activity related to that order. Rene, you violated that order more than fifty times in the two months after that order was issued. Eventually, I called Mercy Ministries' attorney and made clear to him my wish to never hear from him or that organization, again, about a criminal trespass matter involving you. Your persistence in keeping watch over your son demonstrated your profound remorse and concern. You truly showed a mother's love for Daniel." Rene nodded in agreement. Horatio held her hand.

"I never doubted that this day would come, Rene," the judge continued. "In fact, I was so certain that it would, I made my wife a promise. That promise being on the day you proved me to be right, I would commence my retirement from the bench and enjoy my time with family and," he chuckled, "slip in a bit of fishing and golf. I thank you and my family thanks you for your persistence and perseverance. You are a very determined woman."

"You don't know the half of it, Judge Young," Horatio chuckled. Rene blushed.

"Now, please," Judge Young instructed, "take your son and this suitcase and return to your guests. I wish you the very best in everything you do. As for me, I'm going home."

He stood and held the door for Horatio and Rene to leave. Rene kissed him on the cheek. "Thank you, Judge Young," she said. "God bless you."

Unbeknownst to Horatio and Rene, a reception had been prepared at the church. Everyone present returned to Good Shepherd's community room to continue the celebration. Humorous accounts were shared by family members and friends of the covert preparations necessary to keep the plan a secret. Horatio and Rene were incredulous at the level of sacrifice and cooperation that was revealed in the exchange.

"Pastor and First Lady, we love you," Sam called out.

Everyone echoed that sentiment. The celebration ended at nine o'clock. It had been a long and memorable day for so many. Horatio walked his bride next door and, carefully, picked her up and carried her across the threshold. Their parents and Daniel followed close behind. Exhausted, excited, and enthusiastic about beginning their life as husband and wife, mother and father, Horatio and Rene retired later that evening after reading a bedtime story to Daniel. They shared a moment in a prayer of thanksgiving. It was a very good day.

Day 75
February 15th - Saturday

The morning began with the Smiley family sitting at the breakfast table and making plans to transport some of Rene's clothing and personal effects back to the parsonage. Rene and Horatio's mother worked the stove together to prepare a breakfast of hash browns, bacon and eggs. Horatio recalled the breakfast time he shared with the Willises, a few months earlier in his kitchen. He never expected that God would bless him with a family of his own to enjoy that experience, every day. He laughed until he began to weep, realizing how wonderfully God had blessed him. God had taken him from a season of loneliness and doubt to a place of wedded bliss and fatherhood.

Thank you, Lord, for my family and your precious love.

Before long, Deacon, Mrs. Brock, Kelli and Sam had joined them at the breakfast table. After breakfast, a caravan of vehicles departed to gather Rene's belongings.

Two hours later, they returned home. After several boxes had been off-loaded and brought inside the house, Horatio noticed a familiar-looking object sticking up from one of the boxes. "Rene, is that your calendar?"

"Calendar?" Rene wasn't certain of what he was referring to.

"Yeah, the calendar you received during the New Year's Eve Watch Meeting," he reminded her.

"It could be."

"Is it okay if I show it to my parents? Mine is at the church and I'd like to show it to them."

"Of course, dear. Can you get to it okay?"

"Got it," he said, as he reached over and retrieved it from the box.

"Rene, you never opened it," he observed. "It's still wrapped in cellophane."

"It was too pretty to open. I wanted to save it as a keepsake," she explained.

"Is it okay if I open it?"

"Sure. I'd like to see it, too."

Horatio unwrapped the calendar as Rene and his parents looked on. Prefacing the unwrapping with a chronicling of events experienced by others with respect to their blotch date, his parents and Rene inspected the calendar with a heightened sense of curiosity.

Consistent with everyone else's response to the photography, they oohed and aahed as they flipped the pages. Horatio stood to the side until they had finished.

"Did you notice anything unusual about it during your inspection?"

"Unusual like what, Son?" his father asked.

"The reddish blotch I mentioned. Did you see it anywhere on the pages?"

"I didn't notice any blotch," his mother said. "It's a very beautiful calendar, though."

"I didn't see anything, either," Rene confirmed.

"It has to be there," he continued. "It's always there. You just have to look for it. Am I right, Sam?"

"Every time, Pastor," Sam acknowledged.

"Let me take a look. Please, everyone," Horatio summoned, "gather around the table and observe."

He laid the calendar flat on the table and inspected it. The January page was perfect. No blotch. He turned to the second page, February, and inspected it. Everyone gasped at what appeared. The crimson blotch, in the shape of a cross, rested squarely on the fifteenth of February. Everyone's mouth fell wide open.

"Oh, my God!" Rene exclaimed. "This can't be. Yesterday was the fifteenth. The best day of my life," she said. "What calendar company could possibly know this much about anyone's future?" she questioned.

"That's what I've been wrestling with," Horatio continued. "At first, I believed it was something demonic. But now, considering the way God moved in our circumstance yesterday, it makes perfect sense. The Lord sent these calendars to make clear to us that he knows our beginning, our end, and everything in between. I believe with all of my heart that what the Lord tells us in Psalms 139 is true."

"Glory to God. You can say that again, Pastor. You can sure say that, again," Sam acknowledged, as he lifted his eyes heavenward.

The End